Crisis and Consensus in British Politics

From Bagehot to Blair

Michael Williams
Lecturer in Politics and Public Policy
University of Hertfordshire

First published in Great Britain 2000 by
MACMILLAN PRESS LTD
Houndmills, Basingstoke, Hampshire RG21 6XS and London
Companies and representatives throughout the world

A catalogue record for this book is available from the British Library.

ISBN 0–333–77571–6

First published in the United States of America 2000 by
ST. MARTIN'S PRESS, LLC,
Scholarly and Reference Division,
175 Fifth Avenue, New York, N.Y. 10010

ISBN 0–312–23274–8

Library of Congress Cataloging-in-Publication Data
Williams, Michael, 1949–
Crisis and consensus in British politics : from Bagehot to Blair / Michael Williams.
p. cm.
Includes bibliographical references (p.) and index.
ISBN 0–312–23274–8 (cloth)
1. Great Britain—Politics and government—20th century. 2. Capitalism—Great Britain—History—20th century. 3. Capitalism—Great Britain—History—19th century. 4. Great Britain—Politics and government—1837–1901. 5. Great Britain—Economic conditions—20th century. 6. Great Britain—Economic conditions—19th century. 7. Bagehot, Walter, 1826–1877. 8. Blair, Tony, 1953– I. Title.

DA566.7 .W53 2000
941.082—dc21

00–042060

This book is printed on paper suitable for recycling and made from fully managed and sustained forest sources.

10 9 8 7 6 5 4 3 2 1
09 08 07 06 05 04 03 02 01 00

Printed and bound in Great Britain by
Antony Rowe Ltd, Chippenham, Wiltshire

To the memory of my mother Mary and father Jack:
the twentieth century was theirs as well as mine

Contents

Preface

This book seeks to chart the movement between crisis and consensus in British politics during the twentieth century against the background of the development of the British state and British capitalism since the Industrial Revolution. The main focus is upon the breakdown of the post-war consensus in what has been called 'the crisis of the mid-1970s' and the emergence of a new consensus during the 1990s.

Much of the book, therefore, is cast in the form of a history of my own time. I grew to political awareness in the early 1960s just as Harold Macmillan's modernisation strategy foundered in a welter of scandal. As a sixth-former and undergraduate in the last half of the 1960s, I watched the disintegration of the Wilson Government and then, as a research student in the early 1970s, the more dramatic collapse of the Heath Government.

I entered the civil service in 1974 at the height of the mid-1970s crisis and watched it unfold from the vantage point of the secretariat of an inquiry into local government finance which interpreted its remit widely to include the whole system of public finance which was central to the crisis. The Winter of Discontent found me supporting a top official at the Department of Transport in his negotiations with the General Secretary of the Transport and General Workers' Union about permits for lorries delivering vital supplies. The 1980s were spent as an involuntary foot-soldier in what has been called the 'Thatcher Revolution', serving in the Department of Transport and the (now privatised) Property Services Agency, while the beginning of the Major years found me in the Department of the Environment helping to pick up the pieces from the most egregious failure of the Thatcher years by developing a replacement for the Poll Tax. Tony Blair had been elected leader of the Labour Party and the Conservatives fatally riven over Europe by the time I left the civil service in 1995. Since then I have watched the final collapse of the Major Government and the first years of the Blair Government from the vantage point of a university lecturer in politics and public policy.

Every book is a collective product even though the title page may bear only one name. Thanks in this instance are due above all to my old friend and present colleague Alan Hooper with whom I have honed the ideas and arguments in this book over 30 years of constantly stimulating talk. Alan read two drafts of the book and made a great many valuable suggestions. The weaknesses of the book are my responsibility; the qualities owe much to him.

Thanks also are due to Ben Pimlott, for introducing me to the study of British politics in his seminars at Birkbeck College and for encouraging me to publish my own thoughts; to Sara Arber at the University of Surrey for giving me a free hand when commissioning the series of lectures on British politics from which this book has grown; to Geoff Andrews and Mark Perryman and other members of the Signs of the Times group for helping me to refine my thoughts on managerialism; to Martin Hewitt for reading and commenting on a novice's account of welfare reform; to the civil service for endowing me with skills which I have learned to appreciate since I left its portals; and to students at the University of Hertfordshire and elsewhere who have been a lively and stimulating audience as I developed the ideas in the book. Finally, thanks are due to Marguerite and the boys for their forbearance during hours spent in the study: 'Scribble, scribble, Mr Gibbon'; 'tap, tap on the pc, Mr Williams'.

MICHAEL WILLIAMS

Introduction

'I can't bear Britain in decline, I just can't. We who either defeated or rescued half Europe, who kept half Europe free when otherwise it would be in chains. And look at us now' (cited British Broadcasting Corporation, 1991). The words were Margaret Thatcher's, delivered in heart-felt tone in a party political broadcast in 1979. But much the same could have been said by almost any British politician since the early 1960s. Tony Benn, for example, was just as concerned as Thatcher about reversing Britain's relative economic decline, as may be seen from the account in his diary of a major speech on this theme given, in his own words, 'on every possible occasion' (cited Panitch & Leys, 1997: 45, 283).

The question of Britain's relative economic decline first entered the awareness of a large part of the governing elite in Edwardian times; it has been the dominant issue in British politics for the last forty years. This is not yet another book about Britain's relative economic decline but it does form the essential backdrop to my main theme, which is the movement between crisis and consensus during the twentieth century – the product of successive challenges to the traditional governing elite and a conception of Britain's place in the world which was formed in the age of Walter Bagehot in mid-Victorian times and remains unresolved today under Prime Minister Tony Blair.

Britain entered the twentieth century at a time of growing crisis resulting from the political challenges mounted by the labour movement and Irish nationalism at home and the economic (and potentially military) challenges from the USA and Germany. The threat from the labour movement was overcome by the defeat of the General Strike in 1926 and by the taming of the Labour Party between 1924 and 1931 while the threat from Irish nationalism was overcome by partition in 1921. Britain chose to conciliate the USA as the price of being able to defeat the more immediate and threatening challenge from Germany (Gamble, 1994: 58–63). Thus a tacit consensus was achieved by the late 1920s and reinforced by the National Government after 1931. Britain would not be ruled by single party government again until 1945.

The inter-war consensus collapsed in the crisis of 1940 which laid the foundation for a new consensus consolidated by the Labour Government after 1945 and largely accepted by the incoming Conservative Government in 1951. The post-war consensus (sometimes called the post-war settlement) is commonly conceived to consist of a bipartisan agreement on the boundaries between the public and the private sector, a commitment to full employment maintained through Keynesian techniques of macro-economic management, the conciliation of the trade union movement, and universal welfare services (Kavanagh & Morris, 1994: 4–5). The existence of this consensus has been challenged by some historians (see, for example, Pimlott, 1988), but most of Britain's governing elite took it for granted at the time and the notion has been accepted by enough commentators to render it still useful. Mark Mazower has pointed to parallel developments in the rest of post-war Western Europe (1999: 294–6).

The post-war consensus came under increasing strain during the 1960s and 1970s as a result of a succession of political and economic failures culminating in what Samuel Beer has called 'the crisis of the mid 1970s' (1982: 95). Conservative victory in the 1979 election signalled an end to consensus and the beginning of a period of social and political conflict which did not begin to abate until after the fall of Thatcher in 1990. The conflicts of the 1970s and 1980s have been replaced in the 1990s by what an increasing number of commentators have seen as a new consensus – Blaijorism in Colin Hay's coinage (1996: 163).

As will be clear from the Preface, this book has been written from the standpoint of one who spent 20 years as a policy adviser in Whitehall following an intellectual training as a historian. This background may explain the essentially top-down account of successive challenges to the British governing elite and the focus in the later, policy-oriented chapters on the changing role of the state. Mine is essentially a state-centred account, albeit in the context of long-term changes in British society. Readers will have to judge the extent to which I have succeeded in my ambition of combining the perspectives of the historian, political scientist and policy analyst in an account of the onset of Britain's relative economic decline and its delayed – but explosive – impact on British politics since the 1960s.

The first five chapters are broadly historical, offering an account of British politics 'from Bagehot to Blair' in the words of my subtitle. Chapter 1 looks at the development of British capitalism since the Industrial Revolution, identifying six phases of which the third – from the 1870s until 1914 – was crucial as the one in which Britain as the first great industrial power began to be overhauled by Germany and the USA. This third and crucial phase in the development of British capitalism coincided with the transition to mass democracy which is the subject of Chapter 2. This chapter charts the emergence of modern party politics in the 1860s and 1870s and the gradual expansion of the electorate during the next half-century until votes were granted in 1928 to all women aged over 21. It examines the strategies adopted by the two main parties – Liberals and Conservatives – in the competition for support from the expanding electorate, and seeks to explain why the Liberals were replaced by the Labour Party at the end of this period.

The onset of full democracy (in terms of adult male and female suffrage) coincided – in Britain as in Germany, France and the USA – with what Eric Hobsbawm (1994) has described as the Age of Catastrophe from 1914 to 1945. Chapter 3 examines the way in which the British governing elite met the twin challenges from labour and external enemies, and charts the connection between warfare and welfare in the creation of the welfare state, which spanned the period from the aftermath of the Boer War in the early 1900s to the onset of the Cold War in the late 1940s. The Age of Catastrophe gave birth to the post-war consensus which was sustained by economic prosperity through what Hobsbawm (1994) has described as the Golden Age from the late 1940s until the early 1970s. Chapter 4 looks at the factors leading to the collapse of consensus, focussing on the political and economic failures of the 1960s and early 1970s and the accompanying collapse of the deferential political culture which Bagehot had seen as the precondition for British politics. It follows the trajectory of Thatcherism from the 1970s to the collapse of the Major Government in the 1990s and concludes by raising the question of whether Thatcher's apparent success in eliminating the threat of socialism, while no doubt welcome to British capital, might not be fatal to the Conservative Party as an instrument of government.

The crisis of the 1970s was, above all, a crisis for the Labour Party which was closely associated with the main components of the post-war consensus – full employment sustained by Keynesian macro-economic management, universal welfare services, a large public sector and conciliation of the trade unions. Each came under sustained challenge during the 1980s and 1990s, and none has survived unchanged. Chapter 5 looks at the gradual and painful end of the old Labour Party and the emergence of New Labour as the vehicle for a new consensus in the 1990s.

The next six chapters focus on public policy, seeking to illustrate the general argument about the movement between crisis and consensus through an examination of six policy areas focussing particularly upon the impact of the mid-1970s crisis on the British state and the way in which it has been restructured since then. The central government machine still bears the mark of William Ewart Gladstone, probably the greatest of nineteenth-century British politicians. The main component of the reforms undertaken by him as Chancellor of the Exchequer in the 1850s and early 1860s and then during his first period in office as Prime Minister from 1868 to 1874 was the reform of the civil service along lines adumbrated in the Northcote–Trevelyan Report of 1854 which he commissioned. Chapter 6 describes the way in which Gladstone conceived of the reformed civil service as a means of preserving the power of the traditional governing elite in an age of democracy. Indeed, the civil service assumed its classic form, which endured until the 1970s, in 1920, on the morrow of the 1918 extension of the vote to all adult men and to women over 30. However, a central part of the crisis of the mid-1970s was a collapse of confidence both *within* the civil service, among many senior officials, and a collapse of confidence *in* the civil service on the part of many politicians, Conservative and

Labour alike. Another thing that Margaret Thatcher had in common with Tony Benn was an acute suspicion of a defeatist caste of senior officials. The crisis of confidence of the 1970s was followed in the 1980s and 1990s by the biggest changes in the civil service since the early twentieth century, to the point where it is fair to talk about a 'managerial revolution', echoing the title of a famous book by James Burnham (1941). The civil service has been the testbed for managerial reforms that have been extended throughout the public services, just as the Northcote–Trevelyan model was in its day.

Another element of the crisis of the mid-1970s was a crisis of confidence in the operation of the nationalised industries that had accounted for a large part of the British economy since the 1940s. Trade unions in the nationalised industries were responsible for many of the strikes which undermined the Heath Government in the early 1970s, while the investment and pricing decisions of the industries were distorted by political intervention. Chapter 7 describes how the Conservatives entered office in 1979 with a commitment to 'rolling back the frontiers of the state' but only gradually moved towards privatisation as a means of solving the perceived problems of the nationalised industries. As well as describing the development of the policy through the 1980s and into the 1990s, this chapter examines the consequences for managers, workforce, shareholders and the public. It also looks at methods of regulating the privatised utilities. It argues that privatisation is a central aspect in the development of a new kind of state – a regulatory state.

The mid-1970s crisis was also a crisis in the role of the state in managing the economy. Chapter 8 describes how the First World War destroyed the liberal world economy which had been dominated by the City of London, a domination expressed through the Gold Standard which was suspended on the outbreak of war. British macro-economic policy since the 1920s can be seen as a series of attempts to restore the *rentier* capitalist paradise which had been lost in 1914. The attempt to restore pre-war 'normalcy' by returning to the Gold Standard in 1925 broke down in 1931 in the first of the great sterling devaluation crises that have punctuated British history since then. The post-war consensus depended upon a benign combination of sustained economic growth with full employment and low inflation which seemed to validate the ideas about managing the economy associated with J. M. Keynes. The gathering problems of the 1960s and 1970s seemed to discredit these ideas and to lend force to the alternative so-called monetarist ideas with which the Conservatives entered office in 1979. Events were to show that these ideas in practice involved a wholesale assault on the trade unions – a form of class struggle from above described more surgically as shock therapy. This shock therapy laid the foundations for a gradual retreat from discretionary management of the economy to a rule-based approach, first adumbrated by Chancellor Nigel Lawson in the 1980s and fully accepted by Chancellor Gordon Brown, with the support of his Conservative predecessors, in the 1990s.

In 1979 the incoming Conservative Government described public expenditure as being 'at the heart of Britain's present economic difficulties' (Lawson, 1992: 37). Chapter 9 looks at the reasons for the growth of public expenditure in the twentieth century and attempts to explain the apparent loss of control over public expenditure which lay at the heart of the mid-1970s crisis. It seeks to demonstrate that the problems confronting the Labour Government in 1974 were inherited from the Heath Government and had been largely overcome by the time of the intervention of the International Monetary Fund in 1976. It goes on to examine the record of the Conservative Government in an attempt to explain why they were unable to realise their ambitions to achieve real reductions in the level of public spending. At the end of the 1990s, both main parties seem to agree that there is no scope either for reducing or increasing public spending as a proportion of national income. The last decade has seen the emergence of a new consensus about the role of public spending and public services in contributing to the competitiveness of the British economy. This new consensus on national competitiveness in a global economy has been described by Bob Jessop (1994) in terms of a Schumpeterian Workfare State, just like the post-war consensus was based on a Keynesian Welfare State which seemed to break down in the mid-1970s crisis.

The mid-1970s crisis was also a crisis in the relations between the constituent nations of the United Kingdom and in the UK's relations with the other main Western European countries in the EEC. Chapter 10 looks at the crisis of territorial governance within the UK as the product of a long process of agglomeration. It shows how the transition to mass democracy in the late nineteenth and early twentieth centuries was accompanied by a crisis in the relations between the constituent peoples of the UK, associated above all with the Irish Question. This crisis seemed to be resolved by partition in 1921 but it resurfaced in the late 1960s, along with strong nationalist parties in Scotland and Wales, and reached a climax in the mid-1970s. The Conservative Government was obliged to concede a southern dimension to the problem of Northern Ireland but resisted any change in the position of Wales and Scotland in the Union – at the eventual price of the loss of all Conservative representation from these countries in the House of Commons in 1997. By establishing a Scottish Parliament and a Welsh Assembly the Blair Government has recast the territorial settlement within the UK with long-term effects that cannot be predicted.

Chapter 11 looks at the European dimension to the movement between crisis and consensus charted in this book. Harold Macmillan's application to join the EEC in 1961 was a central part of his modernisation strategy, and de Gaulle's veto was an important contributory factor to the decline in the self-confidence of the British governing elite during the 1960s. Britain eventually entered the EEC in 1973 on the threshold of an enveloping economic crisis which would not be resolved until the 1980s. In the short term, the incoming Labour Government in 1974 was torn by divisions over membership of the EEC which were only partially resolved by the referendum of June 1975. Differences over Europe played an important part in the division between the Labour Party and the Social Democratic Party in the 1980s, and since the late 1980s similar differences have undermined the Conservatives. Paradoxically, however, the differences within the Conservative Party over Europe have contributed to a realignment on the left which has resulted in a wider consensus over Europe than has existed in the past.

The conclusion focusses on the Blair Government in the context of the movement from crisis to consensus which is the main theme of this book. It borrows Harold Perkin's argument that the post-war consensus may be understood in terms of the rise of professional society based on the acceptance of the professional ideal of functional service to the community, and that the crisis of the 1970s can be understood in terms of 'the bifurcation of the professional ideal' between the private and public sector professions (Perkin, 1989). It seeks to extend

Perkin's analysis by arguing that the emergence of a new consensus in the 1990s is based upon the common acceptance of a managerial ideal and an emerging managerial society in which wealth and power are based upon the possession of marketable skills. Thus we are seeing the emergence of a new kind of state – the regulatory state or the Schumpeterian Workfare State – presiding over a new kind of society – managerial society, with New Labour – with its stress on work, education, partnership and pragmatism – as the vehicle, and likely main beneficiary, of a new political consensus.

As a 'history of my own times' this book offers a personal interpretation of British politics since the 1960s which I hope will be of interest to readers who lived through this period and to younger readers seeking to make sense of it. By setting recent events in the context of the development of British capitalism and the British state since the late eighteenth century I hope the book will be useful for students of modern British history and politics and also for students of public policy who wish to locate their subject in its proper political setting. It owes a considerable debt to a large body of literature on 'the politics of decline' but seeks to build upon this literature by charting in detail the emergence of a new political consensus based on a new phase in the development of British society whose lineaments are only just beginning to emerge.

1
Britain in Decline: Structural Change in British Capitalism since the Industrial Revolution

Introduction

The Industrial Revolution which began in Britain in the late eighteenth century has been aptly described as 'the most fundamental transformation of human life in the history of the world recorded in written documents' (Hobsbawm, 1969: 13). As Harold Perkin remarked, 'Modern society ... has its roots in the Industrial Revolution' (Perkin, 1969: 1). Britain's pioneering role in this transformation has left lasting marks on its subsequent history. In particular it helps to account for the characteristic combination of archaism and modernity in its culture and institutions. Norman Stone in the early 1980s described England as 'the last of the *ancien regimes*' (Stone, 1983: 18), and 'modernisation' has been a recurring motif in political discourse for the last forty years. We cannot hope to appreciate the problems facing British politicians in the twentieth century without some understanding of the development of British capitalism over the last two centuries.

This chapter traces the process of structural change in British capitalism and its political ramifications through six phases since the onset of the Industrial Revolution. These phases show links with so-called long waves in economic development first identified by the early Soviet economist Kondratiev and elaborated upon by Schumpeter, and with developments in world history, for one of the distinguishing features in the history of British capitalism has been its close integration with the world economy. This chapter seeks to explain why the problem of relative economic decline should have loomed so large in British politics since the early 1960s and concludes with a brief consideration of the extent to which the Conservatives can claim to have overcome this problem during their period in office from 1979 to 1997.

Phase 1: the Industrial Revolution

By convention the onset of the Industrial Revolution is dated from around 1780 and the first phase of industrialisation can be said to have been completed by 1850. The great question which has aroused generations of economic historians is why the Industrial Revolution began in Britain rather than elsewhere. This is not the place to attempt a definitive answer but three factors seem to be particularly important.

First, Britain in the eighteenth century was already a market society, and had been so for several centuries – perhaps since the late Middle Ages. Whereas in most of Europe the majority of the population were peasants who produced most of what they consumed, in Britain the majority of people had to sell their labour in order to buy the products which they consumed. Britain had a large middle class of manufacturers and artisans estimated at around one-third of the population as early as 1688 (Perkin, 1969: 21). Britain was also the most urbanised major country in Europe and one where laws protected property rights. A large home market provided an essential base for the cotton industry which was at the leading edge of the Industrial Revolution. David Willetts made the point nicely in a review of David Cannadine's *Class in Britain* (Cannadine, 1998): 'It is not that Britain had the industrial revolution and then became a capitalist society. It is because we were already the first capitalist society that we were then ripe for the industrial revolution' (Willetts, 1999).

Second, Britain in the 1770s was at the centre of a world economic system without a significant rival following the defeat of France in the Seven Years War which ended in 1763. France's attempt to challenge Britain's position in the War of American Independence reduced the Monarchy to bankruptcy and precipitated the revolution which resulted by 1815 in the eclipse of France as a serious rival to British world hegemony. The world economic system dominated by Britain and policed by the Royal Navy involved the production of raw cotton in the southern states of the

USA by slaves transported from Africa in British ships and then the import of raw cotton to Britain to be turned into manufactures for sale at home and in Africa and India (where the indigenous cotton industry had been destroyed).

Third, these exceptionally favourable conditions, at home and abroad, were not the product of accident, unassisted by political action. They were instead the achievements of governments dominated by a commercially minded aristocracy with close ties to the City of London. At home these governments relied on inaction: 'There was from 1660 onwards an almost complete absence of government interference with innovating enterprise, which amounted to effective *laissez-faire* in internal trade and industry a full century or more before it was put forward as a conscious object of policy' (Perkin, 1969: 11). Abroad this governing class was, in Hobsbawm's telling phrase, 'both businesslike and warlike' (Hobsbawm, 1969: 26). Since the Commonwealth of the 1650s, with only a brief interruption under Charles II and James II, this oligarchy had waged aggressive war for predominantly commercial reasons. By the early nineteenth century – at the end of the Napoleonic Wars – Britain had eliminated its last important commercial rival.

The Industrial Revolution coincided with the French Revolution, together constituting what historians have described as the 'dual revolution': 'If the economy of the nineteenth-century world was formed mainly under the influence of the British Industrial Revolution, its politics and ideology were formed mainly by the French' (Hobsbawm, 1962: xv, 76). Industrialisation brought an immense disruption of traditional working patterns well-documented by Edward Thompson in his classic *The Making of the English Working Class* (1968). These changes were accelerated by a dismantling of what remained of paternalistic controls on prices and, following the New Poor Law of 1834, the end of relief for the poor in their own homes. They also involved 'a decisive shift in the distribution of income' from wages to profit of between 6 per cent and 14 per cent of national income (Perkin, 1969: 138). No wonder, then, that 'a high wind of social discontent ... blew across Britain' in these years: 'At no other period in modern British history have the common people been so persistently, profoundly and often desperately unhappy' (Hobsbawm, 1969: 73).

The aristocratic Whig factions which had governed Britain since the early eighteenth century met the challenge of revolution abroad and discontent at home by coalescing in the 1790s under the leadership of William Pitt. They were no simple reactionaries: Pitt had signed a free trade treaty with France in 1786 and Edmund Burke was a follower of Adam Smith as well as the leading critic of the French Revolution. Once the storms of the years between Waterloo (1815) and Peterloo (1819) had been weathered, Pitt's younger disciples like Canning, Peel, Huskisson and Goderich presided over a series of administrative and commercial reforms that did much to remove the grievances of the emerging provincial industrial bourgeoisie. The Pittite coalition finally dissolved in 1829 over the question of extending civil rights to Roman Catholics, thus opening the way in 1830 to a reforming Whig ministry which met the political grievances of the provincial bourgeoisie through the Reform Act of 1832, incorporating the middle class within the political nation the better to resist working-class demands for the vote through Chartism. The Conservative Government's repeal of the Corn Laws in 1846 involved a recognition of the primacy of industry and a commitment to free trade. A series of Factory Acts marked an attempt to meet working-class grievances about conditions of work. 1848 found Chartism at its last gasp while most of mainland Europe was convulsed by revolution.

Phase 2: the Workshop of the World

The Great Exhibition of 1851 symbolised the economic prosperity and new-found political stability of Britain at the outset of what has become known as 'the Age of Equipoise' (Burn, 1964). This was an equipoise founded on the brief moment from about 1850 until the mid-1870s in which newly industrialising countries like France, Germany and the USA provided expanding markets for British coal, steel and manufactured goods while not yet offering a serious challenge to British primacy. The Industrial Revolution had been based mainly on cotton. This next phase was based on the railway and the stimulus that it offered to coal, iron and steel and engineering, as well as the reduction in transport costs. Britain 'had surmounted the original crisis of the early Industrial Revolution, and had not yet begun to feel the crisis of the pioneer industrial country which ceases to be the only "workshop of the world"' (Hobsbawm, 1969: 119–20). For a short time Britain enjoyed a dominant position, producing two-thirds of the world's coal, half of its iron, five-sevenths of its steel, half of the cotton goods produced for sale, and 40 per cent of other industrial products (Hobsbawm, 1969: 134). Economic growth reached a peak of an average 3.6 per cent a year in the decade from the early 1860s to the early 1870s (Perkin, 1989: 36). Living standards rose and commentators began to point to an emerging labour aristocracy.

This period saw the disappearance of the main challenges to aristocratic political power. The challenge from the working class disappeared with the collapse of Chartism after 1848, and the Anti-Corn Law League failed to lay the foundation for an independent middle-class radical party. Both were among the currents that flowed into the Liberal Party that emerged in the 1860s under the leadership of William Gladstone, a former High Tory and later disciple of the Conservative Prime Minister Robert Peel who had divided his party over the Repeal of the Corn Laws. The Second Reform Act of 1867 extended the suffrage to the skilled working class of the cities who were no longer judged to be revolutionary. The General Election of 1868 was the first in which working men formed the majority of electors in urban areas.

Phase 3: the onset of decline

British industrial supremacy was bound to be temporary; Britain was bound to lose ground to a united Germany and a continental USA if only because of their larger populations. By 1890 the population of Germany was 50 million and the population of the USA was 63 million, compared with Britain's 37 million (Kennedy, 1988: 199). Larger populations meant larger home markets from which to compete in world markets. The figures in Table 1.1 for percentage shares of world manufacturing output show the way in which Britain was overhauled by the USA and Germany: Britain had been overtaken as a manufacturing power by the USA by 1900 and Germany by 1913.

But Britain's loss of ground to emerging competitors was not just a matter of bigger populations and bigger home markets. Annual

Table 1.1 Shares of world manufacturing output (percentages)

	1860	*1880*	*1900*	*1913*
Britain	20	23	19	14
USA	7	15	24	32
Germany	5	9	13	15

Source: Kennedy, 1988: 149, 202.

growth of the British economy failed to match the growth rates achieved by its rivals. During the decisive period 1870–1913 British productivity (defined in terms of Gross Domestic Product per man-hour – GDP being the usual measure of national income and output) rose by an average of 1 per cent a year compared with averages of 2 per cent a year in Germany and the USA (Gamble, 1994: 17). The real question, therefore, is why Britain failed to achieve comparable growth rates in the face of the challenges from the USA and Germany.

Just as the Industrial Revolution was associated with cotton and the period in which Britain could plausibly be described as the Workshop of the World was associated with the railway, this third phase was associated with the emergence of new industries based on organised scientific and technological knowledge such as chemicals or the electric industry (where Germany took the lead) and mass production for a mass market (where the USA took the lead, epitomised by the names of Henry Ford and Frederick Taylor, pioneer of scientific management). No longer was it possible to rely upon unschooled technical expertise and incremental improvements as in earlier phases in which Britain had taken the lead.

For at least a century, since Britain's relative economic decline first began to impinge upon the minds of Britain's political and industrial elites, there has been controversy over the reasons for this decline (Gamble, 1994). 'This sudden transformation of the leading and most dynamic industrial economy into the most sluggish and conservative, in the short space of thirty or forty years (1860–90/1900) is the crucial question of British economic history' (Hobsbawm, 1969: 178). A whole literature has grown up around this question of Britain's relative economic decline. Some authors have attributed it to a snobbish disdain for trade; others to hidebound schools and universities; yet others to an enfeebled political class, archaic institutions or entrenched sectional interests (Anderson, 1964, Barnett, 1972, Wiener, 1981, and Olson, 1982, set the main parameters of the debate). Probably the most plausible explanations are economic and political: because capital already invested in traditional industries offered an adequate return and because Britain was able to use its political and military power to consolidate captive markets for traditional products such as cotton and manufactured goods, 'When faced with a challenge, it was easier and cheaper to retreat' (Hobsbawm, 1969: 191). The consolidation of traditional overseas markets under the banner of Empire was associated with conservatism at home, involving a crucial loss of dynamism that later governments sought in vain to rekindle.

As we shall see in Chapter 2, the main concerns of the British governing elite in the late nineteenth century were the internal challenges posed by a predominantly working-class electorate and an increasingly militant Irish nationalism. Only in the aftermath of the Boer War of 1899–1902, which revealed a whole range of military, educational and administrative deficiencies, did the British political class become aware of external economic and military challenges which the country was ill-equipped to meet (Searle, 1971). The ensuing sense of crisis engendered an all-party movement for 'national efficiency' which prompted provisions for the expansion of state secondary education contained in the 1902 Education Act and the foundation of a string of civic universities as well as the end of Late Victorian 'splendid isolation' through an alliance with Japan in 1902 and the *entente cordiale* with France in 1904.

This sense of crisis produced two main strategies to meet the challenges from external competitors as well as from an increasingly assertive labour movement. The first – the programme of tariff reform and imperial federation associated with the Unionist Joseph Chamberlain – was effectively defeated in the 1906 election which resulted in a landslide victory for the Liberals. The Liberal victory was followed by a programme of welfare reform coupled with free trade based on Britain's traditional pre-eminent position in the world economy. Externally, the commitment to the maintenance of an open world economy required cooperation with the USA and rendered more likely a clash with Germany, the other main challenger to Britain's world position. Domestically, the Liberal

Government's programme of social reform and Home Rule for Ireland failed to meet the challenges from labour and Irish nationalism. Rising social tension was overtaken by the outbreak of the First World War which effectively removed the question of Britain's relative economic decline from the political agenda for half a century.

Phase 4: the Age of Catastrophe

Eric Hobsbawm and Robert Skidelsky, in two masterly and complementary surveys of the twentieth century, have identified three distinct phases (Hobsbawm, 1994; Skidelsky, 1995). The first, from 1914 to 1945, they have described as 'The Age of Catastrophe' or 'The Age of Wars' – with obvious justification. Both have described the period from the late 1940s to the early 1970s as 'The Golden Age', Skidelsky shrewdly comparing it to the mid-nineteenth century 'Age of Equipoise' encompassing almost exactly the same years (Skidelsky, 1995: xiv). The final phase, from the 1970s until the present, Hobsbawm has characterised as 'The Landslide', dominated by the descent into poverty and insecurity of large parts of Africa and Latin America as well as the successor states to the Soviet Union and Yugoslavia, whereas Skidelsky has characterised the same period in terms of 'Shock Therapy' needed to correct the supposed ills of collectivism which came to a head in the 1970s. The rest of this chapter follows this periodisation in examining economic developments and their political ramifications in Britain.

The Age of Catastrophe began with the First World War which involved the breakdown of the liberal world economy centred upon Britain and a transformation of Britain's position in the world. Britain was reduced to financial dependence on American loans by the end of 1916 and during the course of the war the centre of world finance moved across the Atlantic to Wall Street (Kennedy, 1988: 268, 282). The war was followed by the collapse of Britain's traditional industries and the onset of chronic mass unemployment: 'The Victorian economy of Britain crashed in ruins between the two world wars' (Hobsbawm, 1969: 207). The 1930s saw some limited modernisation but not enough to transform Britain's overall economic performance. The Second World War saw the liquidation of Britain's remaining overseas assets followed by the post-war termination of imperial preference under US pressure. The transformation of Britain's position from the centre of global finance and the world's greatest empire in 1914 to dependence on US loans in 1945 constituted an immense decline in absolute power, leaving aside questions of relative decline in economic performance.

The inter-war years were a period of Conservative hegemony as a result of an Opposition divided between the declining Liberal Party (which remained a significant force until 1931) and a rising Labour Party which split in 1931. A sad irony of the time was that only the Liberals (led by David Lloyd George and inspired by Keynes) had serious plans for coping with Britain's economic problems. Labour had none. The Conservatives tried to regain 'normalcy' by returning to the Gold Standard in 1925 but after 1931 fell back on imperial markets with a policy of devaluation and imperial protection. The Second World War, and in particular the formation of the Coalition Government headed by Churchill in 1940, marked a swing to the Left which eventually resulted in the large-scale nationalisation, extension of social insurance and creation of the National Health Service by the Labour Government of 1945 (Addison, 1994). As many following Richard Titmuss have observed, the welfare state and the warfare state developed in tandem (Titmuss, 1958). We shall return to these points in Chapter 3.

Phase 5: the Golden Age

The term Golden Age has been used to describe the long boom from the late 1940s to the early 1970s – from the Marshall Plan announced in 1947 to the first oil price rise in 1973. In the late 1940s Britain was home to the biggest economy in Western Europe, responsible for half of its coal production and 40 per cent of its iron and steel production (Denman, 1996: 182). In the mid-1950s the

Table 1.2 Shares of world exports of manufactures (percentages)

	1950	*1960*	*1970*
Britain	26	17	11
Germany	7	19	20
France	10	10	9

Source: Gamble, 1994: 17.

economic problem seemed to have been solved. In fact it was only in remission. By the late 1950s it was clear that Britain had failed to match its main European competitors, as shown by the figures in Table 1.2 for percentage shares of world exports of manufactures. By 1960 Britain had been overtaken by West Germany and by the late 1960s it was being pressed hard by France.

This relatively poor performance could not be attributed to population and the size of the internal market as in the case of a united Germany and a continental USA earlier in the century: the populations of Britain, West Germany and France were about the same. The relative decline can be attributed to the same reason as in the past: low productivity. Between 1950 and 1976 British productivity rose by an average 3 per cent a year (better than before or since) compared with 6 per cent achieved by West Germany and 5 per cent by France (Gamble, 1994: 17).

Contemporaries attributed this slow growth to continued reliance on traditional Empire/Commonwealth markets, excessive arms spending resulting from lingering great-power pretensions and the high priority given to defending an overvalued currency. By the late 1950s this question of Britain's relative economic decline had forced itself back onto the political agenda for the first time since the 1900s. This awareness formed the backdrop to the modernisation strategy embraced by the Conservatives in 1961 and continued by the Labour Government elected in 1964. It explains the application for membership of the EEC and the embrace of indicative planning for growth – what has come to be known as 'hands-on Keynesianism' (Marquand, 1988: 45). By the 1970s the whole project had foundered, as we shall see in Chapter 4.

Phase 6: shock therapy

The background to the last of our six phases in the development of British capitalism since the late eighteenth century was the political crisis of the mid- to late 1970s which followed the failure of the governments led by Harold Macmillan (latterly by Alec Home), Harold Wilson, Edward Heath and Harold Wilson (again) and James Callaghan. Traditional 'one nation' Conservatism was thought to have failed under Macmillan and Heath, and social democracy to have failed under Wilson and Callaghan. The question began to be asked 'is Britain governable?' The 1979 election has come to be seen as a watershed. Mrs Thatcher insisted in her memoirs that 'everything we wished to do had to fit into the overall strategy of reversing Britain's economic decline' (Thatcher, 1995: 15).

What have been the results of shock therapy under Thatcher? The record is a controversial one but the general conclusion is that the Conservatives halted economic decline. Between 1980 and 1989 Britain's GDP grew by an average 2.2 per cent a year compared with 2.1 per cent a year for France and 2 per cent a year for West Germany (Johnson, 1991: 266). Between 1979 and 1991 British labour productivity grew by an average 1.9 per cent a year compared with 2.3 per cent a year for France and 1.4 per cent a year for Germany and 1.6 per cent a year for the advanced economies as a whole (Gamble, 1994: 206). During the 1990s, especially after the departure of sterling from the European Exchange Rate Mechanism in 1992, economic growth in Britain has been above the average for the European Union and unemployment below the EU average.

Britain's position in the world prosperity league (measured in terms of GDP per head), after falling from first place in 1900, through third place in 1950, tenth in 1970, fifteenth in 1975 and nineteenth in 1985, had risen to seventeenth place in 1994 and sixteenth in 1995 (Wolf, 1997; Kuper, 1997). Between 1980 and 1990 Britain had fallen behind Italy in terms of GDP per head whereas by 1998 it had overhauled it by 16 per cent, regaining the relative position in 1970. Britain now stands within 5 per cent of overhauling France and thus recovering its position as the world's fourth largest economic power after the USA, Germany and Japan (Kaletsky, 1999). More subjectively, the neo-liberal World Economic Forum (organiser of the annual Davos Conference) ranked Britain in eighth place in the world competitiveness league published in 1999, down from fourth place in 1998 but well up from fifteenth place in 1995 (*Financial Times*, 14.7.99; Coyle, 1997). There remains a question mark over whether this relative improvement in British performance simply reflects poorer performance among traditional rivals. Britain retains its traditional weakness in manufacturing: a recent OECD study concluded that British productivity had improved in the last decade but was still 'well behind' other countries (*Financial Times*, 14.7.97). The increase in GDP since 1979 has been four times as big as in manufactured output. Slow growth has meant that improvements in productivity have resulted in a more than 40 per cent decline in employment. Since 1994 productivity has barely risen (Wolf, 1999b). Nevertheless even the Marxist Hobsbawm thought that the British economy '*needed a kick in the pants*' (Hobsbawm, 1989: 209, italics in original) – which was duly administered by Thatcher.

Conclusion

The question of relative economic decline has dominated peacetime politics in Britain for much of the twentieth century. In the early nineteenth century Britain was the most dynamic society and economy in the world. In the last decades of the century Britain reacted to the emerging challenges from Germany and the USA by retreating into empire rather than modernising industry. It was able to exploit the world hegemony established during the preceding century in order to build the largest empire in the world and to dominate financial services and shipping. In the twentieth century, 'Alone of the major European nations, England [*sic*] emerged undefeated and unoccupied from two world wars, its social structure untouched by external shocks or discontinuities' (Anderson, 1964: 27). Roy Denman, chronicler of Britain's 'missed chances' in its relations with the European Union, commented: 'Britain never had a serious, house-clearing revolution' (Denman, 1996: 287). Crisis loomed at the beginning of the 1960s as the Empire disappeared and traditional rivals in Western Europe recovered from war.

The Conservatives may have managed to halt the relative decline of the British economy but without remedying its fundamental economic weaknesses. Peter Mandelson and Roger Liddle were still able in *The Blair Revolution* to point to the need to overcome Britain's relative decline (1996: viii, 1, 3, 8, 18). A report commissioned by the Labour Government from the international consultants McKinsey concluded that 'reforms to labour and capital markets in the 1980s and 1990s have halted Britain's relative decline but it still came bottom of the league table of G7 countries [in terms of output per head], and the gap shows no sign of closing' (McKinsey Global Institute, 1998: 5). McKinsey pointed to low labour productivity as the main cause of this comparatively poor performance. Another report found that British firms were investing about a third less than comparable companies in Europe, Japan and North America (*Financial Times*, 9.11.98). The Labour Government's White Paper *Our Competitive Future* published in December 1998 began by pronouncing that 'Britain's goal must be to reverse a century of relative economic decline by raising the sustainable rate of growth' in much the same way as any of its predecessors might have done since the early 1960s (Department of Trade and Industry, 1998: 6). Whether the present Government will be any more successful in addressing this problem remains to be seen.

2
The Impact of Democracy: from Parliamentary Politics to Party Politics

Introduction

Chapter 1 discussed the development of British capitalism since the Industrial Revolution and its political repercussions. It identified six phases of which perhaps the most important was the third – the period from the early 1870s to 1914 which saw the onset of Britain's relative economic decline which has dominated politics since the early 1960s. It concluded by arguing that the Conservatives may have arrested that relative economic decline but had not eliminated the motif from political discourse as the century ended.

This third phase in the development of British capitalism – from the 1870s to 1914 – coincided almost exactly with the transition from the politics of Parliamentary manoeuvring, based on a restricted franchise, to the politics of mass democracy. This change was part of the transition to a recognisably modern society: 'The years between the 1860s and the First World War transformed Britain more swiftly and more profoundly than in any other comparable era' (Shannon, 1976: 11). More recently, Jose Harris has ranked the 1870s and 1880s with the 1960s and 1970s as one of two 'great chasms' in the development of modern British society (Harris, 1994: 252).

Britain in the 1860s would still have been comprehensible to someone born in the eighteenth century, like Lord Palmerston (Prime Minister until 1865). The Census of 1871 showed that it was still a country of small towns:

> Among a population of 31 million throughout the British Isles, nearly two-thirds of the population lived in rural areas or in towns of less than 10 000 inhabitants. Even in England and Wales, rural and small-town dwellers still accounted for 45 per cent of the populace.
>
> (Harris, 1994: 41)

Only the railway had begun to effect substantial change in the urban and rural landscape. By contrast, Britain in 1914 was overwhelmingly urban and suburban: 'By 1911 [the date of the last pre-war Census], out of a total population of 45 million, 40 per cent lived in towns of over 100 000, in England and Wales more than 50 per cent.' London alone contained over 7 million inhabitants (Harris, 1994: 42). Within a few decades Britain had turned into a society of department stores and large industrial establishments, with a rapidly developing service sector. Cars, cinema, radio and aircraft would all have been recognisable to someone born, like myself, in the middle of the century.

The same period – from the 1870s to 1914 – also saw the emergence of a new middle class associated with the increasing scale of industrial and commercial operations and the growth of public-sector employment. As Max Weber observed: 'Bureaucracy inevitably accompanies modern *mass democracy*' (Gerth & Mills, 1948: 224). Employment in the Civil Service grew almost tenfold from around 30 000 in the 1860s to 280 000 by 1914 (Dowding, 1995: 22). This period also saw an immense improvement in working-class living standards: 'Probably the most rapid general improvement in the conditions of life of the nineteenth-century worker took place in the years 1880–95' (Hobsbawm, 1969: 162). It saw the consolidation of what was regarded until recently as the traditional working class – employed in large factories, organised in trade unions. Only in the last two decades has this way of life largely disappeared. In short, the period which saw the onset of Britain's relative economic decline coincided with the emergence of a modern class society. This coincidence helps to explain the governing elite's much greater concern, remarked upon in Chapter 1, with the internal challenge of an emerging democracy than with the external challenge from emerging industrial competitors.

Our concern in this chapter is with the political ramifications of this transformation. It looks first at the development of the party system prior to the 1860s, trying to explain the peculiar strength of party in Britain, where it is probably more entrenched than in any other country. It goes on to chronicle very briefly the transition to democracy between the 1860s and the achievement in 1918 of near universal suffrage. Then it examines the strategies adopted by the Liberal and Conservative Parties in the face of the challenge of an emerging democracy. It attempts, in particular, to explain why the Conservatives survived to dominate government for most of the twentieth century while the Liberals were displaced by Labour as the main party of the Left.

The development of party

As Andrew Marr has observed, 'The party system has been with us for rather longer than democracy' (Marr, 1996: 123). We can identify four stages in what might be called the 'pre-history' of party before the Second Reform Act of 1867 began the transition to democracy.

The first phase took place in what might be called the 'short seventeenth century' – from the accession of James I in 1603 to the overthrow of his grandson James II in 1688 (although some – see Plumb, 1969 – would argue that it was not concluded until 1714 when George I assumed the throne). This phase was dominated by the politics of principle: a life-and-death struggle over the nature of the regime between the proponents of absolute monarchy on the French model and the supporters of parliamentary absolutism. This conflict, which erupted in Civil War in the 1640s, was effectively settled in by the so-called 'Glorious Revolution' of 1688 although not definitively resolved until after 1714. Henceforth the monarch ruled by grace of Parliament not God. The notion of party and the terms 'Whig' and 'Tory' both originated in this period.

The second phase dominated the period from 1688 (or 1714 at the latest) until 1790 when the impact of the French Revolution began to be felt. In this period 'the rage of party gave way to the pursuit of place' (Plumb, 1969: 188). Church and King Tories were driven to the political margins after the failure of the Jacobite rising of 1715, and political parties for most of the rest of the century were reduced to the followings of rival Whig nobles in their manoeuvres for office. Political conflict was mainly about who was to enjoy the spoils of office, not over the nature of the regime or great issues of principle. Cabinet government and the office of Prime Minister emerged during this period.

The third phase from the 1790s until the Reform Act of 1832 involved a renewal of conflict over serious issues of principle centred on parliamentary reform in response to the challenges of the 'dual revolution': 'The way into the nineteenth century led across the battlefield as well as through the cotton mill and the iron foundry' (Briggs, 1959: 129). This period saw the consolidation of the landed interest, regardless of party affiliation, in what Halévy (1937, i: 33) has described as a 'parliamentary dictatorship' led by Pitt while a small minority of Whig reformers were driven to the political margin until 1830. It was brought to an end by the Reform Act of 1832 which involved a redistribution of seats in the House of Commons away from so-called 'rotten boroughs' in the pockets of peers to the emerging provincial industrial cities and a modest extension of the franchise (from 400 000 to 600 000) mainly to the middle class. The Reform Act also, incidentally, established the paramount position of the House of Commons and ended most of the residual powers of the monarch.

The justly entitled Great Reform Act of 1832 ushered in the fourth phase in the pre-history of party which lasted until the Second Reform Act of 1867. This phase saw the gradual emergence of party at the Parliamentary level comprising two main groupings – Conservatives and Liberals. This development, evident in the reconstruction of the Conservatives under Robert Peel in the 1830s, was interrupted by the division of the Party over the Repeal of the Corn Laws in 1846 and the dissolution of both main parties into factions over which Lord Palmerston presided from 1855 until his death in 1865. The death of Palmerston offered an opening for reform which was exploited by the minority Conservative administration led by Benjamin Disraeli in the House of Commons (under Prime Minister Lord Derby) in order to pass a measure of reform with the help of the radical wing of the Liberal Party. The effect of the Act was to create a predominantly working-class electorate in the towns and effectively to extend party politics from Parliament to the country at large in what John Vincent has described, in the case of the Liberal

Party, as a 'mutual convergence of provincial feeling and Parliamentary politics' (Vincent, 1972: 33).

How do we account for the importance of party in the British system of Government? Probably the best explanation is contained in Walter Bagehot's *The English Constitution* (1867), written just as the 'prehistory' of party was drawing to a close. As Ferdinand Mount, one of his shrewdest modern commentators has observed, Bagehot's basic concern is with power: 'He deals and can only deal in the coinage of power – who holds it and how much he holds' (Mount, 1992: 42). Bagehot made a famous distinction between the dignified parts of the constitution – 'those which excite and preserve the reverence of the population' – and the efficient parts – 'those by which it, in fact, works and rules'. For, 'every constitution must first *gain* authority, and then *use* authority; it must first win the loyalty and confidence of mankind, and then employ that homage in the work of government' (Bagehot, 1867: 4).

Bagehot regarded the Monarchy, the House of Lords – and even the House of Commons in some of its manifestations – as the dignified parts of the constitution. He found the main locus of power – the efficient part of the constitution – in the Cabinet. And the source of that power lay in the Cabinet's control of Parliament:

> The efficient secret of the English Constitution may be described as the close union, the nearly complete fusion, of the executive and the legislative powers ... The connecting link is *the cabinet* ... a *hyphen* which joins, a *buckle* which fastens, the legislative part of the state to the executive part of the state.
>
> (Bagehot, 1867: 9, 12)

Bagehot saw the main function of the House of Commons as being to elect the Cabinet (Bagehot, 1867: 115). The purpose of party was to assemble a majority in the House capable of electing the Cabinet and then to retain that majority in order to sustain the Government in office (Bagehot, 1867: 125). Party provided an essential means of disciplining Members of the House of Commons and thus sustaining the executive. Without party, governments would be vulnerable to the shifting allegiances of individual Members. Thus the importance of party in the British system of government is a function of the connection between the executive and the legislature and the need for the one to control the other. Bagehot was the first to identify this 'efficient secret'.

The Second Reform Act altered the rules of the political game in which governments were made and unmade in the House of Commons and the main skill of the Prime Minister (as under the French Third and Fourth Republics) lay in assembling and maintaining a majority in the House of Commons. The General Election of 1868 was the first in which the government was effectively chosen by the electorate in the way to which we have become accustomed. Disraeli created a precedent by announcing the Government's resignation before a vote of confidence in the House of Commons (Shannon, 1976: 74). His action opened the modern era in which most governments were made or broken by the electorate rather than by Parliament. The newly emerging power of the electorate created a need to mobilise party loyalties among the electorate and not just Members of the House of Commons.

The rest of this chapter examines the strategies of the Liberal and Conservative leadership for mobilising support among the electorate. But first let us survey briefly the chronology of the transition to democracy.

1867 The Second Reform Act extended the vote to householders in urban constituencies, increasing the electorate from about 1.4 million to 2.5 million, equivalent to about one-third of the adult male population, making artisans a majority of the electorate in urban areas (Shannon, 1976: 64).

1872 The Ballot Act introduced the secret ballot thus protecting voters from illegitimate pressure.

1884 The Third Reform Act extended the vote to householders in rural areas, thus increasing the electorate from 3 million to 5 million – equivalent to about 60 per cent of the adult male population (Shannon, 1976: 177). This extension of the franchise was followed in 1885 by a redistribution of seats in favour of suburban areas – effectively admitting the principle of equal weight for each vote in constituencies of approximately equal size.

1911 The Parliament Act reduced the delaying powers of the House of Lords to two years (removing them altogether for money bills) and reduced the term of Parliament from seven to five years. It also introduced payment of MPs in response to pressure from the Labour Party.

1918 The Representation of the People Act extended the vote to all men over 21 and all women over 30.

1928 The Equal Franchise Act extended votes to women over 21.

Thus the transition to democracy was a long process. It has often been compared to the gradual admission to a club: in 1867, for example, 'the vote was discussed chiefly as a kind of personal reward or certificate of good character, never as an instrument for changing the social condition of the people' (Vincent, 1972: 285). The franchise was granted only after the putative recipients demonstrated that they posed no threat to the established order.

Adjusting to democracy

Formal democracy may have been delayed until after the First World War but working men formed the majority of the urban electorate from 1868. As Peter Clarke put it: 'household suffrage inaugurated mass politics in Britain. The parties now had to project their appeal beyond Westminster' (Clarke, 1992: 21).

The extension of the franchise aroused great fears among Liberals such as Bagehot as well as Conservatives. In his famous Introduction to the Second Edition of *The English Constitution* published in 1872, Bagehot wrote: 'I am exceedingly afraid of the ignorant multitude of the new constituencies'. He argued that the objective of the established parties in the face of an emerging mass democracy should be to avoid 'a political combination of lower classes, as such and for their own objects', which could only be regarded as 'an evil of the first magnitude'. 'The higher classes' would have to exercise 'the greatest wisdom and the greatest foresight' in preventing that eventuality (Bagehot, 1867: 272).

Managing an emerging democracy was a much more pressing matter for the majority of Britain's political leaders in the late nineteenth and early twentieth centuries than reversing a process of relative economic decline that began to be evident to most of them only around the turn of the century. The rest of this chapter looks at the strategies adopted by key political leaders between the 1860s and the 1920s when the Labour Party emerged as the main opposition to the Conservatives. The purpose is not to offer a blow-by-blow political history of more than half a century but rather to focus on the strategies followed in each of three succeeding phases beginning with the aftermath of the Second Reform Act.

Phase 1: Liberal dominance 1868–86

The Liberals held office for all but 6 of these 18 years (1868–74, 1880–6). They were the first party to develop links with a mass electorate dominated by small shopkeepers and artisans to whom they were able to appeal through their stress on independence and autonomy (Vincent, 1972: 119). We can identify two main strategies for winning power, the first associated with William Ewart Gladstone ('The People's William') and the second with Joseph Chamberlain ('Radical Joe').

Gladstone led the Liberal Party from 1868 until 1894 (although he ceded the formal position after electoral defeat in 1875). He entered the House of Commons as a Conservative in 1832. The Whig *Globe* newspaper described him in 1834 as exhibiting 'the most zealous adherence to the most antiquated and obnoxious principles of his party', while Macaulay famously described him in 1839 as 'the rising hope of those stern and unbending Tories' who chafed under Peel's caution and moderation (Shannon, 1999: 43, 82). He went on to hold office under Peel as President of the Board of Trade before resigning in 1845 over the payment of government grants to the Catholic seminary Maynooth College in Ireland. The origins of his famous rivalry with Benjamin Disraeli lay in the opposing sides which they took over the Repeal of the Corn Laws that split the party in 1846. Disraeli won the House of Commons leadership of the Protectionist rump of the Conservative Party while Gladstone followed his mentor Peel into the centre ground from which he emerged only in the 1860s as leader of the Liberal party following the death of Palmerston. Gladstone's instincts remained aristocratic. As he confided to his diary in 1878: 'I am a firm believer in the aristocratic principle – the rule of the best. I am an out-and-out inegalitarian' (cited Clarke, 1992: 32). His aim, in Clarke's words, was 'to perpetuate the rule of a high-minded liberal aristocracy by founding it upon the secure basis of popular consent' (Clarke, 1992: 40).

Gladstone's strategy for ensuring the continued 'rule of the best' was to focus on grand moral issues capable of mobilising a broad coalition of support from liberal intellectuals such as John Morley or J. S. Mill, through the broad ranks of provincial Nonconformity to small businessmen, artisans and trade unionists. These were issues such as the disestablishment of the Church of Ireland (1868), the immorality of Conservative foreign policy in the Balkans (1880) and Home Rule for Ireland (1885 and 1892). His purpose essentially was to sustain the Liberal coalition by avoiding issues concerning the redistribution of wealth and economic intervention which would be bound to sunder it. As Clarke put it, 'Gladstone's populism was ... the means of avoiding socialism under democracy' (Clarke, 1992: 40).

The weakness of this strategy was that it aroused expectations that could not be met: 'There was always the likelihood, therefore, with Gladstone, that expectation would outrun achievement; that high hopes would end up with disappointment; and this indeed would prove to be the pattern of his administrations' (Shannon, 1976: 70–1). The appeal of moral crusades which offered mainly psychic satisfactions to Liberal voters was bound to diminish as social concerns became more important as a result of the changing character of the working class in the late nineteenth century.

Joseph Chamberlain was a Birmingham businessman who rose to prominence as Lord Mayor in the 1870s and leader of the Liberal extra-parliamentary party organisation. From these bases he became leader of the Radical wing of the Liberal Party until Gladstone divided the party over Irish Home Rule in 1886 and Chamberlain led the Liberal Unionists into opposition. Chamberlain recognised the emergence of a new class politics. In 1882 he argued that 'the politics of the future are social politics' (Clarke, 1992: 67). In a famous speech in 1885 he asked 'what ransom will property pay for the security it enjoys?' (Shannon, 1976: 185).

Chamberlain's strategy was to mobilise the working men who formed a decisive majority of the electorate after the Reform Act of 1884 behind a programme of political and social reform. He fought the 1885 General Election on the basis of the so-called 'unauthorised programme' (often described as the first modern party manifesto) including the old Chartist demands for adult suffrage and payment for MPs as well as various measures of social reform including free elementary education and local authority provision of small-holdings (Shannon, 1976: 185).

This challenge was one of the factors that led Gladstone in 1886 to precipitate the split in the Party over Home Rule. He drove out both Chamberlain and many of his followers on the Left and most of the remaining Whig aristocrats on the Right. Both eventually coalesced with the Conservatives as the Unionist Party. In the short term Gladstone won the Party for his kind of politics but in so doing weakened the Liberals and ensured that they would be out of office for all but 3 of the next 19 years. Gladstone's resignation in 1894 following the House of Lords' rejection of his Second Home Rule Bill in 1893 marked the final failure of Gladstone's strategy following the frustration of Chamberlain's strategy in 1886.

Phase 2: Conservative dominance 1886–1905

The Liberal division over Home Rule for Ireland allowed the Conservatives to hold power for all but 3 of the next 19 years (1886–92, 1895–1905). The Conservatives developed two main strategies for winning and using power. The first, developed by Benjamin Disraeli (leader 1868–81) and continued by Lord Salisbury (leader 1881–1902) was to establish the Conservatives as the 'national party'. Disraeli was primarily responsible for creating the 'one nation' strand of Conservatism. Salisbury perceived class as the main political divide in an emerging mass democracy and saw that an increasingly radical Liberal Party would arouse opposition that the Conservatives would be able to mobilise.

Salisbury's strategy, therefore, was to conciliate the working class while at the same time mobilising the expanding middle-class, suburban vote behind the Conservatives. As he remarked in 1882: 'I believe there is a great deal of Villa Toryism which requires organisation' (Clarke, 1992: 53). The weakness of this strategy was that the defence of established interests in an increasingly conservative society offered no strategy for arresting Britain's relative economic decline which began to be perceived as the key issue by the time he resigned in 1902 (to be replaced by his nephew Arthur Balfour).

The alternative strategy was developed by Joseph Chamberlain in his Unionist phase. The fact that he was responsible for devising forward-looking strategies for both of the two main parties marked him as one of most creative of all British politicians. Winston

Churchill described him, in a famous phrase, as 'the one who made the weather' in the early 1900s (Clarke, 1992: 2). Chamberlain's strategy in the 1890s and early 1900s was to attempt to forestall class polarisation with a new form of political mobilisation by the Right that anticipates elements of thc fascist programme advanced by Oswald Mosley in the 1930s (Clarke, 1992: 77–81; Gamble, 1994: 165–6). In the 1890s he was the first to advocate old age pensions, as a way of winning working-class votes. By the early 1900s he was advocating a programme of tariff reform to bind the empire together in the face of the external challenge from the USA and Germany and meet the internal challenge from Labour with social reform. The opportunity to implement these ideas was lost following the decisive defeat of the Conservatives in the 1906 General Election. Chamberlain was incapacitated by a severe stroke shortly afterwards and died in 1914. Tariff Reform split the Conservative Party and contributed to their landslide defeat in 1906. They did not form their own government again until 1922, by which time the opportunity perceived by Chamberlain – to build an imperial power to rival the USA – had passed.

Phase 3: the death agony of Liberalism 1906–22

Let us begin with three snapshots which encapsulate the precipitous decline of the Liberal Party. The first portrays them in 1906 following the landslide victory which returned 377 Liberal MPs flanked by 83 Irish Nationalist and 53 Labour MPs, the first contingent to enter the House of Commons in any numbers, plenipotentiaries of an increasingly organised and assertive working class (Shannon, 1976: 378). The second portrays them in 1910 after the two General Elections of that year reduced the number of Liberal MPs to 272, the same as the Conservatives, thus making the Liberal Government dependent on the Irish Nationalists (who would disappear from Parliament following the General Election of 1918 when Sinn Fein won the majority of seats in Ireland and refused to take their places at Westminster) and Labour (40 seats) (Shannon, 1976: 400). The third portrays them after the 1918 Election which returned only 26 Liberal MPs opposed to the Coalition headed by David Lloyd George, placing them second to the Labour Party whose 59 MPs now formed the Official Opposition (Taylor, 1970: 175). This debacle was the result of the wartime split between the respective adherents of Herbert Asquith and Lloyd George who replaced him as Prime Minister in 1916. The Liberals went on to make a limited recovery in the 1920s but never won more seats than Labour and after 1931 ceased to exist as a significant force in British politics until the 1970s.

One of the great questions in modern British political history is how to explain what one historian famously described as 'The Strange Death of Liberal England' (Dangerfield, 1935). The key agent in the decline of the Liberal Party, and the most creative politician of the early twentieth century, was David Lloyd George (Chancellor of the Exchequer 1908–15, Minister of Munitions 1915–16 and Prime Minister 1916–22). Perhaps the best way to understand Lloyd George is as the heir to Joseph Chamberlain in his radical phase. He advanced two distinct strategies for sustaining the Liberal Party in the face of the challenge from the Labour Party.

The first, seen most clearly during his early years as Chancellor of the Exchequer, involved promoting social reform as an alternative to socialism which emerged suddenly as a bogey following Victor Grayson's victory in the Colne Valley by-election in 1907 (Shannon, 1976: 392, 397). Lloyd George's speech at Newcastle in 1909 echoed Chamberlain by threatening the moneyed classes with revolution if they did not submit to the reasonable imposts of the Liberals (Shannon, 1976: 382). His famous 'People's Budget' of 1909 was designed to mobilise 'the people' behind the Liberal Government in a conflict with the House of Lords controlled by the Conservatives. The main thrust of this most political of budgets was to tax the rich to pay for social reform (in the form of national insurance).

This strategy proved to be self-defeating. Conflict with the Conservatives had the effect of arousing Labour militancy. It led to a series of bitter strikes just before the outbreak of war and contributed to the growing strength of the trade unions. Thus it had the effect of driving the Liberals' middle-class supporters into the arms of the Conservatives. The two General Elections of 1910 fought over the People's Budget and reform of the House of Lords left the Government dependent on the Irish Nationalists and bogged down in a struggle over Home Rule that won few votes among mainland voters.

Lloyd George's second strategy can be seen most clearly during the years from 1918 to 1922 when he headed the post-war Coalition Government sustained by the Conservatives as the largest party in the House of Commons after the 1918 Election fought immediately after the Armistice. Stanley Baldwin famously described these massed ranks of Conservative MPs as 'hard-faced men who looked as if they had done well out of the war' (cited Taylor, 1970: 175). During this period Lloyd George's strategy was to create a Centre party to resist the Labour Party now endowed with a fully socialist platform. Unfortunately for Lloyd George, the Conservative Party was already well-placed to take advantage of widespread fear of Labour among the propertied classes. As A. J. P. Taylor put it,

> The rise of the Labour party, which seemed to disrupt the pattern of politics, paradoxically restored the two party system in a new form. Class became the determining factor in party allegiance, and there was no place for Lloyd George, the man who bounced from one class to another.
>
> (Taylor, 1961: 281)

Lloyd George thrived on crisis and was eventually driven from office in 1922 – once the immediate post-war crisis had passed – by the famous 'revolt of the cabin boys' (as Lord Birkenhead described the Conservative backbenchers). Their leader Baldwin described him as 'a great dynamic force ... a very terrible thing' (Taylor, 1970: 250) – an epithet that might have been applied to Margaret Thatcher who was expelled from office in similar fashion. Lloyd George never held office again. The inter-war period was dominated by the Conservatives led by Baldwin and Joseph Chamberlain's son Neville who were more capable of defending the interests of the propertied classes against the challenge of Labour than an essentially artificial Centre party led by Lloyd George would have been.

Conclusion

The period between the Second Reform Act of 1867 and the First World War marked the onset of Britain's relative economic decline and the transition to mass democracy which plunged both the Liberal and Conservative Parties into prolonged crisis. The Liberals failed to surmount this crisis because they failed to develop a strategy for winning and holding working-class support. The more the party appealed to working-class interests, as over the

People's Budget and social reform, the more it antagonised middle-class supporters and the more it aroused expectations among the working class which the Labour Party, with its links to expanding trade unions (with 4 million members in 1914, rising to 8 million in 1920 – Hobsbawm, 1969: Table 51), was better placed to exploit.

Lloyd George could have retained office in the face of the growing polarisation of British politics in the early twentieth century only by putting himself at the head of a 'Progressive' party containing both Liberal and Labour MPs. But Lloyd George thought in traditional Liberal and Radical terms of 'the people' against 'the classes' (meaning the upper classes). A. J. P. Taylor summed up the problem facing Lloyd George in the following way: 'Where once the typical man of the people had been a shopkeeper (preferably a cobbler [famous for their radicalism in the nineteenth century]), he was now a shop steward. With him, Lloyd George's magic failed to work' (Taylor, 1970: 147). Only the disappearance of the organised working class as a significant political force in the 1980s would permit the rise of a new kind of progressive politics seeking to merge the two traditions on the Left of British politics which bifurcated in the early part of the century. In this sense,'Tony Blair is returning his party to the liberalism of Lloyd George' (Beer, 1998: 24).

By contrast, the Conservative Party was well-placed to benefit from the flight of middle-class voters from the Liberal Party and from their fear of Labour, especially in the aftermath of the Russian Revolution and in the climate of post-war working-class militancy which ended only with the defeat of the General Strike in 1926. But, as we shall see in Chapter 3, the Conservative Party of Baldwin and Neville Chamberlain was ill-equipped to carry out the programme of national reconstruction in the face of relative economic decline as envisaged by Joseph Chamberlain.

3
Warfare and Welfare: the Road to 1945 and the Post-War Consensus

Introduction

Chapter 1 discussed structural change in British capitalism since the Industrial Revolution while Chapter 2 looked at the transition to mass democracy which coincided almost exactly with the onset of Britain's relative economic decline. The gradual extension of the franchise was an essentially conservative process – the vote was given only when the new voters had shown that they could be trusted not to vote for radical change. It was, in effect, the mark of admission to a club of the politically trustworthy. Thus it was no accident that votes for all men and most women had to wait until after a war in which over two-and-a-half million men volunteered to fight (and nearly three-quarter of a million died) and over a million women entered the labour force for the first time, often in jobs previously done by men (Taylor, 1970: 48, 165; Marwick, 1970: 105). War was the key factor in the completion of formal political democracy in Britain (as it was also in Germany).

Britain in the late nineteenth century faced serious economic competitors after almost a century of unchallenged hegemony. However, most of the governing elite were primarily concerned to manage the transition to mass democracy. Then, for most of the first half of the twentieth century – in what Hobsbawm has called the Age of Catastrophe – this elite faced the threat or reality of the even more severe external challenge of war in which victory depended upon their ability to mobilise the mass of the population.

The twentieth century opened with Britain still engaged in the Boer War in which the entire might of the Empire was needed in order to defeat two small republics capable of putting only a few tens of thousands of soldiers into the field. The Boer War also revealed the hostility of other states in Europe. It prompted Britain's first peacetime alliance – with Japan in 1902 – followed by a near alliance with France in 1904 which extended to Russia in 1907. Britain was able to reach agreement with these two other imperial powers in order better to resist the looming threat from Germany.

The First World War was unprecedented in its scale and in the demands which it made upon all of the countries at war. This was a total war in which defeat resulted in political collapse and exhaustion followed victory. It was followed by several years of instability at home and overseas. The threat of war with Turkey precipitated the fall of the Lloyd George Coalition in 1922.

The Second World War could be seen coming since the early 1930s; in March 1932 the Government cancelled the famous ten year rule, adopted in 1919, that no great war need be expected for the next ten years (Taylor, 1970: 292, 450). By the middle of the decade Britain faced potential threats from Japan, Italy and Germany. The eventual war proved to be even more desperate than the First World War.

What came to be known as the Cold War could in its turn be seen coming by the closing stages of the Second World War, as British troops intervened in Greece in December 1944 to suppress the rising led by the Greek Communists. By 1946 Churchill was talking about an 'iron curtain' descending upon Europe from Stettin on the Baltic to Trieste on the Adriatic. Britain played a major role in the creation of NATO in 1949 and rearmed against the threat of a Soviet invasion of Europe at the time of the Korean War in 1950. Only by the mid-1950s did the fear of war begin to lift. The Suez debacle of 1956 exposed the hollowness of British pretensions to great-power status. Conscription was ended in 1958. Only then, on the eve of the 1960s, did the burden of military mobilisation cease to weigh upon the population.

During the same period – the first half of the twentieth century – the British political elite also faced an unprecedented internal challenge from the Labour Party. Here at last was the party of the working class that Bagehot had warned against in 1872. The rise of the Labour Party – from the revival of working-class militancy and the emergence of the first socialist societies (the Fabians and the Social Democratic Federation) in the 1880s to the first majority Labour Government in 1945 – was a long process. The main landmarks were as follows.

1900 The Labour Representation Committee was founded by the Trades Union Congress (TUC) (with Ramsay MacDonald – eventually the first Labour Prime Minister – as secretary) with the aim of securing direct representation of the trade unions in Parliament in order to reverse legal judgments damaging to industrial action. Thus the trade union link was important right from the outset (Shannon, 1976: 295).

1906 Fifty-three Labour Party MPs were elected to the House of Commons where they operated mainly as 'a sectional pressure group, a satellite to the Liberal sun' (Shannon, 1976: 381).

1915 Labour entered government for the first time as part of the first Coalition Government headed by Herbert Asquith. Arthur Henderson, leader of the pro-war majority of the party, served as Minister of Education until he resigned from the War Cabinet in 1917 on the question of Labour Party attendance at the Stockholm Conference of socialist parties to discuss the terms of a negotiated peace. George Barnes took Henderson's place in the War Cabinet while the other Labour Ministers remained in office (Taylor, 1970: 129).

1918 Labour was founded as a national party, with a socialist constitution drafted by Henderson and Sidney Webb. The party broadened its scope and potential electoral appeal by including anti-war Liberal intellectuals as well as trade unionists. Fifty-nine MPs were elected in the 1918 General Election compared with only 26 Asquithian Liberals. Labour now became the official Opposition in Parliament (Taylor, 1970: 130, 175).

1924 Labour formed its first minority government headed by Ramsay MacDonald. Dependent on Liberal support, it lasted less than a year.

1929 Labour formed its second minority government which lasted until the 1931 crisis which led to the fall of the Labour Government and the formation of the National Government led by Ramsay MacDonald. The party split and won only 52 seats in the subsequent election.

1940 Labour entered the Coalition Government under Churchill, with senior posts in the main domestic ministries. Clement Attlee served as Deputy Prime Minister, and his colleagues Ernest Bevin, Herbert Morrison, Stafford Cripps and Hugh Dalton occupied senior posts.

1945 Labour formed its first majority government headed by Attlee. The Government lost its secure majority in the 1950 Election and was defeated in the 1951 Election. Since then the Labour Party has won office with a firm majority on only two occasions – in 1966 (under Harold Wilson) and in 1997 under Tony Blair. No Labour Government has ever served for two whole terms.

Thus Labour formed a majority government for the first time almost forty years after the first Labour MPs entered the House of Commons and after two previous minority governments, of which the first achieved little and the second ended in disaster. The men who led the 1945 Government had already served a long and arduous apprenticeship in office since 1940. Thus by 1945 the challenge from Labour had been thoroughly blunted.

This chapter will argue that the welfare state and what has come to be known as the post-war consensus were the products of the interaction of two challenges – the external challenge of war and the internal challenge from Labour, both the working class in general and the Labour Party in particular. It begins by looking at the origins of the welfare state in the reforms of the last Liberal Government. Then it considers the impact of the First World War with the aim of trying to explain why the Lloyd George Coalition failed to deliver its promise of 'a fit country for heroes to live in' (subsequently transformed into 'homes fit for heroes' – Hennessy, 1992: 168). It goes on to examine the inter-war period, with the aim of trying to explain why successive governments – and notably the Labour Government of 1929–31 – failed to overcome the problem of mass unemployment. Finally it considers the impact of the Second World War with the aim of explaining its role in creating the consensus that endured until the 1970s.

The origins of the welfare state

It would be misleading to think of the welfare state as a distinctively socialist or social democratic creation. It was invented by the German Chancellor Bismarck in the 1880s at the same time as he was trying to suppress the infant Social Democratic Party. Two factors were at work in explaining the origins of the welfare state in Britain in the decade before 1914. First, at the level of political strategy, it can be seen as a device for maintaining working-class support for the Liberals, as discussed in Chapter 2. It had the effect of alienating middle-class voters and therefore polarising politics to the ultimate benefit of the class-based Labour and Conservative parties. Secondly, it can be seen as a means of promoting 'national efficiency' in an age when commercial success – and possibly national survival in war – was increasingly seen to depend upon the physical and intellectual quality of the population as a whole.

The Boer War played a key role in stimulating concern over the physical condition of the working class. One frequently-cited survey found that only 1000 out of 11 000 volunteers for the army from Manchester were fit for overseas service, and only another 2000 fit for home service (Searle, 1971: 60). These findings inspired Beatrice and Sidney Webb's concern to provide a 'national minimum' standard of social services; they were the first to call for a National Health Service (Searle, 1971: 239). Specific reforms included the Conservative Education Act of 1902, setting up a system of secondary education provided by local education authorities created for that purpose, and three notable Liberal measures: the Education Act of 1907, providing for school meals and regular medical tests for schoolchildren, the Old Age Pensions Act of 1908 providing for the first non-contributory pensions and the National Insurance Act of 1911, providing unemployment insurance for some two and three-quarters of a million workers in industries particularly vulnerable to the trade cycle. The first two measures reflect concern for the rising generation characteristic of enthusiasts for national efficiency; the last two reflect pressures from Labour.

The First World War

The First World War led to a massive expansion in the role of the state particularly in the two pillars of the opposing alliances, Britain and Germany. In Britain public expenditure rose from about 15 per cent of national income in 1913 to over 70 per cent in 1918, declining to around 30 per cent by the 1920s, where it remained until the late 1930s (Hicks, 1954: 11). War resulted in the creation of 12 new government departments and 160 new boards of commissioners; the number of civilians employed by central government rose from 325 000 in 1914 to 850 000 in 1918 (Cronin, 1991: 71–2).

> By the end of the war the twenty clerks of the Contracts Department in August 1914 had grown to 65 000 officials in the mighty Ministry of Munitions set up by Lloyd George in 1915, which came to control 2 million workers in 250 government factories, mines and quarries, and another 1.4 million in 20 000 controlled establishments.
>
> (Perkin, 1989: 228)

The First World War enhanced the role of Labour in two main ways. First, it brought the Labour Party into government for the first time (in the interests of national solidarity; the same was true in France and Germany). Participation in government accelerated Labour's emergence as a national party in 1918. Secondly, the experience of full employment and the key role of labour in war production enhanced the role of the trade unions whose officials served on a wide array of committees and advisory bodies dealing with production and the distribution of food and fuel (Cronin, 1991: 48). Lloyd George helped to establish his wartime reputation through his skill in negotiating productivity deals (so-called dilution). On one occasion he told militant Clydesiders, 'I'm as keen a Socialist as any of you' (cited Taylor, 1970: 64). Judging by Glasgow's reputation as a bastion of socialism during the later years of the war and in the 1920s Lloyd George's appeal seems largely to have fallen on deaf ears. Trade union membership reached eight million by 1920 (more than today) (Taylor, 1970: 191). The Russian Revolution also had the effect of enhancing the role of the working class, through the fears which it aroused among the middle class and the political elite as well as the heightened expectations and confidence which it stimulated among the working class.

The Lloyd George Coalition carried out modest reforms on the lines of the pre-war Liberal Government, including a house building programme and an extension of social insurance from less than 3 million to some 12 million people (Taylor, 1970: 198), thus playing a key role in mitigating the social and political effects of unemployment as well as undermining the intended downward pressure on wages from the return to the Gold Standard after 1925.

But – as we saw in Chapter 2 – Lloyd George remained very much a prisoner of the Conservative MPs who formed the bulk of his parliamentary supporters. Once recession set in after 1920 the Government's priority was to cut public spending, which forced an end to Lloyd George's reforming ambitions.

Between the wars

The period from 1922 to 1940 was dominated by the Conservatives apart from the two short-lived minority Labour Governments. The key domestic problem facing governments of this period was unemployment: the so-called 'intractable million', 10 per cent of the working population unable to find work throughout the 1920s. This figure rose to three million by 1932 before falling to one-and-a-half million by the mid-1930s. Full employment was restored only as a result of rearmament after 1938 (Skidelsky, 1970: 15, 423). This problem was the result of the collapse of traditional markets for the staple Victorian industries and an inability to win a leading share in export markets for new products (Skidelsky, 1992: 131).

Both of the main parties – Conservatives and Labour alike – were prisoners of what might be called the 'inter-war consensus' that governments could do little to mitigate unemployment – what Paul Addison has called 'a consensus to prevent anything unusual happening' (Addison, 1994: 14). The Conservatives believed that the solution to Britain's post-war problems was to return to the vanished world of pre-war normality, hence the 1925 return to the Gold Standard at the pre-war parity which simply pushed up export prices and worsened unemployment – and generated a round of wage-cutting that led to the General Strike of 1926. Labour believed that unemployment was the inevitable product of capitalism which could be overcome only by socialism. Unfortunately Labour had no strategy for achieving that goal: 'Socialism was impossible and capitalism was doomed: there was nothing [for Labour] to do but govern without conviction a system it did not believe in but saw no real prospect of changing' (Skidelsky, 1970: 433).

Governments of both main parties failed. The return to the Gold Standard failed to revive British industry and the Conservatives went down to defeat in 1929. The second Labour Government failed to prevent rising unemployment and was driven from power in

1931. The National Government was forced to leave the Gold Standard anyway. These successive failures helped to create the mood of self-doubt and defeatism that nourished appeasement of Hitler in the late 1930s.

Paradoxically only marginal parties and politicians had any constructive ideas for dealing with the problem of unemployment. Lloyd George inspired by Keynes published a manifesto entitled *We Can Conquer Unemployment* in 1929 but the Liberals won only 59 seats in the election. Frustration drove that maverick Keynesian Oswald Mosley out of the Labour Government in 1930 and eventually into the wilderness of fascism. The Independent Labour Party, with their plans for reducing unemployment by boosting working-class purchasing power, carried little weight with Labour Ministers and they left the party in 1932. 'Thus were the "bold" men driven to political suicide, while Britain, complacent and insular, came to the verge of disaster' (Skidelsky, 1970: 424).

The Second World War and after

The outbreak of the Second World War and the disasters of spring 1940 represented a comprehensive defeat for inter-war Conservatism. Churchill's Coalition Government brought the 'bold' men to power. Successful prosecution of the war meant mobilising the masses; it required a shift to the Left.

The post-war consensus was the product of the wartime convergence between four separate streams. First were the Conservative radicals like Churchill, Eden, Macmillan and Boothby who had resisted appeasement. Second was a Labour Party led by men like Attlee, Morrison and Dalton, and supported by a younger generation of men like Douglas Jay, Evan Durbin, Harold Wilson and Hugh Gaitskell, who had been exposed to the influence of Keynes. All were determined to achieve practical reforms after the disaster of 1931. A third factor was the rise to positions of power and influence of middle-class progressive intellectuals such as Keynes at the Treasury and Beveridge at the Ministry of Labour and then head of an inter-departmental inquiry into social security. 1941 saw the publication of the first Keynesian budget and 1942 the publication of the Beveridge Report which held out a prospect of social security for all plus a National Health Service.

A fourth factor was a change in the popular mood compounded of several ingredients. First was a wholesale rejection of the Conservatives who were blamed for the debacle of 1940 – they were the *Guilty Men* in the title of a famous book. Second was the need for planning to deliver the mass mobilisation needed for military victory which allowed Labour to seize the intellectual initiative. It also increased the role of the state: public expenditure rose to over 80 per cent of national income (Hicks, 1954: 11). Third, total war generated social pressure for equality of sacrifice: 'The moral code of a society at war demanded that no-one should benefit unduly from a collective effort in which men were getting killed' (Addison, 1994: 131). The Second World War bore much more heavily on civilians than the First World War had done: more civilians than fighting men died in first three years of war (Titmuss, 1958: 82). A fourth ingredient was the renewal of the traditional industrial working class that had been weakened by the chronic mass unemployment of the inter-war years (McKibbin, 1998: 531). Finally, admiration for the Soviet contribution to victory increased support for planning and socialism and lent weight to the collective aspirations of the working class.

Thus the Labour victory in 1945 should have come as no surprise. It was the product of a conviction that things had to change. The 1942 Beveridge Report sold 635 000 copies; opinion polls showed that the middle class were just as much in favour of universal social security as the working class who would be the main beneficiaries. In 1943 a sceptical Churchill felt obliged to promise 'national compulsory insurance for all classes for all purposes from cradle to grave'. The 1944 White Paper on Employment Policy promised 'a high and stable level of employment after the war' (Addison, 1994: 217, 218, 228, 246).

The change in the public mood is well-illustrated by two quotes. In 1943 the Conservative Quintin Hogg told the House of Commons during a debate on the proposed minimum wage for catering workers: 'If you do not give the people social reform, they are going to give you revolution' (Addison, 1994: 232). Ernest Bevin described a meeting between himself and Churchill and troops about to attack on D-Day:

> They were going off to face this terrific battle with great hearts and great courage. The one question they put to me when I went

> through their ranks was 'Ernie, when we have done this job for you are we going back on the dole?' ... Both the Prime Minister and I answered: 'No, you are not.'
>
> (Addison, 1994: 242)

The Second World War had hardly come to an end when the Cold War began. This was not a desperate war for survival like the First and Second World Wars. It was rather an ideological struggle with a society that promised a new and superior civilisation with free welfare for all – an appeal which endured until the early 1960s while the military threat lasted another twenty-odd years. Therefore Western politicians had to offer their own system of universal welfare as part of this 'great contest'. It is unrealistic to argue, like Correlli Barnett, that the welfare state – what he described contemptuously as 'New Jerusalem' – could have been withheld in 1945 (Barnett, 1995). At least some part of Chamberlain's ransom now had to be paid.

Conclusion

The foundations of the post-war consensus were laid by what Hugh Dalton liked to call 'the Churchill-Labour Government' of 1940–5 (cited Clarke, 1992: 178). Its construction was completed and consolidated by the Labour Government of 1945–51, and largely accepted by the Churchill Government after 1951. The main ingredients in what has been described variously as 'Keynesian social democracy', 'the Keynesian welfare state' or 'the post-war settlement' were the mixed economy (nationalisation of the public utilities while retaining private ownership of most of the economy), full employment, conciliation of the trade unions and universal welfare.

The existence of consensus on these main policy issues does not mean that there was complete agreement between the two main parties. There remained differences over particular policies (for example, over commercial television and iron and steel nationalisation). Each main party drew electoral support from distinct classes, and each had its own distinct political philosophy. The post-war consensus has been well-defined as 'the philosophy of the overlap' between the two main parties (Marquand, 1988: 18). It was essentially 'a Whitehall consensus', 'an elitist exercise' (Addison, 1994: 281, 284).

The crucial weakness of the post-war consensus was that it assumed that the economic problem – the problem of Britain's relative economic decline which had surfaced in the first decade of the century – had been solved. As the Labour revisionist Anthony Crosland put it in *The Future of Socialism* published in 1956: 'I no longer regard questions of growth and efficiency as being, on a long view, of primary importance to socialism. We stand, in Britain, on the threshold of mass abundance.' At that time he was still able to compare Britain's economic performance in the post-war decade favourably with other countries (cited Pliatzky, 1982: 44). Politics for Left and Right alike seemed to be just a matter of distributing the surplus generated by an economic growth that could be taken for granted. Britain's part in defeating Hitler and building NATO bolstered the self-confidence of the governing elite. The strains began to show by the end of the 1950s as Britain's relative economic decline became increasingly obvious and the new post-war generation which grew up in an age of affluence failed to show the same solidarity and conformity as the wartime generation. But that is the subject of Chapter 4.

4

The Great Moving Right Show: the Crisis of the Mid-1970s and the Rise of Thatcherism

Introduction

Chapter 3 argued that the post-war consensus – commonly understood to cover the mixed economy, a commitment to full employment, conciliation of trade unions and universal welfare – was a response to two challenges: the external challenge of war, which dominated the first half of the twentieth century, and the internal challenge posed by the rise of labour in the shape of the Labour Party itself and the growth of trade union membership (from about two million in 1900 to almost ten million in 1950).

The failure of appeasement and the military disasters of spring 1940 discredited the inter-war consensus dominated by the Conservatives. Mere national survival, let alone victory, was seen to depend upon state intervention on an unprecedented scale, conciliation of the trade unions and a commitment to full employment and welfare for all after the war. The foundations of the post-war consensus were laid by the Churchill Coalition, consolidated by the Attlee Government of 1945–51 and accepted by the Conservative Government after 1951.

This consensus was the product not only of wartime exigencies but also of the uniquely favourable economic circumstances of the post-war years – the long boom based on fixed exchange rates under the Bretton Woods agreement reached in 1944, trade liberalisation presided over by the USA, Marshall Aid and the adoption of American industrial techniques. The Conservatives reaped the benefit of rising living standards in the 1950s, winning three elections in a row (1951, 1955 and 1959). This was the era of 'never had it so good'.

Chapters 4 and 5 examine the responses of the two main parties to Britain's increasing economic problems which came to a head in what Samuel Beer has described as 'the crisis of the mid-1970s' (Beer, 1982: 95). This chapter seeks to explain the breakdown of the post-war consensus beginning in the late 1950s with a renewed awareness of Britain's relative economic decline and culminating in the political and economic crisis of the mid-1970s which gave birth to Thatcherism. It examines the course of Thatcherism and the significance of the prolonged Major interlude, and concludes with a discussion of the 1997 Election and future prospects for the Conservative Party.

The return of the economic problem

In an important analysis of the breakdown of the post-war consensus, *The Unprincipled Society*, David Marquand identifies three phases in what he calls 'the thirty-year-long Keynesian social democratic ascendancy' (as he describes the post-war consensus) (1988: 42–7). The initial 'heroic' phase spanned most of the 1940s and included an element of physical planning of manpower and industrial investment which was abandoned by the end of the decade because industry and trade unions disliked it and Whitehall was not up to the job. The second, extending from the late 1940s until the early 1960s, involved what Marquand called the arms-length management of the economy through the levers of interest rates and tax and public spending which could be readily pulled by the Treasury. The last phase, extending from the early 1960s until the final breakdown in the so-called 'Winter of Discontent' of 1978–9, involved an increasingly interventionist, or 'hands-on', approach to economic management – the 'growthmanship' or 'hubristic Keynesianism' inaugurated by Macmillan in the early 1960s (Beer, 1982: 38). The rest of this section examines the reasons for the failure of both 'arms-length' and 'hands-on' Keynesianism.

The post-war Labour Government abandoned its aspirations to physical planning by the late 1940s and steadily reduced rationing and other controls. Stafford Cripps's first budget in April 1948 has generally been taken to mark the inauguration of a reliance upon what came to be regarded as the traditional Keynesian techniques of demand management for steering the economy: a combination of fiscal policy (tax increases and reductions) and monetary policy (increases or reductions in bank rate which determined interest rates in the economy as a whole). This sort of 'arms-length' economic management suited the Conservatives after 1951 (hence the famous expression 'Butskellism' which combined the names of Hugh Gaitskell, the last Labour Chancellor, and R. A. Butler, the first Conservative Chancellor). Manipulation of aggregate demand by fiscal and monetary levers was perfectly consistent with a reliance on the market for allocating resources within the economy. The Conservative Governments of the 1950s were the first to master the black arts of manipulating the economy for electoral advantage, through tax cuts and interest rate cuts ahead of elections followed by increases afterwards. Edmund Dell has described the outcome of the 1955 Election as 'the first Keynesian election victory' (Dell, 1997: 199). The Conservatives managed to repeat the trick in 1959 but narrowly missed in 1964.

However, the continued commitment to maintaining the exchange value of sterling meant that any surge in imports or increase in inflation had to be choked off by increases in tax or interest rates in order to avoid a run on sterling. This practice led in turn to the problem of repeated 'stop–go' episodes which were eventually seen to have undermined investment and economic growth (Dell, 1997: 285). This practice was one of the factors blamed for Britain's relatively poor economic performance which began to be apparent by the late 1950s. It gave rise to a spate of books described by Christopher Booker as 'the What's Wrong With Britain movement' (Booker, 1970: 157).

This spate of books began soberly enough with the prosaically titled *British Economic Policy since the War* (Shonfield, 1958). The rising panic is conveyed by the titles of subsequent volumes, from *The Establishment* (Thomas, 1959), through *The Stagnant Society* (Shanks, 1961) and concluding with *Suicide of a Nation?* (Koestler, 1963). Samuel Brittan's *The Treasury under the Tories* (1964) was a more prosaic but equally critical and influential analysis of the Conservative Government's record.

Shonfield's seminal book set out the harsh facts in a table which compared economic growth in Britain and the six members of the

European Economic Community (set up in 1958) during the years 1952–6. It showed Britain, with a 15 per cent increase in national output, in fifth place behind West Germany (38 per cent), the Netherlands (27 per cent), Italy (26 per cent) and France (20 per cent), with only Belgium and Luxembourg performing worse than Britain with 13 per cent (1958: 14). Shonfield's recommendation was for a British Five Year Plan on the French model supported by exchange controls and a wages policy. For him,

> It goes without saying that a Government which embarked on the plan of expansion would have to be prepared to intervene directly, by orders, by threats, by incentives, and by exhortation – whichever happens to be the most promising technique – in the private sector of the economy.

He envisaged an entirely new role for the Government in overcoming what he described as 'resistances' to economic growth (294). Thus was the agenda set for the switch to 'hands-on' management of the economy.

The frustrations of modernisation

The first steps in this direction were taken by Macmillan in the early 1960s with the explicit objective of 'modernisation'. Macmillan himself presided over fortnightly meetings of the progress-chasing Steering Committee on the Modernisation of Great Britain (Lowe, 1997: 611). The main fruit of this modernisation drive was the establishment in 1962 of the National Economic Development Council (NEDC), based on the French model of indicative planning, at the same time as Britain applied to join what was then called the Common Market. The NEDC's purpose was to bring together trade unions and business in tripartite talks with Government in order to plan for growth, seen as dependent on restraining demand through an incomes policy agreed with the TUC. An expansionary budget in 1963 – Chancellor Reginald Maudling's 'dash for growth' – failed to win the 1964 election for the Conservatives but succeeded in sucking in imports which created familiar balance of payments problems for the incoming Labour Government.

Labour inherited the same modernisation agenda which had been promoted vigorously in opposition by Harold Wilson. Wilson set up the Department of Economic Affairs in order to bypass the supposedly dead hand of the Treasury and to produce a National Plan to boost economic growth from around 3 per cent to 4 per cent a year. The National Plan foundered rapidly as a result of the priority given to defending the exchange rate and the resulting need to restrain demand by cutting public spending and raising interest rates. Thus was economic growth once again sacrificed in the interest of defending sterling which was in any case eventually devalued in 1967. An abortive attempt to legislate to curtail the powers of the trade unions served only to divide and discredit further an already weakened government which went down in defeat in the 1970 General Election.

The Conservative Government of Edward Heath was elected with a commitment to raise economic growth by allowing freer rein to market forces and curtailing trade union powers. The resulting Industrial Relations Act of 1971 foundered on the rock of trade union resistance while rising unemployment (reaching the ominous figure of one million by January 1972) prompted a notorious U-turn entailing Government intervention to restructure industry combined with another dash for growth (cuts in tax and interest rates and increases in public spending) supported by a statutory incomes policy. This third attempt to raise Britain's economic performance (following Macmillan's and Wilson's abortive modernisation plans) was cut short by the combined deflationary and inflationary effect of the oil price rise in 1973 and electoral defeat in 1974 brought on by another confrontation with the trade unions in the shape of the miners' work to rule and eventual strike.

Thus by 1974 three successive attempts to improve economic performance had ended in failure. The trade union leaders who conferred with ministers and business leaders appeared unable to curb their members who were unwilling to accept the curbs on personal incomes that were needed to transfer resources to profits and thus to raise investment and improve economic performance. Governments committed to full employment were unwilling to allow unemployment to increase to levels needed to undermine trade union resistance.

The decay of deference

Bagehot was perfectly clear that Britain's governing elite ruled 'by their hold, not over the reason of the multitude, but over their imaginations and their habits' (Bagehot, 1867: 239). Government of this kind was possible only in what he described as '*deferential* nations' – ones in which

> the numerous unwiser part [of the population] wishes to be ruled by the less numerous wiser part. The numerical majority – whether by custom or by choice, is immaterial – is ready, is eager to delegate its power of choosing its ruler to a certain select minority. It abdicates in favour of its *elite*, and consents to obey whoever that *elite* may confide in .... England is the type of deferential countries'.
>
> (1867: 235)

'The mass of the English people', Bagehot wrote, 'are politically contented as well as politically deferential.' He warned, however, that such a community was unstable; there might come a time when the mass of the people were no longer content to defer to an elite (238).

We have seen in Chapter 2 how the need to sustain the support, in the case of the Liberals, or the acquiescence, in the case of the Conservatives, of the newly enfranchised working-class voters in the last decades of the nineteenth and the first decades of the twentieth century shaped the political strategies of the two contending parties. By 1945 Labour had adjusted itself to the prevailing political culture. Ramsay MacDonald became famous for seeking the company of elderly duchesses and it was one of Attlee's ministers who pronounced that the gentleman in Whitehall knew best. The post-war consensus has been described as an affair of elites; it depended upon what Beer has described – in terms that Bagehot would have recognised – as a 'civic culture' characterised by 'the survival of a responsible and able governing class into the era of popular government' and 'adherence to a nonideological and pragmatic mode of intercourse in the context of wide-ranging debate and adaptive government' (Beer, 1982: 113).

It was this deferential polity, this civic culture, that began to come under increasing strain as the evidence of comprehensive economic and political failure mounted, and abortive attempts at modernisation from above encountered increasingly urgent demands for participation from below (Hooper, 1999). Christopher Booker has traced the first signs of what he described as 'the revolution in English life in the fifties and sixties' back to 1956 when the Suez crisis exposed the emptiness of British pretensions to great-power status.

> Outwardly it seemed that little had changed. Deep in the national psyche, however, was the knowledge that a real watershed had been passed. Attitudes to the outside world and to authority, the relations between class and class [and, one might add, between the sexes and between generations], England's fundamental view of herself – a whole complex of sentiments and assumptions that had been built up over hundreds of years – had been irreparably undermined. The dam had burst.
>
> (Booker, 1970: 119)

This is not the place to chart the social and cultural changes that ensued in what has been described as the long sixties commencing in 1956 and ending in the crisis of the mid-1970s (see Marwick, 1998, and Andrews *et al.*, 1999). Familiar landmarks are: the Angry Young Men, CND and the Teddy Boys of the late 1950s; the *Lady Chatterley* trial, the satire boom (in which Booker played a prominent part) and the emergence of the Beatles in the early 1960s; 'Swinging London', mods and mini-skirts in the mid-1960s; and the Vietnam Solidarity Campaign, student unrest and the so-called 'pay explosion' driven by rank-and-file pressure in the trade union movement in the late 1960s. Powellism on the Right and the New Left alike pointed to the collapsing political consensus. The notion was scorned by both. By the early 1970s the old culture of deference had gone for good. To some extent this collapse of deference in Britain was fuelled by specific political and economic developments, but contemporary events in France, Germany, Italy and the USA show that it was part of a worldwide phenomenon – the transition from a hierarchical, aristocratic society to an egalitarian, individualistic democratic society described with acute prescience by Alexis de Tocqueville in the 1830s (Williams, 1999).

The mid-1970s crisis and the emergence of Thatcherism

By 1974 a cloud of uncertainty hung over the future of capitalist democracy in Britain. The Hudson Report published in November of that year pointed to 'virtually unanimous agreement' that

> the country is in its worst economic situation since the war – and perhaps since the Great Depression. There is something more: a universal sense ... that the economic crisis is linked to a severe deterioration in the country's social and political health. Popular confidence in the competence of government is very low. A tiny minority (seven per cent, according to a poll taken before the [October 1974] election) believes that the political leadership is capable of mastering Britain's problems.
>
> (Hudson Institute, 1974: 1)

A few weeks later, in a lecture delivered to students at Birkbeck College in January 1975, Eric Hobsbawm described the current state of affairs as 'the most serious crisis of this country ... since the post-Napoleonic period and perhaps even before then ... It is difficult to think of a situation in which the regular institutions of Britain have been so much in doubt'. Hobsbawm looked forward to a real prospect for socialism (Hobsbawm, 1975: 11 – I owe this reference to Alan Hooper). In October 1975 in *New Society*, Robert Skidelsky argued that capitalism was in the process of being replaced by corporatism: 'I would suggest that the Keynesian state will be, is being, replaced by the Corporate State – a system in which collective decision-making in the economic field is shared out between government and the major producers' (Skidelsky, 1975).

By this time inflation was running at 25 per cent, unemployment was rising, stock market values collapsing and public expenditure thought to be out of control. The crisis of the mid-1970s prompted a second spate of books on the condition of Britain comparable to the one launched by Shonfield in 1958. The Hudson Report was among the first, followed by the first edition of Robert Moss's *The Collapse of Democracy* (1975). This was the context in which

Margaret Thatcher was elected leader of the Conservative Party. Her election was followed by another spate of books comparable to those of the early 1960s – such as *Why Is Britain Becoming Harder to Govern?* (King, 1976), based on three television programmes shown in February 1976, *What's Wrong with Britain?* (Hutber, 1978), *Right Turn* (Cormack, 1978), *Britain in Agony: the Growth of Political Violence* (Clutterbuck, 1978) and *The Coming Confrontation: Will the Open Society Survive to 1989?* (Seldon, 1978) – in the approach to the next General Election due by October 1979.

Thatcher's election as Conservative leader in early 1975 represented the capture of the party by the New Right. There were two factors behind this swing to the Right. Perhaps first was the sense of political failure which in the mid-1970s was strongest among the Conservatives who had lost four out of five elections (1964, 1966 and February and October 1974) within ten years. The Labour Party seemed to have an inbuilt advantage because of its links with the trade unions so long as both parties remained committed to full employment and were unwilling to confront the power of the trade unions based on that commitment – or to face the political risks associated with rising unemployment (the reason for Heath's U-turn in 1972). The monetarist focus on controlling the money supply and releasing market forces offered an alternative method of economic management that would allow a Conservative Government to dispense with the need to conciliate the trade unions (Bulpitt, 1986: 33).

Second was the accumulated sense of economic failure. By the mid-1970s both forms of Keynesian economic management – at 'arms length' from the late 1940s to the early 1960s and with 'hands on' since then – seemed to have failed, as the evidence of rising unemployment, declining productivity growth and rising inflation – so-called 'stagflation' – seemed to demonstrate. What came to be known as monetarism associated with Milton Friedman, Friedrich von Hayek, the Institute of Economic Affairs and influential journalists like William Rees-Mogg and Peter Jay of *The Times* and Samuel Brittan of the *Financial Times* offered an explanation of repeated economic failures and proposed an apparently coherent set of remedies in tune with traditional Conservative prejudices against state and trade union power.

The secret of the New Right's appeal to Mrs Thatcher and her associates was that it offered a means of recovering the

Government's freedom of manoeuvre lost through 'hands on' Keynesian economic management – a strategy of 'the free economy and the strong state' in place of 'a weak state and a fettered economy' (Gamble, 1988: 28, 95). The only difficulty with the new strategy was that it required the abandonment of the commitment to full employment and a trial of strength with the trade union movement that had been responsible for undermining Wilson in the late 1960s and Heath in the early 1970s.

However, it would be wrong to regard the 1979 Conservative victory as a foregone conclusion. Following the sterling crisis of 1976 the Labour Government managed to regain authority with the help of a loan from the International Monetary Fund and continued agreement on a voluntary incomes policy. In a famous speech to the Labour Party Conference in October 1976 Prime Minister James Callaghan renounced the policy of seeking to contain unemployment by cutting taxes and boosting government spending. The Government introduced money supply targets and imposed the largest ever cuts in public spending. By 1978 the economy was growing again and unemployment and inflation falling. What turned out to be decisive was Callaghan's decision in October 1978 to postpone the expected election until 1979 and to seek to impose a 5 per cent pay curb. This provoked the revolt of the trade union rank and file in the Winter of Discontent when Labour lost the key asset of good relations with the trade unions and therefore opened the way to Conservative victory.

Thatcher in power

Thatcher defined herself in opposition to consensus. Anthony Parsons, then Britain's ambassador to Iran, described a meeting with her in 1978 in which he said that he, like most people in Britain, believed in consensus. She replied, 'I regard them as traitors, as Quislings' (cited Young, 1993: 223). Speaking before the 1979 election she 'compared herself to Old Testament Prophets who did not say "Brother I want a consensus"' (Kavanagh, 1985: 529–30).

No-one should underestimate the Messianic element in Thatcher (Cannadine, 1998: 171): her memoirs quote William Pitt the Elder: 'I know I can save this country and that no one else can' (Thatcher, 1995: 10). She had two key objectives. The first was to reverse

Britain's relative economic decline: 'everything we wished to do had to fit into the overall strategy of reversing Britain's economic decline' (Thatcher, 1995: 15). The second was to destroy the challenge from socialism at home in the form of the Labour Party and overseas in the form of Soviet Communism.

This chapter focusses on Thatcherism as a political strategy. Later chapters will discuss the Conservative Government's impact in key policy areas such as the reconstruction of the civil service, privatisation and public spending. In terms of political strategy it is possible to distinguish four distinct stages.

The first stage, during Thatcher's period as Leader of the Opposition from 1975 to 1979, involved the development of what Stuart Hall has described as 'the politics of support' – building a new 'hegemonic project' by exploiting popular discontent with Labour by deploying themes such as rising crime, immigration and family breakdown, as well as developing issues such as deteriorating education which had already been raised by Callaghan. Thatcher sought to forge a link between accumulating popular grievances and free-market radicalism: a 'conversion of hard-faced economics into the language of compulsive *moralism*' (Hall, 1979: 31). Martin Jacques, editor of the influential journal *Marxism Today*, described this combination of neo-liberalism and moralism as 'authoritarian populism' (Jacques, 1979: 53). This was the period in which she and her closest colleagues like Nicholas Ridley and John Hoskyns developed detailed plans in 'Stepping Stones' for defeating the trade unions (Ridley, 1992: 67; Cockett, 1995: 272).

The second stage, during her first term in office from 1979 to 1983, involved the acquisition of what Jim Bulpitt has called 'a necessary degree of governing competence in office' in the face of the problems which in large part her Government brought upon themselves (and the country) through the adoption of the economic policies described as monetarism (Bulpitt, 1986: 21). That governing competence was demonstrated by defeating strikes by public sector unions that had undermined previous governments, by bringing the Civil Service to heel, by implementing the first trade union legislation, by defeating the challenge from the 'one nation' Tories in her Cabinet and – most of all – through victory in the Falklands War of 1982. Victory in the 1983 General Election was made possible by division on the Left following the foundation in 1981 of the Social Democratic Party coupled with the first signs of economic recovery and the reputation for firmness acquired over the previous four years.

The third stage, during her second term of office from 1983 to 1987, saw the high point in what Bob Jessop and his colleagues called 'the politics of power' (Jessop *et al.*, 1984: 33). By this term they had in mind her use of state power to build electoral support based on a 'two-nations' rather than the traditional 'one-nation' strategy, exploiting the division between home owner and council tenant, between private and public sector workers, between south and north, and between those in employment and those dependent on state benefits. This 'two nations' strategy was associated with the privatisation of the public utilities and the long conflict with the so-called 'loony Left' in Labour-controlled local authorities and with the National Union of Mineworkers – 'the enemy within' – led by Arthur Scargill. The continued division on the Left – between the Labour Party and the Liberal/SDP Alliance – ensured a third General Election victory in 1987 – the high tide of Thatcherism.

The fourth and final stage, during her third term of office from 1987 until the coup that removed her in 1990, was a classic example of hubris leading on to nemesis. Over-confidence born of persistent success resulted in the invitation to disaster represented by the Poll Tax (adopted against strong opposition from her Chancellor Nigel Lawson) and conflict over Europe (leading to the resignation of former key henchmen Lawson and Geoffrey Howe in 1989 and 1990 respectively). Her defeat in the 1990 leadership contest was the result of back-bench concern about mounting unpopularity (first demonstrated in the 1989 elections to the European Parliament) and the riots over the Poll Tax in 1990. Rising discontent threatened defeat in the next General Election due by spring 1992. Rejection by Cabinet colleagues following the first round of voting sealed her fate.

The Major years

An illuminating way of understanding the transition from Margaret Thatcher to John Major – and its bitter legacy to the Conservative party – is in terms of 'the routinisation of charisma'. As Max Weber put it, 'Emotional revolutionism is followed by the traditionalist routine of everyday life; the crusading leader and the faith itself fade away or, what is even more effective, the faith becomes part of the conventional phraseology of political Philistines and banausic [mechanical] technicians' (Gerth & Mills, 1948: 125). The paradox of the period is one of continued radicalism under a bureaucratic guise: a change of form but not content. Kenneth Clarke described John Major's Government as 'Thatcherism with a human face' (cited Kavanagh, 1994: 9), Hugo Young as 'Thatcherism pursued by non-Thatcherite means' (Young, 1994: 23). The rest of this section looks at elements of change and continuity.

On the one hand, Major adopted a more conservative, more routinised and bureaucratic policy style. Examples of this approach included greater use of Cabinet and Cabinet Committees and a retreat from the presidential style associated with Thatcher, a more conciliatory approach to Cabinet-making shown by greater readiness to tolerate different strands within the party (albeit united on the central Thatcher agenda), and by greater openness illustrated by the publication in 1992 of *Questions of Procedure for Ministers* and the membership of Cabinet Committees.

But this more conciliatory, more consensual style was accompanied by an increased radicalism in substantive policy terms. As Colin Hay put it: 'Major's managerial and bureaucratic mask hides a more radical series of policy initiatives' (Hay, 1996: 166). Major presided over the privatisation of parts of the public sector not touched by Thatcher, including railways, nuclear electricity generation and what remained of the coal industry. He continued with the reform of central government begun by Thatcher, making increased use of consultants, out-sourcing of computer services and launching the Private Finance Initiative for involving the private sector in public investment. In the field of social security Major's Government began moves towards workfare through the Jobseeker's Allowance and the extension of Project Work obliging claimants to work for benefits (*Financial Times*, 6.11.96).

With justice, Hay has described Majorism as 'a subterranean radicalism, albeit one born more of economic pragmatism within the neo-liberal straitjacket than of ideological fervour or the realisation of a coherent project' (Hay, 1996: 166). Major's real triumph has become ever clearer since his defeat in 1997: to have obliged Labour to make a full adjustment to the Thatcherite policy agenda following his victory in 1992 and the election of Tony Blair as leader in 1994. Jonathan Hill, Major's Political Secretary from 1992 to 1994, drew this conclusion in a review of a biography of his former master: 'by winning those extra five years of Conservative government, Major changed the political terms of trade for good, and made Tony Blair possible' (*New Statesman*, 7.11.97). Thus Major was more than just a footnote to Thatcher, a prolonged interregnum between her and Blair.

Conclusion

There remain two final questions: first, to explain the catastrophic defeat of the Conservatives in 1997; second, to consider the long term prospects for the Party.

The first question is easy enough to answer. Defeat was above all the result of a failure in statecraft, a breakdown in governing competence, shown most dramatically by the forced exit of sterling from the European Exchange Rate Mechanism in 1992 and more insidiously through internal divisions over Europe and continuing revelations of sleaze. By the mid-1990s, as the General Election approached, the Government had acquired an ineradicable reputation for corruption and incompetence. Meanwhile the transformation of the Labour Party under Tony Blair ensured that a 'safe' alternative – one that accepted the changes wrought by the Conservatives – was waiting in the wings.

The second question is obviously much more difficult to answer. The Conservatives have rebounded from other heavy defeats, in 1906, 1945 and 1974. Both the party leader William Hague and Michael Portillo as the main pretender to the position have shown a certain degree of flexibility on moral and social issues and a readiness to accommodate the new political agenda. But perhaps this time the challenge is greater. As we have seen, the traditional Conservative appeal, going back to Disraeli and Salisbury, was based on the defence of established institutions like the Church of England, the Monarchy, the BBC, civil service and judiciary, on the unity of the Kingdom itself, on the defence of property and on national independence – 'state, union, property and empire', with the characteristic ideological themes of 'constitutionalism, unionism, anti-socialism and imperialism' (Gamble, 1995: 9). Thatcherism has been corrosive of all of these causes and themes.

Conservative reforms of the public sector, including the Civil Service, the BBC, the universities and the judiciary, did much to estrange the Party from former allies in the Establishment. The alliance with Ulster Unionism was lost in the 1970s and 1980s as a result of the search for a settlement in Northern Ireland, and the 1997 Election robbed the Party of all representation in the House of Commons outside of England. The trade unions no longer represent the challenge to capital that they did in the 1970s and successive Labour leaders since the mid-1980s have made strenuous efforts to woo business and weaken the old ties with the trade unions. Labour no longer represents any threat to property and there is no longer any basis for the division between Liberals and Labour which was the basis for the Conservative hegemony between the wars and again between 1979 and 1997.

More than half-way through the life of the present Parliament, the Conservative Party still conveys the impression of an exhausted, traumatised party, engaged in their own private debate in which the electorate as a whole shows little interest. The majority of party members are over 65 at a time when Blair has been proclaiming Britain a 'young country'. The thought has begun to dawn upon the Conservatives that Thatcher may have won the battle to establish a new pro-market consensus at the cost of destroying the instrument of that victory, the Conservative Party itself. As Tessa Keswick, Director of the Centre for Policy Studies founded in 1974 by Thatcher and Keith Joseph, recently remarked, Thatcher's 'victories were so complete that she left the Conservatives without their raison d'etre' (Keswick, 1999).

Perhaps in time the internal disputes over Europe will come to resemble the divisions over the Corn Laws in 1846 which deprived the Conservatives of a majority in the House of Commons until 1874. Perhaps the Conservatives have barely begun their wanderings in the wilderness of the kind endured by Labour after 1979. A sobering thought for Hague is that Blair was not elected to the House of Commons until 1983. Perhaps the next Conservative Prime Minister has still to be elected. Who knows? Much will depend upon the success of Blair in building a new post-Thatcher but still Thatcherite hegemony and in demonstrating the kind of 'governing competence' which so signally eluded Major. If Blair does succeed in winning a second term in the next election due by 2002 then the Conservatives are likely to be faced with a series of *faits accomplis* on Europe by the time of the following election, rather as Labour was by the late 1980s on trade union reform and privatisation. Their internal disputes will be settled for them by Labour, as Thatcher settled Labour's internal disputes in the 1980s.

5

Crisis on the Left: from Labourism to New Labour

Introduction

Chapters 3 and 4 focussed on the construction and collapse of the post-war consensus. Chapter 4 discussed the role of the Conservative Party in overthrowing the consensus while this chapter focusses on the crisis into which the end of consensus plunged the Labour Party and the transformation which it needed to undertake in order to win power again in 1997.

The Labour Party played a major role in shaping the post-war consensus. The Labour Chancellors Hugh Dalton, Stafford Cripps and Hugh Gaitskell developed the techniques of arms-length Keynesian economic management (described briefly in Chapter 4 and discussed at more length in Chapter 8) that would be exploited by Conservative Chancellors after 1951. Labour held office for most of the 1960s and 1970s when Governments of both parties undertook their unsuccessful experiments in hands-on Keynesian economic management (discussed in Chapter 4) in order to try to raise economic growth while containing inflation and unemployment. The perceived failure of these experiments by the late 1970s and the ensuing abandonment of consensus by the Thatcher Government plunged the Labour Party into its deepest crisis since 1931.

This chapter focusses on the prolonged crisis of the Labour Party which was surmounted only in the mid-1990s and consummated in the great election victory of 1997. First it examines the nature of the Labour Party at the time of its foundation as a national party in 1918. It identifies two main tensions that remained unresolved for the next sixty years before coming to a head after 1979. Then it looks at various attempts to resolve these tensions during the 1960s and 1970s under the leadership of Harold Wilson and James Callaghan, in order to understand the eventual breakdown. Next it looks at the explosion of internal tensions after 1979 and the process of gradual recovery after 1983. It concludes with reflections on the nature of the Labour Party in the aftermath of its greatest victory in the 1997 election, delivering 419 Labour seats, more even than the 393 seats won by Labour in 1945 and the 377 won by the Liberals in 1906.

The nature of the Labour Party

It is important to understand two unique features of the Labour Party which help to explain its subsequent history. First is the link with the trade unions which explains why it was called the Labour rather than the Socialist or Social Democratic Party and why it has always been open to accusations of Labourism – that is, for serving as the political vehicle for the purely sectional interests of the working class within a capitalist society.

Chapter 3 stressed that the Labour Party began life in 1900 as the Labour Representation Committee founded by the TUC as a means of promoting the interests of the trade unions. The Labour Party differed from other European socialist parties of the late nineteenth and early twentieth centuries which developed separately from and often in advance of the trade union movement in countries such as France or Germany. These parties tended in the main to be led by intellectuals, usually Marxist, with the declared aim of transforming their societies in a socialist fashion. As such they mounted an explicit challenge to Liberal parties committed to the defence of capitalism. By contrast, the British Labour Party before the First World War operated primarily as a ginger group on the Left of the Liberals, which in turn had been obliged by the need to win working class votes to move beyond the mere defence of *laissez-faire* capitalism.

Even after the Labour Party was constituted as a national party in 1918 it remained common to talk about the two wings – political and trade union – of a single movement, and the unions continued to play an important role for most of the succeeding decades. Until very recently they provided the main source of funding for the Party. Many MPs, especially in the middle years of the century, were former trade union officials; some (notably Ernest Bevin) served as ministers; many other MPs were sponsored by trade unions. Until very recently the unions wielded the great majority of votes (the so-called block vote) at annual party conferences. The TUC played an important role in devising policies while the Party was in opposition, and maintained a special right to be consulted when the Party was in government – in 1931 over the public spending cuts that precipitated the fall of the Government, and in the 1940s, 1960s and 1970s over incomes policies.

Obviously the link with the trade unions meant that the Labour Party was vulnerable to the accusation that it was the party of a sectional or class interest, not a party of the nation or the people. This accusation was not a serious problem when the industrial working class and the trade unions were growing in size and numbers, as they were until the late 1970s. It became an increasing problem when the traditional industrial working class began to contract and trade union membership began to fall in the 1980s.

The second unique feature of the Labour Party is the extent to which it has operated as a coalition of political tendencies which in other countries were represented by distinct, often large, political parties. The nature of the Labour Party as a coalition is partly a product of the British political system itself, notably the first-past-the-post voting system which notoriously favours a two-party system, with a bias against third parties and a consequent severe penalty upon party division (suffered by the Liberals in the 1920s and by Labour in the 1930s and again in the 1980s). Arguably, however, it was mainly a product of the circumstances surrounding the foundation of the Labour Party in 1918 – a point that needs to be explained in rather more detail.

By 1914 Marxist socialist parties were well-established in most other European countries – such as Germany, Italy, France and Austria – although usually with revolutionary and reformist wings. During the First World War these parties divided over support for the war. In most belligerent countries some socialists joined governments of national unity while others opposed the war. Opponents of the war, usually on the radical Left before 1914, formed the nuclei of the post-war Communist Parties; supporters of the war, usually but not invariably on the Right before 1914, reconstituted themselves after 1918 as Socialist or Social Democratic parties, committed to the gradual development of socialism within the framework of the liberal democracies which they had defended in war (Sassoon, 1997).

In Britain, the war divided both the Labour and Liberal Parties. In August 1914, two Liberal Cabinet Ministers resigned and in September 1914 Liberal intellectuals founded the Union of Democratic Control to secure control over the secret diplomacy that was thought to have caused the war. By 1916 and 1917 senior Liberals were among the main advocates of a compromise peace, and leading Liberal intellectuals such as Bertrand Russell and J. M. Keynes were strongly opposed to the war. On the Labour side the bulk of MPs and the overwhelming majority of union leaders supported the war but some of the more important parliamentary leaders such as Keir Hardie and Ramsay MacDonald opposed it. In 1915 the new Labour leader Arthur Henderson joined the first coalition government as Minister for Education and eventually took his place in Lloyd George's War Cabinet.

After Lloyd George displaced Asquith in December 1916 the Liberals divided between the supporters of the two rival leaders but the dissident followers of Asquith continued to support the war, thus depriving Liberal critics of the war of any political home. Only by opposing the war and calling for a compromise peace could the Asquithian Liberals have asserted the leadership of a progressive bloc including Labour. Asquith's failure to provide the necessary leadership opened the way for Labour to displace the Liberals. Meanwhile Arthur Henderson's resignation from the Government over his attendance at the Stockholm Conference in 1917 permitted reconciliation with the Labour opponents of the war led by Ramsay MacDonald and attracted support from anti-war Liberal intellectuals and some MPs. This combination of middle-class Liberal and socialist opponents of the war provided the basis for a new progressive national party distinct from the Liberal followers of Lloyd George and Asquith.

The war itself gave a great impulse to socialism, through the increased role of the state, the growth in trade union membership, and the example of the Russian Revolution. Such was the background to Clause 4 of the Party Constitution drafted in 1918 by Arthur Henderson and the Fabian Sidney Webb:

> To secure for the workers by hand or by brain the full fruits of their industry and the most equitable distribution thereof that may be possible upon the basis of the common ownership of the means of production, distribution and exchange, and the best obtainable system of popular administration and control of each industry or service.
>
> (Cited Anderson & Mann, 1997: 27)

Opposition to the war attracted many former Liberals (like Tony Benn's father) to the Party while its vague socialist aspirations attracted many who, like members of the Independent Labour Party, would have joined the Communist Party in other countries. Clause 4 was vague enough to satisfy all shades of socialist opinion without repelling Liberals who were drawn to the Party more by opposition to war. The link with a unified trade union movement helped to prevent the kind of division of the working-class movement that ensued in other countries. In short, in Britain the division on the Left was between Liberals and Labour rather than between Socialists and Communists. From the outset the Labour Party contained a much wider range of opinion than other socialist parties. It included many who would have joined the Communists in Germany, France or Italy. Consequently the Communist Party of Great Britain remained marginal to the Left as a whole.

Labour and Keynesian social democracy

The 1920s found the Labour Party committed to a vague socialism without any clear conception of how it would operate and thus without any strategy for achieving it. The emptiness of the vague aspirations of leaders like Ramsay MacDonald and Philip Snowden was cruelly exposed by the collapse of the second Labour Government in 1931. During the 1930s and early 1940s Labour acquired a practical programme in the form of a mix of Keynesian economic management, welfare reform, nationalisation, and aspirations to physical planning inspired by the Soviet Union and the wartime Coalition Government's experience.

All shades of Labour opinion could agree on the programme of the Attlee Government – for the Right, the programme involved essential reforms to capitalism which were acceptable to 'social liberals' like Keynes and Beveridge as well as Labour intellectuals like Gaitskell and Jay. For the Left, represented notably by Aneurin Bevan, the foundation of the NHS, the expansion of public housing and the nationalisation of the commanding heights of the economy could be seen as a first instalment in the transformation of capitalism into socialism.

Problems began in the last years of the Attlee Government when the main programme of reforms was largely completed, leading to the conflict between Gaitskell and Bevan over cuts in public spending which helped to bring down the Government in 1951 and continued during the 1950s when the Party was in opposition. There were clear parallels with the 1980s: the rank and file in the constituencies supported Bevan; the parliamentary Party supported the leadership, first under Attlee and after 1955 under Gaitskell. The main difference was that in the 1950s the trade union barons wielded the block vote on behalf of the party leadership whereas in the 1970s and 1980s they were divided, with many inclining to the Left. The internal divisions of the 1950s contributed to three successive defeats, in 1951, 1955 and 1959. The Labour vote fell from a post-war peak of 49 per cent in 1951 to 46 per cent in 1955 and 44 per cent in 1959. Labour seemed to have failed to come to terms with the 'affluent society'.

Gaitskell died suddenly in 1963 and Harold Wilson was elected by Labour MPs in his place. Wilson commanded formidable political skills: he won four out of five elections and resigned at the peak of his prestige in 1976 (proving an exception to Enoch Powell's dictum that all political careers end in failure). Wilson's strategy essentially was to identify socialism with the modernisation of the economy which would generate the faster economic growth needed to finance higher public expenditure designed to produce the more egalitarian society which Anthony Crosland had redefined in *The Future of Socialism* as the objective of socialism. Just like Tony Blair and Gordon Brown in the 1990s, Wilson sought to forge a link between equity and efficiency, only then efficiency was associated with planning on the French – or even Soviet – model rather than with the free market.

Thus in the early 1960s it was still possible to present modernisation in vaguely socialist terms, as Wilson did in his famous speech to the 1963 Party Conference.

> In all our plans for the future, we are re-defining our Socialism in terms of the scientific revolution. But that revolution cannot become a reality unless we are prepared to make far-reaching changes in economic and social attitudes which permeate our whole system of society. The Britain that is going to be forged in the white heat of this revolution will be no place for restrictive practices or for outdated methods on either side of industry.
>
> (Cited Pimlott, 1993: 304)

As we saw in Chapter 4, Wilson's attempt to reverse Britain's relative economic decline by hands-on Keynesian economic management ended in failure. In particular, it foundered on resistance by the trade union rank and file which Labour – because of its links with the trade unions and opposition from the left within the party – was unable to overcome. In 1966 the National Plan which lay at the heart of the Government's economic strategy was undermined by a national seamen's strike which precipitated a run on sterling which prompted a deflationary package of spending cuts and tax increases which curbed expansion while failing to prevent eventual devaluation in 1967. In 1969 Wilson was obliged to withdraw the restrictions on unofficial strikes proposed in the Government White Paper *In Place of Strife* in the face of opposition from the TUC, from the Labour Left and from James Callaghan and others within the Cabinet itself. These frustrations contributed to electoral defeat in 1970. The culminating irony was the defeat of Callaghan's own incomes policy in the Winter of Discontent in 1979. Thus did he and the TUC leadership pay the price of undermining Wilson's earlier proposals for trade union reform.

Disaster strikes

The emergence of Thatcherism was one aspect of an increasing polarisation of politics as the economic crisis deepened during the 1970s. It was accompanied by a shift to the Left within the Labour Party. Both were responses to the perceived failure of Keynesian social democracy.

There were two main factors behind this shift to the Left. First was a growing rank-and-file militancy within the trade unions as a result of slow economic growth and rising taxes coupled with a shift to the Left by some trade union leaders who could no longer be relied upon either to support the Labour Party leadership or to curb their members. Second was a growing political radicalism within the constituency parties under the influence of the 1960s New Left and the revival of revolutionary socialism as well as various New Social Movements emerging from the New Left in the 1970s. Left-wing criticism of the failures of the 1974–9 Labour Government was the mirror image of Thatcher's and Joseph's criticism of the failures of previous Conservative Governments. The one was accused of betraying socialism just as the others were accused of betraying Conservatism.

Electoral defeat in 1979 gave the Labour Left the opportunity to seek control over the Party, just as two election defeats in 1974 gave the Conservative Right an opportunity to win control over their Party. Led by Tony Benn, the Labour Left sought to enable constituency parties (often dominated by small groups of radicals in public-sector, middle-class professions) to win control over the parliamentary Party through mandatory re-selection of MPs, the election of the party leader by an electoral college consisting of local activists and the trade unions as well as Labour MPs, and the right of Conference to draw up the Party manifesto. Their objective was to ensure that any future Labour Government would be committed to implementing what was described as the Alternative Economic Strategy, intended to reverse Britain's relative economic decline through import controls, planning agreements with major firms and withdrawal from the EEC.

These objectives were more plausible then than they seem now. In 1980 the Left managed to secure the election of Michael Foot against the Right's Denis Healey, and only narrowly failed in 1981 to secure the election of Tony Benn as deputy leader (and thus heir-apparent to the elderly Foot). Meanwhile Thatcher was plumbing the depths of unpopularity in 1980–2, with a divided Cabinet, rising unemployment and inner-city riots. In 1981 François Mitterrand, leader of the Socialist-Communist electoral bloc, was elected President of France on the basis of an aggressively socialist policy which promised a break with capitalism (Sassoon, 1997: 546).

The prospects for success were undermined by several factors. First of all, Michael Foot fell far short of Mitterrand in political skill and electoral appeal. Second, the decision to establish an electoral college to elect the party leader prompted the foundation in early 1981 of the breakaway Social Democratic Party which included some two dozen former Labour MPs and quickly attracted 30 per cent plus support in opinion polls. A third factor was the acceleration in the early 1980s of long-term social changes, including the decline of the traditional industrial working class, the reduction in trade union membership and an increase in home ownership, which undermined the electoral appeal of Left-wing policies. A final factor was the political recovery of Thatcher after the 1982 Falklands War.

These factors combined to explain the Party's disastrous defeat in the election of 1983. The party's vote dropped to 28 per cent – only 2 per cent ahead of the SDP–Liberal Alliance and down from 37 per cent in 1979. The party was saved only by a voting system which awarded the Alliance 23 seats to Labour's 209. The Left's attempt to win control over the Party had resulted in the worst general election result since 1935. The Alternative Economic Strategy was discredited in its turn by Mitterrand's abandonment of a similar strategy of reflation in one country, and his embrace of economic liberalism, following a major political U-turn in 1983 which Donald Sassoon has compared with the abandonment of Keynesianism by the Labour Government in 1976 (1997: 561).

The long road to recovery

Labour would require 14 years and another three general elections to recover from the debacle of 1983. Three stages can be identified in this process. The first was from 1983 to 1987 and can be summed up in terms of repackaging Left policies more attractively. Foot resigned immediately after the 1983 election and Neil Kinnock, identified with the so-called 'soft Left', was elected in his place. Kinnock began building bridges to the right by purging members of Militant who had secured a grip on several inner-city constituencies, notably in Liverpool, and distancing himself from the Miners' Strike led by Arthur Scargill and from so-called 'loony Left' councils. The defeat of the miners' strike and the Government's assault on local government in 1984–5 undermined the trade union Left and the urban Left in the same way as the 1983 election defeat undermined the hard Left in the party. Kinnock improved the packaging of party policy by appointing Peter Mandelson as Director of Communications to such an extent that commentators judged that Labour 'won the campaign but lost the election' in 1987 (Jenkins, 1989: 342). Labour decisively established its primacy on the Left by winning 31 per cent of the vote compared to the SDP–Liberal Alliance's 23 per cent.

The second stage in this process of recovery – from 1987 to 1992 – can be summed up in terms of the abandonment of Left policies and a return to traditional social democratic values (public spending to promote social equality). Kinnock launched an extensive policy review which resulted in the acceptance of formerly contentious Conservative policies such as trade union reform and privatisation, and internal reorganisation designed to weaken the constituency Left and assert the leadership's command over the Party. The outcome of the 1992 Election has been described as 'defeat snatched from jaws of victory' (Heffernan & Marqusee, 1992). In particular, Shadow Chancellor John Smith's commitment to raise income tax to spend more on public services exposed the Party to Conservative propaganda about 'Labour's tax bombshell'. Labour won 34 per cent of the vote compared to 18 per cent for the Liberal Democrats. But traditional Labour values had failed to attract sufficient voters to unseat the Conservatives.

The third stage – from 1992 to 1997 – can be summed up in terms of an attempt to reposition the Party beyond both traditional social democratic values and Thatcherite neo-liberalism. Kinnock resigned immediately after the 1992 election, to be succeeded first by John Smith and then (after Smith's sudden death in 1994) by Tony Blair. What is interesting about this process of renewal is the extent to which Blair and close colleagues such as Gordon Brown and Peter Mandelson drew upon ideas developed outside the ranks of the Party in a flurry of books reminiscent of similar flurries in the early 1960s ahead of Wilson's victory in 1964 and in the late 1970s ahead of Thatcher's victory in 1979. Notable among these books was Will Hutton's *The State We're In* (1995) which topped the best-seller charts and sold 150 000 copies in hardback (Crewe, 1996: 434). Others included David Marquand's *The Progressive Dilemma* (1992), advocating the reconstitution of a progressive alliance between Labour and the Liberal Democrat heirs to the Liberal Party of Lloyd George and Asquith; John Gray's argument in *After Social Democracy*

(1996) for an advance beyond social democracy and neo-liberalism; and Andrew Marr's popularisation of ideas for constitutional reform in *Ruling Britannia* (1996). Some of the ground for Blair's new course had been prepared by Marxist intellectuals such as Eric Hobsbawm and Stuart Hall writing in *Marxism Today* since the early 1980s (Andrews, 1999b; Williams, 1999). David Willetts sensed in his assessment of 'Blair's Gurus' (1996) that the Conservatives were losing the battle of ideas. The result of the 1997 General Election seemed to vindicate Blair's 'New Labour' strategy: the Party won 44 per cent of the vote, the same as in 1964 but less than the 47 per cent achieved in 1966.

Conclusion

This chapter has argued that the problems of the Labour Party resulted from two factors: first, an unresolved tension between the industrial and political wings of the Labour movement – the unions and the Party; and, second, an equally unresolved ambiguity about the Party's long-term objectives and its attitude to capitalism. The link with the trade unions allowed opponents to portray Labour as a sectional interest party, while the vague commitment to socialism embodied in Clause 4 allowed them to portray it as anti-capitalist. Both charges became increasingly damaging as trade union members declined as a proportion of the workforce and as socialism became increasingly discredited during the 1980s. To what extent has Tony Blair managed to resolve these two problems?

First, consider the trade union link. The trade unions have been much reduced as an economic and political force by 18 years of Conservative government. Unemployment and legislation have reduced their bargaining power; the decay of manufacturing industry and the privatisation of large swathes of the public sector have reduced trade union membership. Overall numbers have fallen from 13 million (about half the workforce) in 1979 to 8 million (about 30 per cent of the workforce) in 1999. In growing areas of the private sector trade unionism is nearly extinct: unions account for only 5 per cent of workers in hotels and restaurants, only 8 per cent in real estate and business services, 11 per cent in wholesale and retail trade and 14 per cent in construction. The highest level of trade union membership is in public administration (60 per cent), followed by the privatised utilities (58 per cent), education (53 per cent) and health (46 per cent) (*Financial Times*, 8.7.99). Trade union members are aging: they account for fewer than 25 per cent of workers aged under 30 but 40 per cent of workers over 40. They are now concentrated among public-sector professionals rather than industrial workers as in the past (*New Statesman 1998 Trade Union Guide*). Thus unions once again are no more than a sectional pressure group; they cannot plausibly claim to speak for a homogeneous working class as they could even as late as the 1970s when Labour was last in office.

Blair has accelerated the loosening of the trade union connection which began under Kinnock. In 1995 he warned that there would be 'no repeal of all Tory trade union laws. Strike ballots are here to stay. No mass or flying pickets'. He insisted that there would be no privileged role for the trade unions: a Labour government would listen to them just like it listened to business: 'But the decisions must rest with us. We will govern for the whole nation – not any vested interest' (*The Guardian*, 13.9.95). This approach was well summed up in the phrase 'fairness not favours' which Blair used on the Jimmy Young radio show on the day that he was elected as party leader (Anderson & Mann, 1997: 324). It has been generally accepted by the TUC under its General Secretary John Monks. The TUC offered no public endorsement for Labour in the 1997 General Election campaign (even while providing behind-the-scenes help).

Blair has also presided over a dramatic reduction in the Labour Party's financial dependence upon the trade unions. By 1998 they provided less than 30 per cent of Labour Party funds, down from 40 per cent in 1997 and 76 per cent in 1986 (*Financial Times*, 13.11.97, 14.10.98, 9.9.99). Instead the Party has come to rely increasingly on funding from members (14 per cent in 1998) and businessmen (38 per cent in 1998) (*Financial Times*, 9.9.99). A leaked document revealed that the party was expecting to raise £5.47 million from businessmen in the first half of 1999, including £2 million from Lord Sainsbury, one of Blair's ministers (*Financial Times*, 6.9.99). The same document revealed that Lord Gavron, chairman of Guardian Media Group, had given the party £500 000 within weeks of being made a working peer in June 1999 (*The Guardian*, 6.9.99).

Finally, there has been a relaxation in the organisational link between the Party and the trade unions. The union share of the electoral college for the party leader was reduced from 40 per cent to 33 per cent in 1993. The unions' block vote at the party conference has been reduced from 90 per cent to 70 per cent and finally to 50 per cent as party membership reached 300 000 in 1995. Sponsorship of individual MPs has gone and there were only 54 former manual workers among Labour MPs elected in 1997 (Criddle, 1997: 205).

Thus it seems fair to conclude that the Labour Party is no longer the political wing of a unified Labour Movement with pretensions to speak for the majority of the population. Over the last decade or so it has come to resemble the French Socialist Party which attracts support mainly from public sector workers and seeks funds where it can find them.

Second, what has happened to the socialist objectives enshrined in Clause 4 of the Party's constitution agreed in 1918? In fact the Party's vague socialist aspirations have had only a negligible effect on its policy and practice. The policies pursued by the Attlee Government of 1945–51 were derived mainly from the ideas of 'social liberals' like Keynes and Beveridge. The policies pursued by the Wilson Government of 1964–70 were inspired by Crosland's argument that capitalism had been tamed and that social equality was the appropriate goal, best pursued by higher public spending. But Clause 4 remained a totem for the Left and a target for critics.

Blair's decision to drop Clause 4 was wholly symbolic but nonetheless important. It represented a break with socialism redefined as 'social-ism'; a focus on values rather than policies. Blair explained his ultimate objective in an interview in early 1997: 'I want a situation more like the Democrats and the Republicans in the US. People don't even question for a single moment that the Democrats are a pro-business party. They should not be asking the same question about New Labour' (*Financial Times*, 16.1.97).

Thus Blair seems to have achieved a real break with the past which offers advantages and potential dangers. On the one hand, the abandonment of an anti-capitalist rhetoric has enabled Labour to win the centre ground. A study of the 1997 Election results shows that the swing to Labour was much higher among voters on the Centre-Right than on the Left (for example, 18 per cent among mortgage payers, 19 per cent among graduates, 25 per cent among non-manual workers, 28 per cent among share owners compared with only 2 per cent among council tenants and unskilled manual workers) (Davies, 1998). It also opens the way to building a coalition with the Liberal Democrats, thus healing the division on the Left that opened in 1918.

On the other hand, this strategy runs a risk of eroding the Party's core support among the poor. Electoral turnout in 1997 was only 72 per cent compared with 78 per cent in 1992 and was lower in Labour than Conservative seats (68 per cent compared with 74 per cent) (Davies, 1998). A survey of over 14 000 electors in late 1998 showed that Labour had gained ground among the most prosperous sections of society at the expense of lost ground among its traditional core supporters such as council tenants, semi-skilled and unskilled workers and the unemployed (Kellner, 1998). The warning signs were evident in the results of the elections to local councils and the devolved assemblies in Scotland and Wales in May 1999 and in elections to the European Parliament in June. Labour failed to win the expected majority of seats in the Welsh Assembly and lost badly to the Conservatives in the European Elections, provoking increasing concern on the Left and among the trade unions that, as the then junior Welsh Office Minister Peter Hain put it in an interview in the *New Statesman* on 7 June 1999, the Government had 'got itself into the dangerous situation where [it] appears as if it is being gratuitously offensive to its own natural supporters'. Reliance on business funding runs risks of accusations of sleaze which, as in the case of Bernie Ecclestone's donation of £1 million in 1997 and Lord Sainsbury's donation of £2 million in 1999, the Conservatives will be quick to exploit. An odour of corruption surrounding his links with business was a key factor in undermining Lloyd George in the early 1920s.

Blair was quick to discount any intention of altering course by declaring that the New Labour message about 'the importance of business and ambition' remained '100 per cent proof' (*Financial Times*, 23.6.99) but the dangers were evident in these mid-term elections. A reduction in core support exposes the Government to a more volatile centre ground which could easily transfer support to the Conservatives if Labour fails to demonstrate a crucial governing competence. As the *New Statesman* editorialised, 'The Euro election results show exactly how Labour could lose the next general election: through mass abstention among its traditional supporters, while Middle England, finding the Tories refreshed, returns to its natural home' (21.6.99). By the late summer of 1999, as Blair's thoughts turned increasingly to winning a full second term in office that had eluded previous Labour governments, private polls were showing increasing scepticism among voters about Labour's performance in government (*The Independent*, 15.9.99).

6

Whitehall's Managerial Revolution: Reconstructing Central Government

Introduction

Previous chapters have told how Britain's relative economic decline emerged as an issue at the turn of the nineteenth century after several decades (since the Second Reform Act of 1867) in which the governing elite were concerned mainly with the more pressing task of adjusting to an emerging mass democracy. Concern about 'national efficiency' following the Boer War prompted a series of important social reforms before the attention of the governing elite was distracted yet again by the Irish Question and then by war. The next thirty years were to be dominated by the internal challenge of Labour and the external challenge of war. The post-war consensus was essentially the product of these two challenges. However, the problem of Britain's relative economic decline which had lain dormant since Edwardian times revived in the late 1950s and rapidly became the dominant factor in British [illegible] in the mid-1970s under the impact of persistent economic and political failure. The rest of the book follows this process through six main policy areas, beginning with the central state machine.

The British state machine was the product of the same period – from 1870 to 1920 – which saw both the beginning of Britain's relative economic decline discussed in Chapter 1 and the transition from parliamentary government to mass democracy discussed in Chapter 2. Recall Weber's comment: 'Bureaucracy inevitably accompanies modern *mass democracy*' (Gerth & Mills, 1948: 224). The government department and the multi-purpose local authority were as much the products of the late nineteenth and early twentieth centuries as the big industrial corporation; both were hierarchically organised bureaucracies.

British central government began to develop its characteristic form in the early nineteenth century as the political class bifurcated into two distinct categories – professional politicians subject increasingly to the whims of an expanding electorate and permanent officials. We in Britain tend to take this distinction for granted, but it did not apply in the eighteenth century and does not apply, for example, in modern France where many leading politicians (such as President Jacques Chirac and Prime Minister Lionel Jospin) began their careers as civil servants.

This chapter begins by describing the origins of the modern British civil service in the recommendations of the Northcote–Trevelyan Report of 1854 which were only gradually implemented over more than half a century. It then looks at the civil service – at what has been called the 'Whitehall model' (Campbell & Wilson, 1995: xii) – in its classic period from the 1920s to the 1970s. It goes on to examine the Fulton Report of 1968 – an important part of Wilson's policy of modernisation – which mounted the first main assault on the traditional civil service and set the agenda for the Conservative reforms after 1979. It then considers the extent to which these reforms can be taken to have fulfilled the Fulton agenda and the extent to which they went beyond it. Our conclusion will be that the Conservatives accomplished a veritable 'managerial revolution' in Whitehall which, like other Conservative policies, is set to be continued and built upon by Labour.

Northcote–Trevelyan and after

In a sense the history of the modern British civil service can be described as a tale of three reports. The founding document was the Northcote–Trevelyan Report of 1854 (Northcote–Trevelyan, 1854), reprinted as Appendix B of the second of our three reports, the Fulton Report of 1968 (Fulton, 1968). The Report was commissioned by Gladstone, Chancellor of the Exchequer in Lord Aberdeen's Coalition Government of Whigs and followers of Robert Peel (who died in 1850) who left the Conservative Party following the Repeal of the Corn Laws in 1846. Stafford Northcote was a former official at the Board of Trade, then serving as Gladstone's Private Secretary, who went on to lead the Conservative Party briefly in the early 1880s. Charles Trevelyan was head of the Treasury (known confusingly as Assistant Secretary but equivalent to a Permanent Secretary today) and the main author of the Report (Hennessy, 1989: 38).

The Report was the culmination of Trevelyan's drive, begun in the 1840s, to reform the civil service to enable it to cope with what he described as the 'great and increasing accumulation of public business' (Northcote–Trevelyan, 1854: 108). In Gladstone he found a sympathetic political master. The crucial paragraph stressed the need for

> an efficient body of permanent officers, occupying a position duly subordinate to that of the Ministers who are directly responsible to the Crown and Parliament, yet possessing sufficient independence, character, ability, and experience to be able to advise, assist, and to some extent, influence, those who are from time to time set over them.
>
> (Northcote–Trevelyan, 1854: 108)

This statement has been described as 'Whitehall's equivalent of Lincoln's Gettysburg address' (Hennessy, 1989: 38). Note especially the statement that officials should be able to exercise influence over their political masters.

The Report recommended the creation of a career civil service based on recruitment by competitive examination and promotion according to merit instead of patronage as hitherto. Merit was to be ascertained on the basis of general education. The objective, in the words of the companion report written mainly by the historian Macaulay (Trevelyan's brother-in-law) and Benjamin Jowett, Master of Balliol College, Oxford, was 'to elicit young men of general ability, which is a matter of more moment than their being possessed of any special requirements' (Macaulay, 1854: 114).

The traditional view of the Northcote–Trevelyan Report, current in the early twentieth century, was that its purpose was to modernise the state machine in the image of the emerging manufacturing middle class (Gowan, 1987: 7). Today it can be seen as one component in a comprehensive strategy for '*strengthening* the hold of the landed classes on political power' in an emerging age of democracy (Gowan, 1987: 18). We have already noted Gladstone's commitment to aristocracy. He was convinced that the tendency of the proposed reforms would be to 'strengthen and multiply the ties between the higher classes and the possession of administrative power'. He described them as '*my* contribution to parliamentary reform' in so far as it removed the ability of politicians to make administrative appointments (Shannon, 1999: 280–3). Trevelyan agreed: 'The tendency of the measure will, I am confident, be decidedly aristocratic', he wrote. As Asa Briggs put it, 'the reformers did not wish to throw open the civil service to the middle classes but rather to the new educational *élite* of the public schools and universities. Whitehall was not to be surrendered to Manchester, but to Oxford' (Briggs, 1965: 117). Geoffrey Searle has demonstrated how the Government's embrace of Northcote–Trevelyan represented a defeat both for expert administrators like the Benthamites Chadwick, Kay-Shuttleworth and Simon and for Radical advocates of bringing businessmen into government (Searle, 1993: 124–5). Other elements in a strategy for maintaining the hold of the traditional elite upon the levers of power included the reform of the ancient universities and the public schools undertaken during the 1850s and 1860s.

Northcote–Trevelyan's recommendations were gradually implemented over more than half a century after 1854. The Civil Service Commission responsible for overseeing recruitment was established in 1855 while competitive examinations were established as the primary means of recruitment in 1870. The author of this reform was Gladstone's Chancellor Robert Lowe, a leading opponent of the Second Reform Act and now 'working to create a privileged elite, a new aristocracy of talent, to counter the democratising tendencies of the day' (Searle, 1993: 123). However, even in Edwardian times it was still possible for Ministers to make personal appointments to senior positions, as Churchill appointed the young William Beveridge to the Board of Trade to introduce the new Labour Exchanges (Harris, 1994: 188). Political control over appointments was eliminated only in 1920, with the Order in Council creating a unified civil service under Treasury control (Hennessy, 1989: 71). Note the timing – following the extension of the vote to all adult men and to women over 30, when Labour had already displaced the Liberals as the Opposition in the House of Commons. Meanwhile over the preceding half-century the number of central government officials had grown from 54 000 in 1870 to 317 000 in 1922 (Dowding, 1995: 22).

The Whitehall model in its heyday

The next half-century – from the 1920s to the 1970s – was the heyday of Whitehall's prestige and power. The civil service claimed credit for its part in victory in the Second World War and in the creation of the welfare state in the late 1940s. But it began to encounter increasing criticism from the late 1950s as a result of the renewed awareness of British relative economic decline. The question began to be asked: were men educated in the Classics at Oxbridge really up to running the country in the last half of the twentieth century?

What were the main components of the Whitehall model in its heyday? First of all, civil servants held permanent appointments – that is, they could not be removed by politicians. Because of this security of tenure, therefore, they were independent and able 'to speak truth unto power'. Despite this independence and despite having to serve governments of varying political hues, they still had to be politically sensitive; not non-political but 'politically promiscuous', as Richard Rose put it (cited Campbell & Wilson, 1995: 17). The senior official, in short, had to be capable of providing legitimate governments of all political complexions with objective advice and then loyally implementing government decisions. This doctrine was pithily summarised by *The Times* of 15 February 1977 as: 'Civil servants propose. Ministers decide. Civil servants execute' (cited Campbell & Wilson, 1995: 23).

It is important to stress at this point that only a minority of civil servants work in Whitehall and only a minority have regular dealings with ministers. Of some 470 000 civil servants only 2800 belong to the Senior Civil Service set up on 1 April 1996.

What were the conditions for the success of the Whitehall model? First of all, this was a period of broad consensus between the front benches on both sides of the House of Commons, one shared with senior officials in Whitehall and their interlocutors in City boardrooms and St James clubs and Oxbridge common rooms – the Establishment, in a word. Second, it was based on relations of partnership and trust between officials and ministers – relations based upon the traditional relationship between the gentleman and his gentleman (in the case of most Conservative ministers) or the gentleman and his deferential social inferior (in the case of Labour ministers not educated in public school and Oxbridge). A third factor was the clear line of accountability (supposedly demonstrated by the case of Crichel Down in 1954) in that ministers took the rap for the misdeeds of their officials. (The facts of Crichel Down were rather different but what counted was appearance rather than reality.) Fourth, the civil service was left to regulate its own affairs, based on general public confidence in its integrity as a high status profession. Finally, the civil service held a virtual monopoly of policy advice. Distinguished and energetic outsiders recruited during the world wars departed afterwards and both the Lloyd George Coalition and Attlee's Labour Government missed opportunities to reform the British civil service as de Gaulle did the French civil service in 1945 by founding the celebrated *Ecole National d'Administration*. External policy advice was channelled through Royal Commissions and Committees of Inquiry whose members were selected from among 'the great and the good' and whose reports were largely drafted by Whitehall officials.

This complacent world is epitomised by Attlee's comment: 'The Civil Servant forms part of a service unequalled in all the world – one of the causes of just pride in his fellow-countrymen' (cited Balogh, 1959: 87). It was a world that was about to be shattered by the renewed awareness of Britain's relative economic decline of which Balogh's famous essay on 'the establishment of mandarins' (the source of the quotation from Attlee) was an important expression. The burden of Balogh's argument was that the mismanagement of the British economy could be laid at the door of Treasury officials without an education in economics. His was merely the first and most influential assault on the civil service. The American author of a book on industrial management in Europe published in 1962 characterised British senior civil servants as 'amateurs', Professor Brian Chapman criticised their 'luxuriant amateurism' in an essay published in 1963, and the anonymous authors (thought to include senior officials) of a Fabian Society pamphlet of 1964 repeated the charge and called for wholesale reform (Garrett, 1972: 31–3). Reform did not have to wait upon Fulton: one important product of Macmillan's modernisation drive was the introduction of the public expenditure planning system following the publication in 1961 of a report of officials chaired by Edwin Plowden (one distinguished wartime recruit who remained in Whitehall) (Lowe, 1997).

Fulton and after

Balogh was an old friend of Wilson from his time as a research assistant to William Beveridge at Oxford in the late 1930s. His essay on Whitehall was an important influence in shaping Wilson's modernising agenda in opposition in the early 1960s, and Wilson brought him into No. 10 as a personal adviser after the 1964 election (Pimlott, 1993: 116, 275, 277–8, 339). His was a major influence behind Wilson's appointment in 1966 of John Fulton (a fellow wartime civil servant and then Vice-Chancellor of the newly founded Sussex University) to chair a Committee of Inquiry into the running of the civil service. Apparently Wilson was hoping for 'a modern equivalent' of the Northcote–Trevelyan Report (Pimlott, 1993: 516–17).

The opening words of the Fulton Report published in 1968 have become famous: 'The Home Civil Service today is fundamentally the product of the nineteenth-century philosophy of the Northcote–Trevelyan Report. The tasks it faces are those of the second half of the twentieth century.' The Report went on to castigate 'the cult of the generalist' or 'the philosophy of the amateur' which it denounced as 'obsolete at all levels and in all parts of the Service'. Its main recommendations were intended to remedy its complaint that 'too few civil servants are skilled managers' (Fulton, 1968: 9, 11, 12).

In the longer perspective, Fulton's recommendations to improve civil service management proved to be most important in setting an agenda for change that would be available for any government with an inclination and will to carry it forward. The Report recommended that the civil service should contain 'a strong force of highly-qualified professional accountants', including a management service unit in each department to promote efficiency. The service should introduce 'accountable management', by which individuals and branches could be held responsible for 'objectively measured performance'. It should 'distinguish those [staff] within departments whose primary responsibility is planning for the future, from those whose main concern is the operation of existing policies or the provision of services'. Fulton concluded that 'large-scale executive operations cannot be effectively run by government departments and [therefore] should be "hived off" wherever possible to independent boards [which] would be wholly responsible in their own fields within the powers delegated to them' (Fulton, 1968: 51, 55, 61–2).

Wilson's Government had lost much of its modernising impetus by the time the Report was published in 1968 and Heath soon became bogged down in the conflict with the trade unions which culminated in electoral defeat in 1974. Both Wilson and Heath were largely content to leave the Report's implementation to senior officials who adopted those recommendations that they favoured while shelving the more threatening ones. However, by 1974 the civil service had been hit by an unprecedented collapse of confidence within its own ranks and was about to be hit by a similar collapse of confidence in its integrity and ability among politicians of both main parties. Much of the blame for the economic crises of the 1970s was laid at the door of senior civil servants who began to be seen as the main obstacles to the radical reform needed to reverse Britain's relative economic decline. The collapse of confidence both *within* the civil service and *in* the civil service was an important component of the crisis of the mid-1970s. In these years, Peter Hennessy has claimed, the civil service 'became the scapegoat for national failure' (Hennessy, 1989: 260).

The collapse of confidence

Proverbially a fish rots from the head. The collapse of confidence within the civil service was most evident in the case of Sir William Armstrong, the service's head. As events bore down upon him in 1973 and 1974, Heath turned increasingly to Armstrong for support and advice – to the point where Armstrong appeared alongside him at press conferences and began to be described as 'deputy prime minister' (Hennessy, 1989: 238). Douglas Hurd, Heath's political secretary, has offered a vignette of Armstrong in his account of a weekend at Ditchley Park in January 1974 as Heath pondered how to escape from the crisis enveloping his Government: 'The atmosphere was Tchekovian. We sat on sofas in front of great log fires and discussed first principles while the rain lashed the windows. Sir William was full of notions, ordinary and extraordinary' (Hurd, 1979: 131). Campbell Adamson, then Director General of the CBI, has recalled being harangued by Armstrong about the same time: 'We listened to a lecture about how Communists were infiltrating everything. They might even be infiltrating, he said, the room he was in ...' 'Downing Street insiders' describe him as 'really quite mad at the end ... lying on the floor and talking about moving the Red Army from here and the Blue Army from there' (cited Whitehead, 1985: 110). He collapsed in early February and, after going on sick leave, took early retirement when Wilson took office in March (Hennessy, 1989: 240).

The Treasury was hit particularly hard by the recurrent economic crises of the time. Jock Bruce-Gardyne and Nigel Lawson, future Treasury ministers under Thatcher, noted in 1976 how the Treasury 'took the rap' for economic failure in the 1960s and 1970s and 'its power and influence dwindled with the purchasing power of the pound' (Bruce-Gardyne & Lawson, 1976: 164). The tough-minded and resilient Leo Pliatzky, second permanent secretary in charge of public expenditure, has described the impact of the oil price rise in late 1973: 'At times it seemed that a whole civilisation and way of life based on cheap and plentiful oil was under threat'. Christmas parties that year were held by candlelight because of power cuts caused by the miners' work to rule. The following passage gives a vivid picture of rising panic.

> To be part of the government machine coping with this situation and striving to keep things going gave a sense of awful but impotent responsibility. Housman's epitaph on an army of mercenaries who saved the sum of things for pay came recurrently to mind. To compare this situation with the time when the earth's foundations fled may now seem overdramatic. A little while afterwards, talking to one of my opposite numbers at the top of the Ministry of Finance in Paris, when I said that I felt we had just pulled back from the brink, he said scornfully, 'Brink? What brink? You had a strike. You had an election. No one was shot.' However, there was a good deal of stress at the time, which

> played a part in the illness which put William Armstrong out of action at one stage during these events.
>
> (Pliatzky, 1982: 119–120)

For about eighteen months – from Heath's confrontation with the miners in early 1974 until the referendum on Britain's membership of the EEC in June 1975 – officials served Ministers engaged in almost continuous electoral campaigning. Only in the summer of 1975 were Labour ministers ready to address the economic problems that had been accumulating since 1973.

Those problems also undermined politicians' confidence in officials. Two things stand out from this criticism. First was the extent of common ground among critics of the civil service on the right of the Conservative Party and on the left of the Labour Party. Margaret Thatcher was as critical as Tony Benn of the defeatist mentality among the higher reaches of the civil service and their readiness to conspire to frustrate radical ministers' intentions. Brian Sedgemore, later Benn's Parliamentary Private Secretary at the Department of Energy, found an ally in Nicholas Ridley when they served together on the House of Commons' Expenditure Committee's inquiry into the civil service in 1976–7 (Sedgemore, 1980: 27–8). Sedgemore was as critical of the political role played by William Armstrong under Heath as he was of the conduct of senior officials at the Departments of Industry and of Energy under Tony Benn (32, 81, 123, 140). Nicholas Ridley, dismissed by Heath in 1972, had already concluded that the civil service 'virtually controls the Departments', with Ministers reduced to 'but the public and parliamentary relations officers of their Departments'. He described civil servants as 'a political party of monolithic view' which had prevented Heath from carrying out aspects of Conservative policy just as they had prevented Wilson's Government from carrying out a socialist programme. His remedy for asserting ministerial control was very close to the policy recommended by Fulton and carried out by the Conservatives after 1988 of turning 'selected functions of each Ministry ... into administrative agencies, organised more or less on business lines' (Ridley, 1973: 3–6).

Second was the extent to which consensus-minded politicians in key positions lost confidence in senior officials. Richard Crossman's diaries of the 1964–70 Government published in three volumes between 1975 and 1977 were decisive in dispelling the myth of dispassionate civil servants loyally supporting their Ministers. Douglas Hurd concluded on the basis of his experience of the Heath Government that a Conservative Government which believed in reducing the power of the state 'will always face serious problems with civil servants at all levels', simply acting from self-interest rather than party-political loyalty. Nor could senior officials be relied upon to give sound advice at critical times (Hurd, 1979: 29–30, 117–18). James Callaghan suspected that Treasury officials were conspiring with their opposite numbers in the IMF and the US Treasury to frustrate British government policy during the IMF crisis in 1976 (Burk & Cairncross, 1992: 62). Denis Healey could not forgive Treasury officials for misleading him and previous Chancellors about the true level of public spending (Healey, 1990: 402). Edmund Dell, Paymaster General at the Treasury and effectively deputy Chancellor until he entered the Cabinet as Secretary of State for Trade in 1976, has criticised the divisions among Treasury officials and their 'naive' advice to Healey (Burk & Cairncross, 1992: 25; Dell, 1997: 405). Finally, Joel Barnett, Chief Secretary in charge of controlling public expenditure from 1974 to 1979, recalled 'many instances ... when Ministers suspected the motives of senior civil servants' and the development of a 'them and us' attitude between Ministers and officials (Barnett, 1982: 188).

Prevailing perceptions of the civil service in the late 1970s are well captured in the titles of two important books of the period. The first, *Your Disobedient Servant*, described how senior officials at the Property Services Agency (responsible for Government property management) frustrated the efforts of the author, when director of PSA Southern Region, to introduce cost-saving reforms (Chapman, 1978). The second, *The Civil Servants: an Inquiry into Britain's Ruling Class*, by Norman Hunt, a leading member of the Fulton Committee and a junior education minister after 1974, and the journalist Peter Kellner, described how senior civil servants manipulated ministers from both parties and undermined Fulton's recommendations for reform (Kellner & Crowther-Hunt, 1980). The popular television comedy series *Yes, Minister* caricatured only very slightly this portrait of manipulative mandarins and pliant politicians.

Conservative reforms

The perceived problem of over-mighty senior officials was one that Mrs Thatcher was determined to address as part of her self-proclaimed mission to reverse Britain's relative economic decline. Her contempt for the cadre of top officials which she inherited is well-captured in her description of the famous dinner which she gave for her Permanent Secretaries in 1980 as 'one of the most dismal occasions of my entire time in government' (Thatcher, 1995: 48).

Thatcher's priority was to reassert political control over the civil service which she did by appointing the managing director of Marks & Spencer Derek Rayner as her personal adviser on efficiency (and effective head of the civil service), by imposing an immediate freeze on new recruitment, by ending so-called 'pay comparability' (by which civil service pay was fixed in relation to pay in comparable private sector occupations) thus permitting a gradual reduction in civil service pay relative to the private sector, and finally by defeating a long strike called by the civil service unions in 1981 over the ending of pay comparability. Thatcher followed the defeat of this strike with the dismissal of the Minister for the Civil Service, Lord Soames, and the forced retirement of the Head of the civil service, Sir Ian Bancroft, the abolition of the Civil Service Department (CSD) and the transfer of its responsibilities for civil service pay and manpower to the Treasury which could be relied upon to take a suitably tough line. This coup 'symbolised a new era in which the power civil servants had was at Ministers' pleasure' (Foster & Plowden, 1996: 244). So by 1981 there could be no doubt about who was in charge and the scene was set for the most far-reaching changes in the civil service since the decades following Northcote–Trevelyan.

We can discern three stages in the Conservative Government's programme of civil service reform. The first, from 1979 to 1988, involved a series of essentially piecemeal management improvements within the departmental structure inherited from previous governments. The second, at its height between 1988 and 1992 but continuing until 1997 at a lesser tempo, involved a reconstruction of government departments along lines set out in the third of our three reports, the so-called Ibbs Report published in 1988 (Efficiency Unit, 1988). The third stage, from 1992 to 1997, cannot be characterised so easily as the two previous stages but essentially involved the introduction of market mechanisms within the civil service and the out-sourcing of major functions hitherto carried out in-house. Let us look at each of these phases in more detail.

1979–88: piecemeal management reform

This first stage of reforms has been characterised as 'Raynerism' after Mrs Thatcher's first adviser on efficiency who served from 1979 until 1982 (when he was succeeded by Robin Ibbs from ICI) (Hennessy, 1989: 589). Perhaps most important was the series of so-called 'efficiency scrutinies' undertaken by middle-ranking officials of areas of departmental work with a view to effecting savings by management improvements. These scrutinies included the development in the Department of the Environment of prototype management information and management accounting systems (MINIS and MAXIS respectively) which were subsequently disseminated throughout Whitehall under the aegis of the Financial Management Initiative (FMI) launched in 1982. A growing army of management consultants helped to introduce these changes, which would not have been possible without cheap and powerful desktop computing which became available in these years (Williams, 1996b). Other connected managerial changes included the introduction of a notional rental system for government offices and early experiments in performance-related pay.

Despite these changes the majority of civil servants continued to serve in large, multi-functional departments, with a common grade structure and common pay scales negotiated centrally by the Treasury (after the abolition of the CSD in 1981). These changes can be seen as fulfilling the Fulton agenda, with its stress on better management. They were driven very much by Thatcher's enthusiasm and the Treasury's drive to reduce public expenditure. But during the course of the 1980s they generated a cadre of younger, managerially-minded civil servants with a career interest in the continued extension of these reforms. In retrospect these piecemeal changes can be seen as providing a necessary springboard for later, more radical changes.

1988–92: wholesale structural reform

This stage was launched by the publication in 1988 of the Efficiency Unit's Report *Improving Management in Government: the Next Steps* (often called the Ibbs Report after the Unit's head). This report, the third in our tale, has a claim to be regarded as the single most important document concerning the civil service since Northcote–Trevelyan.

The Report's main conclusions were that senior civil servants were more concerned with policy than management, that it was unrealistic to expect ministers to be ready to answer for the detailed management of services, and that the civil service was too big and diverse to be managed as a single entity (Efficiency Unit, 1988: 3–5). Its main recommendation was to divide the civil service between 'a relatively small core engaged in the function of servicing Ministers and managing departments' and 'a range of agencies employing their own staff ... and concentrating on the delivery of their particular service, with clearly defined responsibilities between the Secretary of State on the one hand and the Chairmen or Chief Executives of the agencies on the other' (15). The link with Fulton's recommendations for 'hiving off' executive functions was pointed in relevant extracts cited in an Annex to the Efficiency Unit's Report. The aim was to clarify accountability so that ministers were responsible for setting policy while Agency Chief Executives were responsible for implementation – a distinction that was easier in theory than in practice.

The process of 'unbundling' departments into their policy-making cores and agencies responsible for service delivery was well under way by the time of the 1992 election. By January 1997, there were 138 agencies employing over 330 000 staff of whom some 305 000 were civil servants. Another four units (including the Inland Revenue and Customs and Excise with over 70 000 staff between them) were organised along similar lines. Some 383 000 civil servants, 80 per cent of the total, were employed in agencies (Cabinet Office, 1998: 303–4). The Department of Social Security was typical, with 2000 staff in Whitehall and another 80 000 spread among six agencies (mainly in the Benefits Agency, Contributions Agency and Child Support Agency).

1992–97: introducing market mechanisms

This stage involved a reversion to the piecemeal approach of the first stage and included a variety of different strands which are probably best summed up in terms of introducing market disciplines of one kind or another. The first and probably best-known of these market mechanisms, because of its close identification with John Major, was the Citizen's Charter, launched in 1991 but not seriously under way until after the 1992 election (Major, 1991). The purpose was to stimulate pressure from the public service's 'customers' (including those of the new executive agencies) to raise standards as a complement to managerial pressure from above in the form of a battery of performance targets.

A second market mechanism (also launched near the end of Major's first term in office but not seriously under way until after the 1992 election) was the programme for introducing greater competition into the public service under the sobriquet of 'Competing for Quality'. This initiative involved a shift in culture from bureaucratic to contractual relations within the public sector as a whole (HM Treasury, 1991: 2). For the civil service it involved putting services such as property management and computing out to tender, the privatisation of several of the recently established executive agencies where similar services were already provided by the private sector, and more open competition for senior posts, especially in the new agencies or for more specialist posts in the core departments.

A third strand, launched by the White Paper *The Civil Service: Continuity and Change*, involved a wholesale restructuring of the core departments, hitherto largely immune from major change, and a radical programme of delegation of management functions such as pay, grading and recruitment from the centre to departments and agencies (Cabinet Office, 1994). These changes were accompanied by a programme of departmental reviews which typically resulted in cuts of around a quarter in the number of senior officials by 1996 when the 2800 who remained were transferred to a new Senior Civil Service (SDS), all on individual contracts and pay. By then the SCS was all that remained of the unified civil service established in 1920 as the culmination of the programme of reform initiated by Northcote–Trevelyan.

Assessing the impact

How are we to assess the impact of these changes which amount to a revolution in the management of the civil service? Let us look first at the impact on the delivery of services such as tax collection, benefit payment and logistic support for the armed forces in which the great majority of civil servants were, and still are, engaged. Probably the most considered assessment is contained in *The State under Stress* by two management consultants, Christopher Foster and Francis Plowden, both with decades of experience of work for government clients. They concluded that there had indeed been some improvement in efficiency since the early 1980s but resulting mainly from the management reforms launched by Rayner and the FMI rather than the more recent restructuring following the Ibbs Report (Foster & Plowden, 1996: 166). Recent problems with IT at the Passport Agency and the Contributions Agency have pointed to the dangers of relying on consultants to deliver new IT systems vital to basic government services like the issue of passports or national insurance (Timmins, 1999b).

Foster and Plowden also argued that all was not well among the relatively small number of Whitehall civil servants responsible for advising ministers and coordinating the government machine. They pointed to confusion over accountability for management decisions of the kind illustrated by the Home Secretary's dismissal of the head of the Prisons Agency in 1995 and to the erosion of Whitehall's capability for advising Ministers as a result of cuts in the number of senior officials following the 1994 White Paper (Foster & Plowden, 1996: 178–9, 208). Other seasoned commentators by the mid-1990s were pointing to a growing fragmentation – 'a hollowing out of the state' in a graphic phrase popularised at this time – resulting from the reconstruction of central government (Rhodes, 1994; Richards, 1996; Fry, 1997). Other studies pointed to declining morale among senior officials (Plowden, 1994; Campbell & Wilson, 1995), a finding confirmed by a poll of members of their trade union, the First Division Association, in 1995 (*FDA News*, Aug./Sept. 1995).

In order to understand the reasons for this collapse in morale, we need to recall three key foundations of the Whitehall model: partnership and trust between officials and ministers; the civil service's regulation of its own affairs; and senior officials' virtual monopoly on advice to ministers. All of these foundations have been dramatically undermined since the crisis of confidence in the civil service in the 1970s (although this process can be traced back to the criticisms of Balogh in the late 1950s).

First of all, there has been a breakdown of trust between officials and ministers, beginning in the 1960s under Wilson, accumulating among politicians of both main parties during the crises of the 1970s, rising to a climax under Thatcher in the 1980s and showing no sign of abating in the 1990s. It has been associated with the rise of the career politician with a strong interest in policy (such as Keith Joseph, Nicholas Ridley, Nigel Lawson, John Redwood, Peter Lilley and Michael Portillo among the Conservatives; and Gordon Brown, Peter Mandelson and Patricia Hewitt among Labour) (Riddell, 1996). It has been reflected in the appointment of increasing numbers of political advisers – from a handful under Wilson in the 1960s, increasing under Wilson and Callaghan in the 1970s, continuing under Thatcher and Major and rising further under Blair. At the latest count in July 1999 the Labour Government was employing 68 special advisers compared with about 40 under Major (*The Times*, 9.7.99; *Financial Times*, 26.11.97).

Secondly, the Conservative Government's managerial reforms involved wholesale ministerial intervention in the organisation of the civil service. Ministers also began to intervene in senior appointments. Thatcher admitted to taking 'a close interest in senior appointments in the civil service from the first' (Thatcher, 1995: 46). Nigel Lawson, Chancellor from 1983 to 1989, did the same: 'staff appointments were a matter in which I always took the keenest interest' (Lawson, 1992: 384). There is much anecdotal evidence that this intervention in postings and promotion resulted in officials tailoring their advice to suit Ministers. The definitive study of the Poll Tax attributed part of the blame for this debacle to an 'activist mentality' among civil servants at the Department of the Environment (Butler *et al.*, 1994: 214). Peter Kemp, the Treasury official chosen by Mrs Thatcher as project manager for the creation of executive agencies, has described the change in terms of a 'shift from wait-a-minute to can-do. And can-do man is here to stay ... The genie of real ministerial control is out of the bottle' (Kemp, 1996). During the summer of 1999 the press carried well-informed stories from seasoned commentators indicating mounting ministerial frustration about foot-dragging in Whitehall and a desire to intervene in senior appointments (Hennessy, 1999; Bevins, 1999).

Third, and of course related to politicians' declining confidence in officials, was the civil service's loss of its near monopoly over policy advice. Increasingly politicians have turned to think-tanks for policy ideas, initially the Conservatives who looked to the Institute of Economic Affairs, the Centre for Policy Studies and the Adam Smith Institute, first while in opposition in the late 1970s and then throughout the 1980s and 1990s (Cockett, 1995). The success of the Right-wing think-tanks spawned imitators in the Centre (the Social Market Foundation) and on the Left (Demos, the Institute for Public Policy Research [IPPR] and a revitalised Fabian Society). During the 1980s a spell in a think-tank formed a useful first step for an aspiring Conservative politician (like Michael Forsyth or David Willetts) and the pattern seems likely to be repeated under Labour. David Miliband, head of the No. 10 Policy Unit, served a spell in the IPPR in the early 1990s and Geoff Mulgan, one of his leading colleagues, helped to found Demos. The same is true of some of the fastest-rising MPs who entered the House of Commons in 1997: Patricia Hewitt, Minister of State at DTI, served as Deputy Director of the IPPR from 1989 to 1994 and Malcolm Wicks, Parliamentary Under-Secretary of State at the Department for Education and Employment, headed the Family Policy Studies Centre. Another source of policy ideas has been individual management consultants such as Christopher Foster – memorably described as 'Thatcherism's Dr Strangelove' for his part in devising the Poll Tax and rail privatisation (Jenkins, 1996: 53) – and Alain Enthoven with his ideas for an internal market in the NHS (Timmins, 1996: 458). Management consultancy firms (especially the large accountancy-based firms such as Price Waterhouse, Coopers and Lybrand [now merged], KPMG and Andersens) also played a vital role in implementing a whole series of reforms, from the FMI and the creation of executive agencies to the reorganisation of the NHS and the privatisation of the public utilities (Williams, 1996b). Stephen Timms, another fast-rising member of the 1997 parliamentary intake recently appointed Pensions Minister at the Department of Social Security, previously worked in IT consultancy (*Financial Times*, 26.8.99).

Other factors in the erosion of confidence and capability among senior officials were the reductions in numbers, especially during the mid-1990s, coupled with an increasing span of management control requiring greater delegation to junior staff. Relative pay declined for most of the 1980s and many of the more talented and ambitious younger officials, especially those whose work on the FMI or privatisation brought them into contact with management consultants and merchant bankers, left for richer pastures in the City. In 1996, the then head of the civil service, Sir Robin Butler, admitted that the service no longer offered the security it once did – a security that had provided an essential base from which to deliver the independent advice envisaged by Northcote–Trevelyan (Hencke, 1996).

Conclusion

In the late 1970s the senior civil service could be described by serious commentators as 'Britain's ruling class' (Kellner & Crowther-Hunt, 1980); a study of *The Civil Service under the Conservatives 1979–97* questioned whether they had not become 'Whitehall's Political Poodles' in the words of the book's sub-title (Richards, 1997). This chapter has drawn on a series of studies published in the last years of the Conservative Government which all concluded that the much-vaunted independent power of senior officials had been effectively neutralised by the cumulative impact of the reforms undertaken since 1979. Civil servants are now seen as implementers of policies devised by ministers rather than partners in framing those policies (Foster & Plowden, 1996: ix). Tony Blair testified to this change when he described the strength of civil servants as being confined largely to 'preparing legislation and managing policy' (Blair, 1998c: 10) – and the present head of the civil service, Sir Richard Wilson, seemed to accept the Labour Government's wish for the service to focus more on policy delivery than policy making, recognising that ministers would wish to draw on external advice and research (Timmins, 1999a).

There is no sign that Labour intends to reverse the Conservative reforms of the civil service. David Clark, Tony Blair's first Minister for the Civil Service dismissed in his first re-shuffle in July 1998, announced in a speech in June 1997 that the new Government was not planning 'to turn the clock back'. It intended to continue with the emphasis on management reform and value for money (Drewry, 1999: 169). Tony Blair himself, in his Fabian pamphlet on *The Third Way*, has emphasised the importance of 'the drive to "reinvent government"' (Blair, 1998b: 15) and his Foreword to the White Paper on *Modernising Government* describes this programme as 'vital to the Government's programme of renewal for Britain' (Cabinet Office,

1999: 4). Sir Richard Wilson sees the civil service as standing at 'the beginning of very big wave of a change' (Timmins, 1999a).

More than two years after the 1997 election, following the publication of a long-awaited White Paper on the subject, how are we to assess the distinctive Labour contribution to civil service reform. Borrowing from the title of the 1994 Conservative White Paper, let us look at elements of continuity and change.

The continuities are very evident. We find the same emphasis on economy and value for money, the same focus on the need to learn from the private sector, the same commitment to innovative use of IT and customer service. Harking back to Fulton we find the same stress on the need for more recruitment from outside the civil service and a commitment to performance-related pay. The White Paper is quite frank in acknowledging the value of 'the reforms of the last two decades [which] have done much to develop a more managerial culture' (Cabinet Office, 1999: 55).

What is new is an emphasis on remedying perceived problems of fragmentation which had developed during the last years of Conservative Government. The White Paper contains commitments to focus more closely on results, to improve coordination among government departments and to increase consultation with other public bodies, voluntary organisations and the private sector in developing policy (Cabinet Office, 1999: 15–16). The Government has strengthened its capacity for coordination through the reorganisation of the Cabinet Office as (in Blair's words) 'a corporate headquarters for the civil service'(*Financial Times*, 29.7.98). More recently Blair has followed Conservative precedents in appointing Lord Simon, formerly chairman of BP and Minister at the Department of Trade and Industry, as a special adviser on civil service reform and ways of improving the functioning of government (*Financial Times*, 30.7.99). Thus in this area we can see that Labour has been building on Conservative reforms which can now be seen as part of a new consensus on the primacy of ministers and the essentially managerial rather than policy-making role of civil servants.

7
Rolling Back the State: Privatisation and Deregulation

Introduction

Privatisation entails the transfer of an activity from the public to the private realm – from the state to private agents. It therefore needs to be seen as part of an attempt to reverse the long-term increase in the role of the state in the economy. The proportion of public spending as a percentage of GDP among the advanced capitalist economies has risen from an average of less than 10 per cent in 1900 to around 45 per cent in the late 1990s. Britain, with public spending running at around 40 per cent of GDP, stands approximately mid-way between the EU average of around 50 per cent and the USA at 30 per cent (*Economist*, 20.9.97). Privatisation also raises the question of whether the transfer of assets from state to private hands involves a reduction in state power or simply a change in the way in which the state exercises power.

Privatisation has been defined by one of its advocates (Stuart Butler, co-founder of the Adam Smith Institute) as 'the shifting of a function, either in whole or in part, from the public sector to the private sector' (cited Feigenbaum *et al.*, 1998: 1). One of its main promoters, Nigel Lawson, described it as 'almost the same thing as de-nationalisation ... essentially the transfer of control of a whole industry or firm from the State to the private sector' (Lawson, 1992: 198). Madsen Pirie, another leading proponent of the policy, as co-founder and President of the Adam Smith Institute, argued that privatisation went beyond the mere return of previously nationalised industries to private hands; sometimes it involved establishing 'a complex web of arrangements to create new owners, and in some cases new forms of ownership' (Pirie, 1988: 9).

This chapter concentrates on the privatisation of the nationalised industries and the regulation of the privatised utilities such as British Telecom but also looks at other related developments under the broad rubric of privatisation. It begins by looking at the growth of state ownership of major industries and the problems that had developed by the 1970s. It then looks at the origins and developments of privatisation under the Conservative Government after 1979 and the distinctive British approach to the regulation of privately-owned utilities which involved a significant departure from practice in the USA, hitherto the main model for regulating privately-owned utilities. Then it looks at other aspects of privatisation, broadly defined, before concluding with a brief assessment of developments under Labour and the implications of this process for the nature of the state.

The growth of nationalised industry

Nationalisation in Britain has never formed part of some grand plan for transforming the economy. The Post Office – the last important nationalised industry – has operated within the public sector since it was established as the General Post Office in the early Victorian heyday of *laissez-faire* capitalism. It remained a government department until the late 1960s, headed by a ministerial Postmaster General (Tony Benn was the last). During the late nineteenth century local authorities practised what was then described as 'municipal socialism' by developing gas and electricity supply industries, as well as looking after sewerage and supplying three-quarters of the nation's drinking water. The government rapidly assumed responsibility for regulating the privately-owned railways. Gladstone as President of the Board of Trade under Peel in the 1840s insisted on 'the competency and right of Parliament' to interfere in setting fares, by introducing the so-called Parliamentary train providing third-class carriages at one (old) penny a mile. The same legislation contained powers for the government to purchase railways 21 years after they had been built (Shannon, 1999: 146).

The first state acquisition of private industry was associated with impending war. Winston Churchill as First Lord of the Admiralty in the pre-1914 Liberal Government was responsible for nationalising Anglo-Persian Oil in order to assure supplies for the oil-burning battleships of the Grand Fleet (Churchill, 1938, i: 137). Chapter 3 described the operation of the Ministry of Munitions which directed an industry employing over 3 million workers. The Government also nationalised the pubs in Carlisle in order to limit local munitions workers' access to beer (Taylor, 1970: 65, 68). These pubs remained in state hands until the early 1970s when (with Thomas Cook the travel agents) they were returned to private hands by the Heath Government.

However, these wartime measures were intended essentially as temporary expedients, like the wartime regulation of the railways and coal mining. Between 1918 and the late 1970s it is possible to identify three main phases in the piecemeal growth of public ownership of industry which we think of as nationalisation.

The first phase took place between the wars and involved the nationalisation of natural monopolies (defined as a service or product which can be delivered more cheaply by one firm than by several). In 1926 the Conservative Government of Stanley Baldwin was responsible for setting up the British Broadcasting Corporation and Central Electricity Generating Board (responsible for generating the electricity supplied by the national grid to hundreds of local authority suppliers). In 1931 the Labour Government legislated for the London Passenger Transport Board which was eventually set up under the Conservative-dominated National Government (and run by the London County Council controlled by Labour). In 1939 the National Government nationalised several airways as the British Overseas Airways Corporation (eventually part of British Airways, privatised in the 1980s). Clearly nationalisation between the wars was no partisan measure; most of it was done by Conservative (or Conservative-dominated) governments.

The second phase took place under the post-war Labour Government and involved essentially the assumption by central government of control over the gas and electricity supply industries hitherto run by local authorities as well as the nationalisation of the coal and transport industries which had been run down during the war and required heavy investment. It also included the nationalisation of the Bank of England and Cable and Wireless, responsible for telegraph communications overseas. The motivation behind this programme was varied. For some on the Left of the Labour Party it could be seen as the first stage in the advance towards a planned economy, as socialism was currently conceived under the influence of the Soviet example (whose prestige was at its height during the war and immediately afterwards). For others it could be seen as the essential means of modernising industries that were fundamental to the economy as a whole and in need of investment that only the state could provide. The generous compensation paid to previous owners could be invested much more profitably elsewhere. The limits of the nationalised sector were accepted by the Conservatives in 1951 apart from road freight transport and iron and steel which were returned to the private sector. The Labour Party in opposition after 1951 had no significant plans for further nationalisation apart from returning iron and steel to public ownership. They were more concerned, under the influence of Anthony Crosland, to expand public spending on welfare services in the interests of promoting social equality.

The third phase involved further piecemeal nationalisation by Labour and Conservative governments in the 1960s and 1970s. Labour took iron and steel back into public ownership in 1965. During the economic crises of the 1970s the Conservative and Labour governments nationalised a whole series of ailing industries such as shipbuilding, aerospace and vehicle manufacture. As part of local government reorganisation devised by the Conservatives (and implemented under Labour in 1974) the local authority water and sewerage undertakings were brought under central government control as Regional Water Authorities.

Nationalised industries in Britain were not run directly by government ministers (as in the Soviet Union) but by Boards of Directors appointed by ministers to head so-called 'public corporations'. This model was devised for London Transport by Herbert Morrison, Labour leader of the London County Council in the 1930s, and adopted by the Labour Government of 1945–51 for the other industries taken into government ownership. These industries were supposed to be run as businesses in the interests of the nation as a whole. There were never any plans for workers' control of these industries.

By 1979 the nationalised industries accounted for 11 per cent of GDP; they employed two million workers – 8 per cent of the workforce – and were responsible for over 13 per cent of total investment in the economy (Saunders & Harris, 1994: 7). They included: the major utility services (about 80 per cent of water supply and all sewage disposal, gas and electricity generation and supply, and posts and telecommunications); much of the extractive industries necessary for energy supply (coal mining and much of the oil industry); most public transport (railways, most buses, the main airports and the main national airline and most ports); plus various firms manufacturing ships, steel, cars, aircraft engines and other products operating in competitive markets. For readers who have reached adulthood since the 1970s the range of industries in state ownership must seem difficult to comprehend.

Emerging problems

'During the 1950s and 1960s state-owned industries were judged to have a good record of productivity, investment and management', writes Peter Riddell (1991: 89). Problems began to accumulate under the Conservatives after 1970, as a result of a series of bruising strikes over pay and then as a result of price control as part of the Government's counter-inflation strategy. Long before 1979 the nationalised industries had begun to be perceived as grossly inefficient. First of all, the growth of productivity (output per employee) was below average. Between 1968 and 1979 productivity in British manufacturing industry rose by a not very impressive average of 1.7 per cent a year. Productivity in the electricity industry rose by less than 1 per cent a year during the same period; in the steel industry productivity actually fell by 2.5 per cent and in coalmining by 4.4 per cent a year. Not surprisingly the nationalised industries were running at a loss. In 1979 they earned a gross trading surplus (profit before allowing for depreciation) of £5.5 billion but received subsidy of £1.5 billion and investment of £5 billion. Taken together these figures added up to an overall loss of around £1 billion. Meanwhile the nationalised industries were accused of delivering a poor service to their customers. A survey by the National Consumer Council in 1981 found 'pervasive discontent with declining standards' (Saunders & Harris, 1994: 9).

The nationalised industries were criticised for being run not in the interests of the public or consumers but their employees. Here, as in other parts of the economy, problems of low productivity and poor quality were laid at the door of over-mighty trade unions: 90 per cent of white-collar and manual workers in these industries belonged to trade unions compared with 39 per cent of white-collar workers and 75 per cent of manual workers respectively in the private sector. Bargaining strength based on the trade unions' capacity to inflict discomfort on millions of voters resulted in strikes which led to above-average pay increases and above-inflation price increases (Saunders & Harris, 1994: 9–10).

Privatisation: origins

It has often been observed (see, for example, Jenkins, 1996: 24 and Feigenbaum *et al.*, 1998: 59–60) that the Conservatives hit upon privatisation almost by accident. Mrs Thatcher herself acknowledges that there is some truth in this observation: 'Our 1979 manifesto', she writes in her memoirs, was 'quite cautious on the subject, promising "to sell back to private ownership the recently nationalised aerospace and shipbuilding concerns, giving their employees the opportunity to purchase shares" and selling "shares in the National Freight Corporation to the general public"' (Thatcher, 1995: 677–8).

Nigel Lawson in his memoirs has explained this caution in terms of a lack of detailed policy development work while in opposition and a wish to avoid frightening voters. Nevertheless, he argues that 'privatisation was a central plank of our policy right from the start', pointing to a passage (which he helped to write) in Chancellor Geoffrey Howe's budget speech in June 1979 which stated that 'the scope for sale of assets in the public sector is substantial' and that it constituted 'an essential part of our long-term programme for promoting the widest possible participation by the people in the ownership of British industry' (cited Lawson, 1992: 199). Howe writes:

> Our long-term aim was spelt out in *The Right Approach to the Economy* in 1977: 'to reduce the preponderance of the state in our community'... But our 1979 manifesto was light on specifics... Margaret had been fearful that a more extensive catalogue might frighten the voters.
>
> (Howe, 1995: 253–4)

Nicholas Ridley recalled that the pre-1979 study group which he headed had concentrated on ways of tightening financial discipline rather than disposal (Ridley, 1992: 16).

It is probably fair to conclude that the notion of privatisation was already present among elements of the Conservative leadership as a general intention but that there was no detailed strategy. John Redwood's account of the nationalised industries published in 1980 contains no mention of privatisation as a concept and discusses very briefly only a limited programme of asset sales confined to those nationalised industries (or parts of those industries) already operating in competitive markets. The only remedies for the rest would be a tougher, more contractual relationship with the Government supported by more stringent regulation by the Monopolies Commission (basically what the Government was doing already) (Redwood, 1980: 197–203). Lawson recounts how even in late 1981 a strategy document prepared by John Hoskyns, head of the No. 10 Policy Unit, barely mentioned privatisation and how Leo Pliatzky, one of the ablest senior civil servants of the time, was unable to formulate satisfactory plans for privatisation (Lawson, 1992: 204–5). In the event, the policy developed only gradually: the initial aims for the sector as a whole were simply to tighten financial discipline, reduce subsidy, increase efficiency and to cut the workforce.

Privatisation: the record

Looking back it is possible to distinguish three phases in the development of the Conservative Government's policy on privatisation.

1979–84: asset sales

This first phase, coinciding closely with Mrs Thatcher's first term in office, basically involved the sale of industries (such as British Aerospace, the National Freight Corporation and Cable and Wireless) or parts of industries (such as British Rail's hotels and cross-Channel ferries) that already operated in competitive markets. The results were modest: only about £1.5 billion was raised in this way (Saunders & Harris, 1994: 12–13). Meanwhile the Government tightened financial control over the rest of the sector, brought in tough managers like Ian MacGregor (for British Steel and then British Coal) and John King (British Airways) – the latter described by Nicholas Ridley (1992: 45) as 'the sort of man [Mrs Thatcher] admired, a tough and determined bully' – and (where possible) began exposing them to competition. The sale of the drug company Amersham International in 1982 showed for the first time the potential appeal of asset sales to small shareholders when the share issue was over-subscribed by no less than 24 times, generating an immediate 35 per cent premium (Lawson, 1992: 210).

1984–8: in search of Sid

If the years 1945 to 1950 can be described as the heroic age of nationalisation, then this second phase of privatisation – coinciding closely with Mrs Thatcher's second term in office – may be described as the heroic years of its antithesis. These were the years – from 1984 to 1988 – in which the Conservative Government discovered Sid, the eponymous hero of the vacuous television advertising campaign used to sell shares in British Gas. This second phase – based on the mass marketing of shares – began with the privatisation of British Telecom (BT) in 1984. It continued with British Gas (BG) in 1986, British Airways, the British Airports Authority (BAA) and Rolls Royce in 1987, and British Steel in 1988. It involved selling public monopolies as private monopolies (in the case of BG and BAA) or near-monopolies in order to speed sales and maximise returns. This phase raised about £14 billion (including £4 billion from BT and £5.4 billion from BG) (Lawson, 1992: 241). It also required the invention of new machinery (discussed below) for regulating private monopolies.

1989–97: introducing competition

Broadly speaking the first phase of privatisation focussed on businesses already operating in competitive markets and the second focussed on what were called 'state monopolies' without any significant attempt to introduce the discipline of competition. The third phase, beginning with water and electricity privatisation in 1989 and 1990 under Mrs Thatcher, and continuing with British Rail under Major, involved a preliminary restructuring of the industry in order where possible to introduce competition or to enhance external regulation.

In the case of electricity, this process involved the division of the Central Electricity Generating Board into two companies (Powergen and National Power owning the power stations) for sale in 1991 while a third (Nuclear Electric) was kept in the public sector until it could be privatised as British Energy in 1996. It also involved selling the 12 regional boards responsible for electricity distribution as separate companies, and the national grid as a third component owned by the distribution companies. The privatisation of the water industry in 1989 involved selling nine separate companies responsible for water extraction and supply and for sewage treatment and disposal, while transferring responsibility for regulating the aquatic environment from the former water authorities to a new National Rivers Authority remaining within the public sector. The privatisation of British Rail (BR) involved an even more elaborate reconstruction of the industry into almost 100 different components, including Railtrack responsible for track and signalling, 25 companies responsible for running passenger services and 5 freight operators, with yet more new companies responsible for leasing rolling stock and maintaining track and stock. The entire process involved selling (often to former BR managers) some 70 companies carved out of BR, the public sale of shares in Railtrack and the franchising of 25 regional passenger services. All of these companies are now connected by an elaborate web of contracts. Chris Green, a former BR director who now runs Virgin Rail, one of the main franchisees, has likened the new system to 'an orchestra where 100-odd musicians have individual contracts with the conductor and with each other' (*The Economist*, 3.7.99).

This third phase continued to raise large sums in the early years: £5 billion from the water industry, £10 billion from electricity (Lawson, 1992: 241). Rather less was raised from the sale of British Energy and Railtrack because both nuclear power generation and most rail passenger services continued to require subsidy, however artfully disguised. This phase also saw attempts to introduce competition into British Gas in 1996 by splitting gas distribution and supply. A free market in fuel for electricity power generation meant that gas undercut coal and resulted in the near elimination of coal mining and the sale of the remaining few mines to the private sector.

Privatisation: objectives, mechanisms and outcomes

One main purpose of privatisation was to reduce the role of the government in the economy as part of an overall strategy of 'rolling back the frontiers of the state'. Another was to reduce the power of the trade unions in one of their strongest redoubts. A third was to build popular support for capitalism – 'popular capitalism' – through widening share ownership. As such it represented a logical extension of the Conservative strategy, originating in the 1950s or even earlier, of building a 'property owning democracy'. The political dividends were obvious. Gerry Grimstone, Treasury Assistant Secretary responsible for privatisation policy from 1982 until he joined the merchant bank Schroders in 1986 (Riddell, 1991: 93), has described how, following the sale of BT, Lawson added to the speech which officials had drafted for him the sentence '2.4 million people have put their money on the table, and they have put it on the blue square' (British Broadcasting Corporation, 1997a). Privatisation also had the advantages of generating funds for investment by allowing access to private capital. Finally, the receipts could be used by the government either to maintain public spending at a higher level than otherwise would have been possible at a given level of taxation – or, conversely, to reduce taxation while avoiding the reduction in public spending which otherwise would have been necessary. The new regulatory agencies ensured that public objectives could still be achieved despite the relinquishment of ownership.

The process of privatisation followed a similar pattern in each industry. A first stage was to improve efficiency which could usually be achieved only through large job losses which the trade unions could be expected to resist. The path to market was preceded by bruising strikes in the case of steel, water, coal and the railways. Capital debt might need to be written off and weak regulatory targets set in order to make the industries attractive to shareholders. The big public utilities were sold as monopolies in order to avoid antagonising existing managers such as Dennis Rooke at BG. The initial share price would be set low in order to offer the certain prospect of short-term speculative gain. Only twice would buyers be disappointed: first in 1987 when the stock market crashed just after the price for shares in BP was set, and again in 1996 when for a few weeks the value of shares in British Energy fell below the initial price. The cooperation of senior management could be induced through the prospect of big salary increases and share options, while trade union opposition could be undermined by the prospect of free (or cut-price) shares for the workers.

The results of privatisation have been far-reaching. First of all, it brought huge receipts into the Exchequer – more than £80 billion at 1997 prices (*Financial Times*, 17.1.97). It resulted in a great shift in the balance of the economy: about 50 businesses and almost one million jobs moved from the public into the private sector. Charges for gas, telephones and electricity have risen more slowly than inflation although water charges have risen faster than inflation in order to pay for the increased investment needed to reduce environmental pollution (*Economist*, 9.12.95). While real costs have fallen the quality of service by the utilities has been perceived to improve except for water, where the impact of periodic droughts seems to have become more severe, and railways, where over-crowding has increased and time-keeping worsened since privatisation. For the workforce, there have been big job losses since privatisation: 90 000 jobs (40 per cent of the workforce) in BT had gone by the beginning of 1997; 15 000 (20 per cent) at BG; 12 000 (20 per cent) among the electricity distribution companies and 20 000 (45 per cent) among the generators (*Financial Times*, 17.1.97). The trade unions have been weakened by job losses and the fragmentation of national bargaining arrangements while productivity has risen.

Higher productivity has allowed large increases in directors' salaries and big gains for the holders of shares in the privatised utilities which for most of the 1980s and 1990s out-performed the FTSE All-Share index. In essence the cash saved by sacking workers was used to pay dividends: the share price of British Energy soared after the company announced plans for large job cuts. Privatisation has been a major engine of inequality which has been increasing more in Britain than in any other liberal democracy apart from New Zealand. By 1995 the number of shareholders had risen to ten million from three million in 1979 but half held shares in only one or two companies and the *proportion* of shares held by individuals had fallen from 30 per cent in 1979 to only 20 per cent in 1994 (*The Guardian*, 8.2.96). Politically, privatisation may have encouraged the Labour Party to change its policy but it certainly did not save the Conservatives from defeat. As we have seen in Chapter 5, the 1997 General Election registered a 28 per cent swing to Labour among shareholders (Davies, 1998).

Regulating the privatised utilities

We have distinguished two main categories of nationalised industry: those operating in competitive markets and state monopolies. There was no need to make special arrangements for regulating newly privatised industries in the first category, such as Cable and Wireless, Amersham International and the National Freight Corporation among the earlier firms, and British Airways, British Steel and Rolls Royce among later ones. The need for regulation arose only with the sale of BT as a virtual monopoly provider of telecommunications services. Privatisation was therefore accompanied by the creation of the Office of Telecommunications (OFTEL) as regulator. OFTEL was followed by similar bodies for gas (OFGAS), electricity (OFFER) (merged in 1999 as the Office of Gas and Electricity Markets – OFGEM), water (OFWAT) and railways (the Office of the Rail Regulator and the Franchising Director).

The established US model for regulating utilities (which had always been in private hands) was intended to prevent them from making excessive profits by setting limits on the rate of return from investment. This model was criticised for creating an incentive to over-invest in the assets used in calculating an acceptable rate of return and for offering little incentive to control costs. The British model, devised for BT, involved setting a ceiling on price increases for a period of years, usually expressed in terms of the rate of price inflation minus a factor for efficiency gains to be settled by the regulator following negotiations with the industry. The resulting formula has been expressed as 'RPI (Retail Price Index) minus X' and has been commended for creating an incentive for the industry to deliver efficiency savings greater than the so-called 'X' factor. In the short term any additional savings would pass directly through into profits but the resulting costs savings would provide a basis for assessing potential future savings when the 'X' factor came to be set for the next period, usually after five years.

This British model has been criticised in its turn. Certainly it offers an incentive for the industry to underestimate the potential efficiency gains in negotiations with the regulator, and sets a premium on the regulator's ability to probe the industry's estimates. Occasions have arisen when the regulators have been embarrassed by greater than forecast cost savings which passed straight through into profits – to the benefit of shareholders and senior managers with share options, the notorious 'fat cats' who did so much to discredit privatisation in the eyes of the general public in the run-up to the 1997 election. On the other hand, the scope for windfall savings is bound to diminish over time; and customers benefit from those savings when the 'X' factor comes to be set for the next five-year period. This model has also been criticised for encouraging the industry to economise on investment and to pare staffing to the bone, both potentially at the expense of standards of service. A lively debate on these matters had developed by the time of the 1997 election.

The British regulators are not formally accountable to Ministers but they are appointed by Ministers and they form part of central government broadly defined. They are staffed by civil servants (and sometimes headed by former civil servants such as the former senior Treasury economist Ian Byatt at OFWAT and, until the end of 1998, another former Treasury official Clare Spottiswoode at OFGAS). They maintain frequent contact with officials in the relevant 'sponsor' Departments (such as the Department of Environment, Transport and the Regions for water and railways and the Department of Trade and Industry for telecommunications, gas and electricity). Therefore arguably the privatised utilities remain just as subject to external control as they did when run by supposedly 'arms-length' public corporations subject to all kinds of nods and winks from Ministers. The difference is that the control is now exercised by nominally independent regulators in frequent contact with officials. Simon Jenkins has recalled how Nicholas Ridley (responsible for privatising the water industry) boasted that 'utilities which we have privatised or intend to privatise are more easily controlled when they are in the private sector' (Jenkins, 1996: 39). Thatcher said much the same in her memoirs: 'on regulatory grounds there are good arguments for private ownership as well: regulation which had, when in the public sector, been covert now had to be overt and specific. This provides a clearer and better discipline' (Thatcher, 1995: 677).

Other aspects of privatisation

This chapter has concentrated on the privatisation of nationalised industries but this process forms part of a wider trend which embraces the transfer of former public assets into private hands and the provision of public services by private bodies. The next section examines other examples of privatisation thus broadly understood.

The Right to Buy

The so-called Right to Buy – that is, the right of local authority tenants to buy their homes at subsidised prices depending upon how long they had occupied those homes – was a key pledge in the 1979 Conservative Manifesto. By 1990 it had resulted in the sale of one and a half million council homes, reducing council houses and flats from almost one-third of all homes to less than a quarter and raising £17.5 billion, more than from the sale of any nationalised industry (Johnson, 1991: 151, 153). The policy brought political benefits for the Conservatives so long as the Labour Party remained opposed to the sale of council homes, but it was tarnished by the collapse of the housing market in the late 1980s and early 1990s, and in 1997 mortgage payers swung heavily to Labour (Davies, 1998).

Privatisation of executive agencies

Chapter 6 described the process of unbundling executive agencies from central government departments. One of the incidental advantages of this policy in the eyes of Mrs Thatcher and her Chancellor Nigel Lawson was that it would be easier to sell these agencies once they had been established as free-standing entities. First to go was DVOIT, IT arm of the Department of Transport's Driver and Vehicle Licensing Agency, sold to the large US-based computing firm Electronic Data Services (EDS) (Willman, 1994: 69). By 1997 DVOIT had been followed by a series of Government research establishments, the Paymaster General's Office (renamed Paymaster) responsible for civil service pay and pensions, the Recruitment and Assessment Services Agency responsible for senior staff recruitment, and HM Stationery Office responsible for Government publishing.

Outsourcing peripheral services

One of the orthodoxies of management gurus in the 1980s and 1990s was that companies should 'stick to the knitting' – that is, focus on their so-called 'core' activities while divesting themselves of 'peripheral' activities that could be supplied more efficiently by other firms, sub-contracted for those services. The public sector has followed private sector practice in this area as in others, often under the influence of the same firms of management consultants. Local authorities were forced by Compulsory Competitive Tendering to test the market for an increasingly wide range of services including refuse collection and the management of leisure facilities. The Government wound up the Property Services Agency responsible for managing civil and defence building maintenance and construction during the early 1990s and began to buy in those services from the private sector (Williams, 1996a). It also transferred most of its computing services to big IT companies such as EDS (Margetts, 1996). It even experimented with using private lawyers to prepare tax legislation (*FDA News*, March 1995).

The Private Finance Initiative

The Private Finance Initiative (PFI) was introduced in 1992 as a way of attracting private funds into investment in public assets such as new roads, hospitals and schools. The justification was that the additional cost of leasing those assets from the private sector rather than paying for them through government borrowing would be more than offset by the supposedly greater efficiency with which the private sector would manage those assets (Terry, 1996). Chancellor Kenneth Clarke announced PFI investment amounting to some £4 billion a year by 2000 in his last budget in November 1996. These schemes included four new roads, the Channel Tunnel Rail Link and an extension of the Docklands Light Railway as well as several IT systems (*Financial Times*, 27.11.96).

This list is far from exhaustive. Privatisation can also be taken to embrace liberalisation, that is, the removal of restrictions on access to particular markets such as long-distance coach transport, air routes, conveyancing and the sale of glasses; the wholesale importation of private sector management techniques and private sector managers into public services; and the means testing of services such as dentistry and care of the dependent elderly. In a sense it can be taken to characterise a whole philosophy of governance.

Conclusion

Since 1997 we can see no evidence of significant change under Labour. Labour is just as committed to private-sector values as the Conservatives, as shown by the important role for business people as Government Ministers and in over a hundred task forces. Privatisation remains on the Government's agenda in the form of Public Private Partnerships as with London Underground. The Government has announced plans for privatising the Tote, Air Traffic Control, British Nuclear Fuels and even the Defence Evaluation and Research Agency of the Ministry of Defence. It is as committed as the Conservatives to using the PFI to finance investment in the NHS and has shown signs of extending the Conservative agenda with its plans to bring private contractors into education. It has kept the 'RPI minus X' mechanism put in place by the Conservatives for regulating the privatised utilities and has extended competition in the retail markets for gas and electricity. It has won John Redwood's approval for plans to extend competition in the water industry (*Financial Times*, 6.8.99).

But privatisation no longer forms part of an ideological crusade as it did under Thatcher and Major. Labour is adopting a more pragmatic approach. Privatisation forms just one among other tools of government, not only in this country but also around the globe. For example, the French Socialist government since 1997 has sold more than £12 billion worth of public services – more than any previous Right-wing government (*The Observer*, 7.3.99).

The effect of privatisation has been to shrink the *size* of the state broadly defined to include the public sector as a whole and to transform its *ethos* to the point where there is no longer a clear divide between the public and private sectors. Instead both are in the grip of what Paul Hirst (in an important essay that deserves to be better known) has described as a 'bureaucratic monoculture' (Hirst, 1996: 104 – I owe this reference to Alan Hooper). But the key question remains: has privatisation reduced the *power* of the state?

Perhaps privatisation and the associated emergence of a congeries of regulatory agencies are best understood in terms of a transformation of the state – as *re*-regulation rather than as *de*-regulation. The Italian political economist Giandomenico Majone has distinguished three functions performed by the state. First is redistribution: the transfer of resources from one group to another as well as the direct provision of public services. Second is stabilisation: the management of the economy in order to deliver satisfactory levels of employment, growth and inflation. Third is regulation: the attempt to modify the behaviour of private agents in order to deliver collective objectives (Majone, 1996: 263).

The Labour Government clearly is still engaged in redistribution (as we have seen in Chancellor Gordon Brown's budgets) but (as we shall see in Chapter 8) it has largely withdrawn from macroeconomic management and (as we shall see when we come to look at public spending and welfare in Chapter 9) it is continuing the process of withdrawal from the direct delivery of public services begun by the Conservatives. At the same time the Government has been creating a range of new bodies – part of the extended state but operating at arms length from Ministers – responsible for regulating private agents and public services. What we are witnessing is the development of a new kind of state – the regulatory state. According to that doyen of management gurus Peter Drucker, 'Government is getting more powerful, not through owning but through regulation' (cited Jackson, 1999). More pungently Rupert Murdoch has remarked: 'Socialism is alive and well, and living in regulatory agencies' (*Financial Times*, 28/29.6.97). Paul Hirst is closer to the mark when he describes the modern state as 'a power that regulates and intervenes whilst speaking the fashionable languages of the new *laissez faire*' (Hirst, 1996: 103). What we are seeing is the emergence of a new relationship between the state and private industry to which we shall return in the Conclusion.

8

Steering the Economy: Macro-economic Management from the Gold Standard to EMU

Introduction

It must be a somewhat hazardous undertaking for a mere historian and political scientist to venture upon the territory of the economist and economic historian by attempting a survey of British economic policy since the First World War. However, no survey of modern British politics which takes as a central theme the question of Britain's relative economic decline could overlook the efforts of successive governments to remedy the problem through what has become known as macro-economic management – steering the economy, in Sam Brittan's phrase (Brittan, 1971). Economists may learn something from the historical and political perspective adopted in this book, while readers without formal training in economics may discover some of the political significance of apparently recondite debate among economists.

The story of British economic policy since the First World War can be seen as a tale of paradise lost and successive fruitless attempts to regain that paradise. The lost paradise is of course the era of the Gold Standard and balanced budgets before the First World War – before the onset of the Age of Catastrophe. It should also be stressed that this was a *rentier*'s paradise, and no paradise for working people. That paradise has never been more eloquently described – and perhaps more elegaically recalled – than by Keynes writing in 1919, after it had disappeared in a welter of slaughter. I quote at length, for Keynes was a master of English prose as well as a great economist.

Keynes described this *rentier*'s paradise – the first age of globalisation (what he calls 'internationalisation') – as an 'economic Eldorado', an 'economic Utopia'.

> The greater part of the population ... worked hard and lived at a low standard of comfort, yet were, to all appearances, reasonably contented with this lot. But escape was possible, for any man of capacity or character at all exceeding the average, into the middle and upper classes, for whom life offered, at a low cost and with the least trouble, conveniences, comforts and amenities beyond the compass of the richest and most powerful monarchs of other ages. The inhabitant of London could order by telephone, sipping his morning tea in bed, the various products of the whole earth, in such quantity as he might see fit, and reasonably expect their early delivery upon his doorstep; he could at the same moment and by the same means adventure his wealth in the natural resources and new enterprises of any quarter of the world, and share, without exertion or even trouble, in their prospective fruits and advantages... He could secure forthwith, if he wished it, cheap and comfortable means of transit to any country or climate without passport or other formality... But, most important of all, he regarded this state of affairs as normal, certain, and permanent... The projects and politics of militarism and imperialism, of racial and cultural rivalries ... which were to play the serpent to this paradise, were little more than the amusements of his daily newspaper, and appeared to exercise almost no influence at all on the ordinary course of social and economic life, the internationalisation of which was nearly complete in practice.
>
> (Keynes, 1919: 10–12)

This lost paradise was also the age of British global economic preeminence. In 1914, despite competition from the USA and Germany, Britain was still the wealthiest country in the world in terms of per capita GDP (Wolf, 1997). It was still the largest creditor country with overseas investments worth £4 billion as against less than £5.5 billion owned by Germany, the USA, France, Belgium and Holland put together. And the British mercantile marine still carried about half of the world's trade (Hobsbawm, 1969: 152).

This was a paradise based on several factors that the First World War brought to an end. First of all, the working class had not yet mounted any significant threat to capitalism although the great strikes on the eve of the war can be seen as a foretaste of more bitter struggles in the 1920s (Dangerfield, 1935). Political life was dominated by two main parties – Liberals and Unionists – led by professional politicians still drawn mainly from the professional classes and aristocracy. The Labour Party was no more than a ginger group on the Left of the Liberal Party. Finally, there was no significant ideological challenge to capitalism. If anything, the radical impetus of the Second International had weakened since its foundation in 1889. Few in 1914 had heard of Lenin. Britain's dominant position in the world economy was expressed through the medium of the Gold Standard to which all major currencies were linked.

The First World War changed everything. It transformed Britain's relations with the USA from creditor into debtor; it turned organised labour into a significant industrial force, with over eight million trade union members by 1920 compared with only four million in 1914; it turned the Labour Party into the main challengers to the Conservatives; it led to the foundation of the Soviet Union and the emergence of a global ideological challenge to liberal capitalism; and it resulted in an end to Britain's global pre-eminence symbolised by the suspension of sterling convertibility to gold in 1914.

This chapter looks at successive attempts to recover this paradise lost. First it considers the inter-war efforts to restore 'normalcy' which ended in failure in 1931 when Britain was driven off the Gold Standard to which it had returned in 1925. It goes on to look at the era of Keynesian demand management which was devised to overcome the problems of the Age of Catastrophe but seemed to be ratified by the post-war Golden Age. Then it looks at what has been called the 'economic counter-revolution' spearheaded by the Conservative Government after 1979 and the resulting 'shock therapy'. Just as we need to understand the failures of the inter-war period in order to appreciate the Keynesian revolution, so too do we need to understand the breakdown of Keynesianism in the 1960s and 1970s in order to appreciate the 'monetarist' counter-revolution. Finally we shall examine the successive failures in economic management between 1979 and 1992 which have led in recent years to the emergence of a new consensus foreshadowed in the 1980s under the Chancellorship of Nigel Lawson and brought to fruition by Kenneth Clarke and Gordon Brown in the 1990s. Dare we call it 'Clownism'?

Return to normalcy

The Gold Standard was suspended on the outbreak of war in 1914 but the consensus among Treasury officials, City bankers and orthodox economists – a consensus that politicians had no alternative but to accept – was that the Government should return to the Gold Standard, at the pre-war parity of £1:$4.86, at the earliest opportunity (Skidelsky, 1992: 40, 187). Return to the Gold Standard was seen as essential in order to contain inflation, which accelerated during the war and immediately afterwards, and to restore the international competitiveness of British industry.

What was the significance of the Gold Standard? Put simply it meant that all bank notes, in every country belonging to the Gold Standard (including even the Soviet Union in the 1920s), were backed by gold: that is, banks were obliged to exchange notes for gold. The link with gold served two functions: to correct imbalances between imports and exports and to control inflation. Suppose, on the one hand, a deficit on the balance of payments, with imports exceeding exports. This imbalance would require a net outflow of gold in order to pay for the excess imports. The ensuing reduction in gold deposits would oblige banks to raise interest rates, thus reducing overall demand (including demand for imports) to the point where balance was restored. Suppose, on the other hand, an increase in the general level of prices within a country. Investors would seek to exchange notes for gold which would oblige banks to increase interest rates which would in turn reduce demand. Firms would cut prices in order to stay in business; workers would accept lower wages rather than lose their jobs.

The great merit of the Gold Standard was that it was automatic; it left crucial decisions on interest rates in the hands of bankers responding to changes in the preferences of private individuals. In the words of Lord Bradbury, Permanent Secretary to the Treasury during the First World War, the Gold Standard was 'knave-proof'; it could not be 'rigged for political ... reasons' (Skidelsky, 1992: 200).

As Nigel Lawson was to put it most succinctly in a famous article in 1978: 'Rules rule: OK?' (Lawson, 1992: 67).

In 1925 Britain returned to the Gold Standard at the pre-war dollar parity which implied a 10 per cent reduction in prices (including wages as the price of labour). Keynes warned at the time that workers would resist reductions in money wages. The resulting attempts to cut wages in the coal mining industry (then a major export industry facing fierce competition from other countries) led to the General Strike in 1926. In appearance the strike was a victory for the Government and employers. In fact it was no more than a stand-off. It showed that wages were indeed 'sticky' downwards and that the social cost of trying to impose wage cuts was too high to be borne. Moreover the extension of social insurance granted by the Lloyd George Coalition meant that workers could not be coerced into accepting wage reductions. Thus the price of returning to the Gold Standard was higher unemployment. The attempt to return to 'normalcy' failed.

This failure did not become fully evident until the Great Depression of 1929 raised unemployment from around one million during the 1920s to around three million in 1931. The national insurance fund was no longer sufficient to pay the same level of benefits to the much greater number of claimants. Treasury officials and the Bank of England pressed the Labour Government to cut public spending in order to balance the budget and restore confidence in sterling. The Cabinet divided on this issue and Ramsay MacDonald went into coalition with the Conservatives in the National Government which proceeded to impose cuts in the wages of public employees. But the cuts resulted in mutiny among the sailors at Invergordon which precipitated the very collapse in confidence that they were designed to prevent. Alan Clark tells the story, and points the moral, in inimitable fashion.

> The Invergordon mutiny, in terms of bloodshed, violence or dislocation, was relatively unimportant. But it came at the end of a month-long period of alarm and turbulence in world financial markets... News of the mutiny straddled the world's headlines over the very same days that the confidence debate, and Snowden's emergency Budget, preoccupied the House of

> Commons. Hourly the reserves drained away and the exchange rate against the US dollar shrank. Had not insurrection in both Germany and Russia started, little more than a decade earlier, in their navies? 'Our Navy is us', had pronounced Ramsay MacDonald himself. And so it was. On the very evening that the Fleet slowly and separately steamed out of Invergordon harbour on a southerly course the gold sovereign abandoned for ever its historic dominance of the global exchanges.
>
> (Clark, 1998: 92)

Evidence of insupportable social and political strains produced a flight from sterling which could not be stemmed and obliged the Government to leave the Gold Standard. In effect the Government chose to abandon the centrepiece of its economic policy rather than face the social upheaval that rigorous deflation would have required.

1931 was merely the first of several devaluations. It undermined the old orthodoxy (the so-called 'Treasury view') but did not lead immediately to the triumph of Keynesian economics. Britain during the 1930s enjoyed a gradual economic recovery as a result of the low interest rates permitted by departure from the Gold Standard and imperial protection (both supported by Keynes). Keynes did not complete *The General Theory of Employment, Interest and Money* until 1936. Only in 1939, on the outbreak of war, did he return to the Treasury where he had the opportunity to develop new techniques of macro-economic management during the course of the war. The 1941 budget which was accompanied for the first time by estimates of the effect on national income has been described as 'a critical moment in the process by which Keynesian analysis came to permeate official thinking' (Cronin, 1991: 134–5).

Thus the consummation of the Keynesian revolution had to wait until the Second World War created the necessary political pre-conditions discussed in Chapter 3. As Keynes himself put it: 'It is, it seems, politically impossible for a capitalistic democracy to organise expenditure on the scale necessary to make the great experiments which would prove my case – except in war conditions' (cited Clarke, 1992: 168). The Second World War, followed soon afterwards by the onset of the Cold War, created the need for popular consent for capitalism, and the necessary political consensus, that underpinned the Keynesian revolution.

The Keynesian era

The failure to cut unemployment in the 1920s and the collapse of the Gold Standard in 1931 discredited reliance on market forces. Montagu Norman, Governor of the Bank of England from 1920 to 1942, was widely blamed for callous indifference to the unemployed and for bringing illegitimate pressure to bear on Labour ministers in 1931. Keynes argued for discretionary macro-economic management by an enlightened elite imbued with public spirit in the interests of full employment. The political commitment to full employment recognised the recovery in the strength of organised labour during the war.

The paradise lost in 1914 seemed to be restored during the 1950s and 1960s in the Golden Age of sustained capitalist expansion. Keynes himself had no part in this boom; he died in 1946. To what extent was it the result of the techniques of Keynesian demand management developed during the Second World War?

It is important to emphasise the extent to which the post-war Golden Age involved a return to the Gold Standard albeit rather differently from the way it had operated before 1914. The post-war boom was in large part dependent on the system of fixed exchange rates agreed at the Bretton Woods conference in 1944. All currencies were linked to the dollar and the dollar was backed by gold. British economic policy focussed on maintaining the sterling–dollar exchange rate. The focus on the exchange rate represented a middle way between the detailed physical intervention in the economy that was abandoned by Labour during the late 1940s and Treasury plans for floating sterling (under the code name ROBOT) that were shelved by the Conservatives in 1952.

All was well so long as the USA followed broadly uninflationary policies, as it did under President Eisenhower in the 1950s. In this period, as Lawson pointed out, 'foreign exchange crises served as a proxy for monetary disciplines' (Lawson, 1992: 1050). Cuts in interest rates or a lax fiscal stance (tax cuts or increases in public spending) would suck in imports which would lead to a fall in foreign currency reserves which would oblige the Government to raise interest rates or tighten the fiscal stance in order to curtail demand and attract foreign investors. The system of fixed parities agreed at Bretton Woods worked in much the same way as the Gold Standard, with the USA acting in much the same way as Britain had done before 1914.

Problems began in the 1960s as the US Government chose to finance both the war in Vietnam and the 'Great Society' programme of welfare spending by inflationary means, by increasing the supply of dollars unbacked by gold – so-called Eurodollars available for speculation. The increasing volume of speculative flows resulted in the devaluation of sterling in 1967 and of the French franc in 1969. The dollar left the Gold Standard in 1971; sterling was floated in 1972; and the Bretton Woods system was formally wound up in 1973. The end of the fixed exchange rate system removed an important constraint on national fiscal and monetary policy but Sam Brittan was most prescient when in 1971 he dismissed any notion that a flexible exchange rate offered some kind of 'magic wand': 'Anyone who believes that home demand could then be allowed to rip without disastrous consequences is making a big mistake. Those who labour under any such misapprehension will discover the truth if and when a British government takes the plunge' (Brittan, 1971: 481). Thus by 1972 the economic preconditions for the crisis of the mid-1970s – the removal of the fixed exchange rate constraint and the resulting increased vulnerability of sterling to speculative flows – were in place.

Economic crisis

The crisis began with Chancellor Anthony Barber's budget of March 1972 when, with unemployment topping what seemed to be the politically unacceptable figure of one million in January, the Government increased public expenditure and cut taxation in an effort to stimulate economic growth and cut unemployment. This expansionary budget came on top of a recent relaxation in controls over bank lending which Donald MacDougall, former Chief Economic Adviser to the Treasury, judged to be 'inherently inflationary' and the victory of the miners in a six-week long strike in January and February 1972. Heath hoped to contain inflation by reaching agreement with the TUC on a voluntary incomes policy but was not ready to pay the price of repealing curbs on trade union bargaining imposed by the Industrial Relations Act of 1971. Heath had to settle for a statutory policy, imposed in November 1972, which provided for automatic pay increases in line with inflation (so-called 'threshold payments'). By early 1973 all of the signals pointed to danger: the economy was growing at an unsustainable 10 per cent a year, inflation was rising at a similar rate, sustained by automatic pay increases, while government borrowing was rising to an unprecedented 6 per cent of GDP. Such was the situation when OPEC quadrupled oil prices in late 1973, delivering a simultaneous deflationary and inflationary shock to the economy. A deflationary package of tax increases, public spending cuts and curbs on borrowing announced in December 1973 came far too late to have any effect in restraining a runaway economy (Dell, 1997: 386–99).

The Labour Government which took office in March 1974 inherited a situation of rising unemployment, declining output and rapidly rising inflation. As a minority government, it faced a second election which was held in October and duly delivered only a small majority, followed by a referendum on EEC membership, commonly described as 'the third general election', on which the Cabinet was divided and the leadership was opposed by the bulk of its own supporters. Only after this issue was resolved with the defeat of the Left led by Tony Benn was the Government in a position to face its economic problems which it did in the first place by negotiating a voluntary incomes policy with the TUC. The Government seemed to be recovering its position by early 1976 when sterling began to decline rapidly against the dollar. In September the Government was obliged to apply to the IMF for a loan to restore the depleted reserves. This was the context in which Prime Minister James Callaghan delivered his famous farewell to the Keynesian era in a speech to the Labour Party Conference in October 1976:

> We used to think that you could just spend your way out of a recession to increase employment by cutting taxes and boosting Government spending. I tell you in all candour that option no longer exists and that insofar as it ever did it worked by injecting inflation into the economy. And each time that happened, the average level of unemployment has risen. Higher inflation, followed by higher unemployment. That is the history of the last twenty years.
>
> (Cited Smith, 1987: 65)

In fact the speech was a tactical ploy in Callaghan's negotiations with the German and American masters of the IMF but it has come to be seen as a farewell to the Golden Age which had ended with the collapse of the Bretton Woods system and the first oil price rise. It has also been hailed as signalling the triumph of monetarism – the economic counter-revolution – to which we shall turn next.

Monetarism and after

What do we mean by monetarism? David Smith has identified three components: the apparently self-evident assertions that, first, 'there is something called money, which can be defined and measured', second (as Milton Friedman, American doyen of monetary economics in the 1970s, put it), 'inflation is always and everywhere a monetary phenomenon' and, third, 'governments can and should control changes in the stock of money – the money supply – in order to prevent inflation' (Smith, 1987: 4–5). To this trio may be added two further assumptions: first, that the main economic problem is inflation and not unemployment (thus reversing the priority of the Keynesian era) and, second, that there is no trade-off between inflation and unemployment. Instead, as Callaghan asserted, unemployment will increase as a result of higher inflation and the best way to reduce unemployment is by containing inflation.

How are we to account for the rise of monetarism in the 1970s? The answer is straightforward: it offered an apparently coherent and readily understandable explanation for the successive political and economic failures of the 1960s and 1970s and an equally simple set of remedies which were congenial to City analysts and the IMF and its American and German masters as well as the Right in Britain. The fundamental difficulty – which Keynes perceived in the 1930s – was that it involved an assault on trade union power for which the conditions did not ripen until the Winter of Discontent in early 1979.

We may identify two stages in the monetarist counter-revolution. The first was what Lawson called 'unbelieving monetarism' (Lawson, 1992: 45) under the Labour Government in the late 1970s. As a condition of the loan negotiated with the IMF in December 1976 the Government made use of monetary targets as well as an incomes policy agreed with the TUC in order to contain inflation while attempting to preserve the long-standing commitment to full employment. By 1978 this combination had delivered reductions in inflation (to around 8 per cent) and unemployment (by 100 000) (Smith, 1987: 69). These achievements were destroyed by the Winter of Discontent which seemed to demonstrate that inflation could be controlled only by tolerating a hitherto unacceptable level of unemployment needed to destroy trade union bargaining power.

The second stage was what former Labour Chancellor Denis Healey called 'punk monetarism' or 'sado-monetarism' in the early years of Conservative government after 1979 (Healey, 1990: 491). The irony is that this 'believing monetarism' (in contrast to the 'unbelieving' or sceptical monetarism practised by Healey with some temporary success) resulted in comprehensive economic disaster, at least in the short term. This disaster resulted from a malign combination of factors. First of all, the increase in VAT announced in Chancellor Geoffrey Howe's first budget in 1979 plus the new government's commitment (announced ahead of the election) to accept whatever increases in pay for public sector workers might be recommended by an independent commission set up under Labour led to an increase in inflation from 13 per cent in 1979 to 22 per cent by 1980. The higher interest rates needed to offset the growth in spending power plus the second oil price rise of 1979 which turned sterling into a petro-currency attracted overseas investors and increased the value of sterling by about 20 per cent. Increases in the cost of borrowing coupled with tougher competition in markets at home and abroad led to a wave of bankruptcies and a 13 per cent decline in manufacturing output between 1979 and 1981 – which led in turn to an increase in unemployment from about one and a half million when the Conservatives took office to over three million by 1981. Meanwhile the Government's ability to hit its targets for monetary expansion was undermined by the removal of exchange controls and controls on bank lending (Smith, 1987: 90–1).

By 1982 monetarism had been tacitly abandoned in the face of this comprehensive disaster. In a famous television interview in 1984 Mrs Thatcher told the journalist Peter Jay (one of the doctrine's leading proponents in the 1970s and the reputed author of Callaghan's famous peroration in 1976) that monetarism was 'a theory to which I have never subscribed' (Smith, 1987: 122).

Looking back, Lawson (principal author of the Medium Term Financial Strategy [MTFS] applied after 1979) claimed that the shock was needed to change attitudes – in particular, to restore 'management's right to manage' and undermine trade union power (Lawson, 1992: 57, 437). Alan Budd, a leading monetarist economist and special adviser at the Treasury between 1979 and 1981, observed in an interview for BBC television in 1991 that the whole episode could be seen in Marxist terms as a crisis of capitalism engineered by the Government and its backers in industry in order to recreate a reserve army of the unemployed and raise profits (British Broadcasting Corporation, 1991; see also Cairncross & Cairncross, 1992: 73–4 – I owe this latter reference to Alan Hooper).

Lawson famously claimed in the Chancellor's annual Mansion House speech in October 1985 that inflation was 'judge and jury' of the Government's macro-economic policy (Lawson, 1992: 480). Looking back, he concluded that the reduction in inflation achieved at such a high social and economic cost in the early 1980s was accomplished mainly by the high exchange rate (416). Hence during the mid-1980s he replaced monetary targets with a renewed focus on the sterling exchange rate as the principal means of regulating the economy. In the circumstances of the time he sought to establish a link not with gold either directly or through the dollar but with the Deutschmark (DM) as the currency with the best anti-inflation record (416, 418–19).

We may identify two stages in this 'post-monetarist' period of Conservative macro-economic management. First was the period of informal targeting of the sterling/DM exchange rate (so-called 'shadowing' the DM) which ended in Lawson's resignation in 1989 following his own and Geoffrey Howe's ill-fated attempt to force Thatcher to agree to British entry to the European Exchange Rate Mechanism (ERM) which would have formalised the link. Lawson, true to the principle of a rule-based approach to macro-economic management adduced in his 1978 article, sought the discipline of a fixed exchange rate. Thatcher wished to preserve a degree of discretion that might be deployed for political ends. The dispute with Lawson and Howe, her principal lieutenants for the previous decade, destroyed her Government.

The second stage opened in 1990 with Thatcher's decision to enter the ERM, taken largely for tactical reasons in the midst of recession in order to be able to announce a reduction in interest rates on the eve of the Conservative party conference. Sterling entered at a level of DM2.95, which turned out to be too high when the Deutsche Bundesbank began to raise interest rates in early 1992 in order to offset the inflationary shock to the German economy from reunification in 1990. By the summer of 1992 it had become clear that the only way in which sterling could remain within the ERM would be by persuading the Germans to cut interest rates (or revalue the DM) or to raise British interest rates (or devalue sterling). Having ruled out devaluation and failed to bully the Bundesbank into raising interest rates the Government was left with no alternative but to raise interest rates to a level that would have plunged the economy even further into recession. In a reprise of previous devaluations going back to 1931, the markets failed to be persuaded by a token show of resolve and the Government withdrew from the ERM on what came to be known as 'Black Wednesday' (Stephens, 1996: 193–260).

Like previous devaluations, 1992's 'Black Wednesday' had a lasting impact. First of all, it discredited the Major Government: this was the first time a Conservative Government had been forced to devalue. At one stroke it destroyed the Conservative reputation for economic competence. John Major's second Chancellor Kenneth Clarke has described how he spent his entire period in office, from 1993 until 1997, in 'trying to win back our [the Conservative Government's] reputation for competence, for economic competence, trying to win back our reputation as a trustworthy government' – with a measure of success that was evident in the 1997 election (British Broadcasting Corporation, 1997b). A second lasting effect was to destroy morale in the Treasury which was wholly unprepared to cope with massive speculation against sterling. The combination of the Government's loss of credibility and the Treasury's loss of morale, coupled with the competent performance of the Bank of England in the crisis, led to the creation of a new framework for monetary policy which gave an increased role to the Bank. What became known as the 'Ken and Eddie show' (coupling the names of the Chancellor and Eddie George, Governor of the Bank of England) involved monthly meetings between the Chancellor and Governor to discuss interest rates in the light of the Bank's forecasts of inflation. The Chancellor set the inflation target and continued to take the crucial decisions on interest rates, and therefore remained open to the accusation of acting from political motives, but in a context which was constrained by the Bank's standing with the money markets (Stephens, 1996: 261–96).

Above all, however, 'Black Wednesday' marked the end of an era in which governments could pretend to run an independent macro-economic policy. Those pretensions were washed away in a flood of speculation in 1992 in what proved to be simply the first of several similar crises, beginning with the effective destruction of the ERM in 1993, proceeding through the devaluation of the Mexican peso in 1995, and on to the shockwaves that spread throughout the so-called emerging markets of East Asia, Russia and Latin America in 1997 and 1998. Even speculators such as George Soros who have benefited most from these successive crises have began to call for the regulation of the global capital flows unleashed in a new era of globalisation – what Keynes had called 'internationalisation'.

Conclusion

Since 'Black Wednesday' we can discern the emergence of a new consensus in macro-economic policy as in other areas. The pretensions of governments to run their own macro-economic policy, comprehending both monetary policy exercised through changes in interest rates, and fiscal policy exercised through changes in tax and public spending, appear to have gone for ever. Labour has taken the Conservatives' initiative even further by, in one of its first acts in government in 1997, granting full operational independence to the Bank of England. Under current arrangements the Government sets the inflation target and the Bank sets interest rates at the level it judges necessary to hit that target. Central bankers like Eddie George carry greater trust in the international markets than Finance Ministers like Gordon Brown.

In granting operational independence to the Bank, Brown has followed the recommendations of Nigel Lawson that Thatcher rejected in the interests of maintaining that political discretion over macro-economic policy which led ultimately to the destruction of her own and John Major's governments (Lawson, 1992: 1059–61). Norman Lamont, Chancellor at the time of 'Black Wednesday', reached a similar conclusion after he had left office (Stephens, 1996: 278).

Kenneth Clarke, originally critical of Brown's decision, has come round to support it; and Francis Maude, Michael Portillo's predecessor as Shadow Chancellor, indicated Conservative support for the principle of Bank of England control over monetary policy (*The Observer*, 21.3.99; *Financial Times*, 26.7.99).

The new consensus on macro-economic policy is best conveyed in Lawson's 1984 Mais lecture (Lawson, 1992: 414–15) which in retrospect has come to be seen as important as Callaghan's speech in 1976. For example, Tony Blair took Lawson's lecture as the point of departure for his own Mais Lecture in 1995 on Labour's economic policy which identified 'a coherent framework for a new consensus between economists and politicians [as] the best way forward for Britain in the late 1990s' (Blair, 1996a: 75) and Robert Skidelsky has described Lawson's self-imposed 'world-historical role' as being to turn Keynes's policy the right way up again (Skidelsky, 1996b: 86). Just as Callaghan dismissed the old orthodoxy, so Lawson heralded the new:

> The conventional post-War wisdom was that unemployment was a consequence of inadequate economic growth, and economic growth was to be secured by *macro*economic policy... Inflation, by contrast, was ... seen as a matter to be dealt with by *micro*-economic policy – the panoply of controls and subsidies associated with the era of incomes policy.
>
> The conclusion on which the [Thatcher] Government's economic policy is based is that there is indeed a proper distinction between the objectives of macroeconomic and microeconomic policy, and a need to be concerned with both of them. But the proper role of each is precisely the opposite of that assigned to it by the conventional post-War wisdom. It is the conquest of inflation, and not the pursuit of growth and employment, which is or should be the objective of macroeconomic policy. And it is the creation of conditions conducive to growth and employment, and not the suppression of price rises, which is or should be the objective of microeconomic policy.

The Thatcher Government, continued Lawson, was 'pursuing simultaneously both a macro and a micro policy ... the macro policy is ... directed at the continuing reduction of inflation, with the ultimate objective of stable prices, and ... the micro policy is equally wholeheartedly designed to make the economy work better and thus generate more jobs', (Lawson, 1992: 414–15).

Gordon Brown would find it difficult to disagree. At the same time that he has put monetary policy into commission with the Monetary Policy Committee of the Bank of England, he has also established just the kind of strict, rule-based framework for fiscal policy that Lawson had in mind when framing the MTFS in his own Code for Fiscal Stability, with its 'golden rule' that governments over the economic cycle should borrow only to invest and not to fund current spending, and its sustainable investment rule that the national debt should be kept at a 'prudent' level of less than 40 per cent of GDP. Like Lawson, Brown has attempted to put the management of the economy onto autopilot so that he can concentrate on a range of micro, supply-side reforms of tax and welfare, using the Treasury as a grand policy unit, allowing the Chancellor a 'finger in pretty well every pie in government' (Lawson, 1992: 273) rather than as a machine for 'steering the economy'. So far as macro-economic policy is concerned, in Brown's conception as in Lawson's, 'Rules rule, OK?'

9
Getting and Spending: Public Expenditure and Welfare

Introduction

'Public expenditure is at the heart of Britain's present economic difficulties' pronounced the opening sentence of the Conservative Government's first Public Expenditure White Paper in November 1979. A few months earlier, in his first Budget speech in July 1979, Geoffrey Howe had set out the new Government's guiding principle: 'Finance must determine expenditure, not expenditure finance' (Lawson, 1992: 37).

This chapter attempts to explain why the control of public expenditure came to loom so large in the Conservatives' analysis of what was wrong with the British economy, and considers the extent of their success in containing public expenditure during their 18 years in office. It begins by looking at the reasons for the growth in public expenditure during the twentieth century and the crisis in control of public expenditure which formed such an important part of the mid-1970s crisis. It goes on to look at the record of the Labour and Conservative Governments in controlling public expenditure, demonstrating that effective control was established by Labour and not the Conservatives – that Labour rather than the Conservatives were responsible for the largest ever spending cuts in the aftermath of the IMF visitation in 1976. Then it looks at the ways in which the welfare state has changed since 1979 under the impact of Conservative efforts to control public expenditure. Finally it looks at the legacy inherited by the Labour Government in 1997 and their plans for reforming the welfare state. It concludes by pointing, once again, to the emergence of a new consensus – this time about welfare reform and the management of public services.

Explaining public expenditure growth

Public expenditure has increased dramatically in every capitalist democracy during the last century or so. Figures for OECD countries show that, on average, public expenditure as a percentage of GDP grew from 8 per cent in 1870 to 9 per cent in 1913; then leaped to 15 per cent by 1920 and grew to 18 per cent (excluding Germany) by 1937; and since the Second World War has grown steadily from 28 per cent in 1960, to 43 per cent by 1980, 44 per cent in 1990 and 46 per cent in 1996 (*The Economist*, 20.9.97). So Britain is not alone in experiencing this steady growth.

Perhaps the most arresting general explanation of the growth of public expenditure was offered by Alexis de Tocqueville writing in the 1830s in the first volume of *Democracy in America* (Tocqueville, 1835 & 1840: 208–10). He argued that the level of 'public expenses' would be 'considerably greater' in a democratic republic than in an absolute monarchy. This conclusion was based on the identification of three main types of government, dominated by the three main classes which he termed the rich, the comfortably off and the relatively poor with little or no property.

A government dominated by the rich, he thought, would take little trouble to make economical use of public money because tax would have little effect upon people of substantial fortunes. Arguably this was the position in Britain in the eighteenth and early nineteenth centuries when indirect taxes provided the bulk of government revenue (Cronin, 1991: 20). Tocqueville regarded government by the comfortably off as 'not the most enlightened and certainly not the most generous, but the most economical' form of government. Arguably this was the position in Britain from the 1840s, when Peel reintroduced the income tax first imposed by Pitt in 1799 and abolished in 1816 after the Napoleonic Wars, until Lloyd George raised direct taxes in his 'People's Budget' of 1909 to pay for the social reforms needed to strengthen the Liberals' appeal to working class voters (Cronin, 1991: 21, 54).

Tocqueville's third category – of countries governed by the relatively poor – bears greatest resemblance to Britain in the half-century or so following the 'People's Budget', when most of the electorate were working class with little or no property and exempt from income tax. Such countries, he thought,

> cannot hope for much economy in public expenditure; expenses will always be considerable, either because taxes cannot touch those who vote for them or because they are assessed in a way to prevent that. In other words, a democratic government is the only one in which those who vote for a tax can escape the obligation to pay it.
>
> (Tocqueville, 1835 & 1840: 210)

He argued that

> when the people begin to reflect on their position, they notice a mass of hitherto unfelt wants, which cannot be satisfied without recourse to the resources of the state. For that reason, public expenditure increases with civilisation, and as enlightenment spreads, taxes rise.
>
> (211)

This tendency is reinforced by the way in which political elites in democracies compete for votes by holding out the prospect of an increase in prosperity which 'almost never can be done without money'. Tocqueville was anticipating by more than a century the familiar New Right explanation of increasing public expenditure.

However, he did not think that public expenditure would rise indefinitely.

> There will, however, be less danger of extravagance in an increasingly property-owning democracy, both because the people will less need the wealthy's money and because it will become ever more difficult to contrive a tax which will not touch the people themselves.
>
> (211)

Thus Tocqueville predicted growing resistance to increases in public expenditure as private incomes rose and tax extended beyond what he called the 'rich' and 'comfortably off' – which is what has happened in Britain since the 1950s. Since then the proportion of homes under owner-occupation has risen from 26 per cent in 1945 to 49 per cent in 1969, 55 per cent in 1979 and 67 per cent in 1997 (Adonis & Pollard, 1997: 193). More recently, largely as a result of privatisation, the number of people owning shares in one or more companies has risen from 2.5 million in 1979 to 12 million in 1999 (Saunders & Harris, 1994: 4; *Financial Times*, 5/6.6.99). In the late 1940s a working man on average pay with two children paid no income tax; by the late 1960s a working man on half average pay was liable to income tax (Timmins, 1996: 265). This transformation of Britain from a country in which the majority of voters were (in Tocqueville's terms) 'poor' to one in which they are 'comfortably off' helps to explain changing public attitudes to tax and welfare in recent decades.

Subsequent attempts to explain the secular growth of public expenditure as a share of GDP have added little to Tocqueville's account. We have seen the way in which he anticipated accounts by the New Right: that public expenditure has risen due to a malign combination of self-interest on the part of politicians competing for votes, bureaucrats seeking to expand their empires and interest groups seeking special favours (Dunleavy, 1991). His argument that public expenditure would increase with the growth of civilisation and enlightenment can be taken to anticipate the late nineteenth-century German economist Adolf Wagner's 'law' that public expenditure would inevitably increase as a proportion of GDP because of the growing complexity of social and economic life and the increasing need for government intervention, as well as later economists' explanation in terms of increasing demand for so-called merit goods such as education and health (Likierman, 1988: 19–20). Perhaps only Peacock and Wiseman (1961) have added significantly to Tocqueville by demonstrating the connection between the two World Wars and the growth of public expenditure.

Public expenditure during the Golden Age

Chapter 3 argued that the welfare state developed in response to twin challenges in the form of organised labour and war. The welfare state of the late 1940s was the product of the exceptional social solidarity that had developed during the Second World War as well as a response to the ideological and military challenge from the Soviet Union in the Cold War. By the 1970s it was in crisis. How are we to explain this transformation?

During the 1950s public expenditure in Britain remained stable at around 30 per cent of GDP; as we have seen, the majority of earners did not pay income tax. Between 1960 and 1970 it rose from 33 per cent to 39 per cent of GDP (Skidelsky, 1997: 22); during the same period public spending on housing, education, health and social security rose by 137 per cent (Timmins, 1996: 262).

Several factors help to account for the increasing cost of the welfare state. First was what might be called technological push: the appearance of new drugs (such as Valium) and new treatments (such as transplants) pushed up NHS costs. A second was what might be called demographic pull: the number of pensioners rose from less than seven million in 1950 to over nine million in 1970, pushing up pension costs; the rising number of pensioners aged over 85 made increasing demands on the NHS (Timmins, 1996: 260). Beveridge's proposals for social insurance had been premised upon low unemployment: as Keynes put it, 'look after unemployment and the budget will look after itself' (cited Skidelsky, 1996a). By the end of 1969 unemployment had stood at more than 500 000 for the preceding $2^1/_2$ years whereas during 13 years of Conservative government from 1951 to 1964 it had exceeded this figure for only eight months in total (Timmins, 1996: 269). Two more factors were the expansion of higher education (recommended by the 1963 Robbins Report) and the programme of school building embarked upon by the Labour Government after 1964 as part of its plans for 'modernising' Britain. A final factor was the method of planning public expenditure (introduced following the Plowden Report of 1961) in so-called 'volume' terms, which meant that the Government accommodated price increases, which tended to rise faster in public services than in the private sector because of the smaller scope for raising productivity (the so-called 'relative price effect').

Most important, however, was the deterioration in Britain's economic performance. GDP grew by an average of 2.7 per cent a year during the 1960s compared with an average 3 per cent during the 1950s (Johnson, 1991: 265). Labour made its plans for public spending on the assumption that economic growth would rise to 4 per cent a year in line with the National Plan published in 1965.

This growth failed to materialise. As early as the summer of 1965 – before the National Plan had even been published – Labour had to make the first cuts in public spending in order to sustain the value of sterling. Major cuts were made in 1966, following the seamen's strike, and again in 1968, following the 1967 devaluation. NHS prescription charges abolished in 1964 were reintroduced in 1968 (Timmins, 1996: 262). At the same time ministers began to encounter evidence of growing tax resistance: Secretary of State for Health and Social Security Richard Crossman noted after a constituency meeting in 1968: 'The trade unionists want to see us spending less on social services so there will be more for wage packets.' Opinion poll support for higher spending on social services fell from 77 per cent in 1964 to 43 per cent in 1969 (Timmins, 1996: 262). Difficulties over public spending grew during the 1970s to the point where 'in the financial crisis of 1976 it was public expenditure which was at the heart of the economic debate' (Pliatzky, 1982: 161).

The crisis of public expenditure control

By 1975 public expenditure had risen to 47 per cent of GDP compared with 39 per cent in 1970. The Government faced widespread criticism that public expenditure was out of control, though

> As one commentator, Rudolf Klein observed, it was not a crisis of Treasury control; it was a crisis of political management. The failure to stick to any public expenditure plan had in fact gone a long way towards discrediting the whole process of government.
>
> (Pliatzky, 1982: 137)

Four factors were at work. First was the Heath Government's expansionary budget in 1972 (discussed in Chapter 8). Second was the oil price rise in late 1973 which throttled the economic boom stoked by the earlier expansion. The Heath Government responded by cutting public expenditure and raising taxes but had lost office before these measures could be implemented. Thus the incoming Labour Government inherited a situation of rising public expenditure and declining output – one in which public expenditure was certain to rise as a proportion of GDP simply because of falling tax revenues and rising unemployment benefits (the same problems were encountered by the Conservatives in the recessions of the early 1980s and early 1990s). A third factor was the new Government's commitment under the Social Contract with the TUC negotiated ahead of the election to increase spending on social services and benefits (part of the so-called 'social wage') in return for wage restraint. These commitments included a 25 per cent increase in pensions which in future would match growth in average earnings or inflation, depending on which rose faster (Timmins, 1996: 317). A final factor was the political weakness of a minority Government facing a second election and then a referendum equivalent to an election: 'While there was an election to win, deflationary discipline could not be expected from any Chancellor who valued his occupancy of No 11' (Dell, 1997: 410).

The combination of these factors meant that public expenditure rose by 12 per cent in a single year between 1973 and 1974 while the economy, under the deflationary impact of the oil price rise, shrank by 1.5 per cent (Thain & Wright, 1995: 431; Johnson, 1991: 265). Actual spending in the financial year 1974–5 exceeded plans drawn up in 1971 by £5 billion, equivalent to 10 per cent of the total, even after allowing for inflation (Thain & Wright, 1995: 43). This overshoot – presented by the press in terms of the 'missing five billions' – was the result of planning in volume terms (number of teachers employed, miles of motorway built, etc.) rather than cash. Meanwhile the gap between Government revenue and Government spending, to be bridged by borrowing (the so-called Public Sector Borrowing Requirement, or PSBR), had risen to almost 10 per cent of GDP and inflation had reached 25 per cent (*ibid.*: 23).

The Labour Government responded in two ways. In April 1976 (before the IMF crisis) it took the first steps to reassert control by imposing cash limits on the volume figures for 1976–7 (*ibid.*: 48). Then, in December 1976, as part of the agreement with the IMF, it imposed cuts of 10 per cent (real cuts, after allowing for inflation) in public spending in 1977–8 – the biggest cuts ever made (*ibid.*: 431). By the end of that year (1977–8) public expenditure had been cut back to the same level as in 1973–4 before the crisis broke. These cuts were regarded by the Labour Government as a temporary measure needed to overcome the mid-1970s crisis of public expenditure control. By the end of 1977 the Government was planning for a modest increase in public expenditure in 1978–9 as the economy recovered.

The Conservative record

The Labour Government had been forced into large public expenditure cuts in 1976 as a condition for the IMF loan needed to stabilise the sterling exchange rate. The Conservatives, by contrast, came into office with strong ideological objections to public expenditure as such. These objections were fuelled by the argument mounted by Robert Bacon and Walter Eltis in *Britain's Economic Problem: Too Few Producers* (1976) that the resources consumed by the public sector were 'crowding out' the resources needed for private sector investment in the so-called 'productive' part of the economy. Monetarist economists explained that the PSBR could be financed only by 'printing money' (that is, selling Treasury bills to the banks, thus increasing their capacity to create credit) or by raising interest rates to sell Government bonds (thus raising the cost of capital in the private sector). These more sophisticated criticisms of public expenditure lent force to traditional Conservative suspicion of public sector waste and inefficiency. Hence the Conservative claim that reducing public expenditure was at the heart of their economic strategy.

What has been the impact of 18 years of Conservative government? One of the problems in discussing public expenditure is that governments change the way in which it is defined in ways that would make sense only to members of the public spending community in the Treasury and finance divisions of other departments or specialist commentators. The best-known and most important instance was in 1976 when the Labour Government reduced public expenditure as a proportion of GDP from around 60 per cent to around 45 per cent by altering (quite legitimately) the treatment of local authority housing debt and nationalised industry investment (Pliatzky, 1982: 162–3). On the basis of the definitions employed by the present Labour Government, public expenditure in 1978–9, the last year of the previous Labour Government, amounted to 44 per cent of GDP, compared with 41 per cent of GDP in 1996–7, the last year of the Conservative Government (H M Treasury, 1998: 113). Just to illustrate the room for confusion in this very technical – but also highly political – area, the Conservatives' last budget statement contained figures on the previous definition for public expenditure equivalent to 42.25 per cent of GDP in 1978–9 and a forecast 41.25 per cent for 1996–7 (*Financial Times*, 27.11.96). Thus on their own estimation the Conservatives failed significantly to reduce public expenditure as a percentage of GDP.

The record shows a gradual retreat from their initial ambitions (Thain & Wright, 1995: 423–40). The 1979 White Paper (claiming that public expenditure was 'at the heart of Britain's present economic difficulties') set a target to reduce public expenditure in real terms (as Labour had done just a few years earlier). The recession of the next few years (rising unemployment leading to higher benefit payments and lower tax revenues) resulted in three successive overspends. By the early 1980s, along with monetary targetry, the aim of reducing public spending in real terms had been tacitly abandoned, blown away in a gale of recession.

The goal of reducing public expenditure in real terms was replaced by the target set out in the 1984 Green Paper on Expenditure and Taxation of keeping public expenditure 'broadly at its present level in real terms'. The Government was no more successful in hitting this target than it had been in hitting the earlier, more ambitious, one; by 1985 public expenditure was 14 per cent higher in real terms than it had been in 1979.

The 1986 Public Expenditure White Paper set a third, even more modest, target of reducing public expenditure as a proportion of GDP. This target was achieved in the late 1980s in the course of a short-lived boom stimulated by tax cuts and interest rate reductions which also allowed some modest reduction in real terms (because of rising tax revenues and falling benefit payments). However, during the recession of the early 1990s, with an election approaching, public expenditure was allowed to rise again – only to fall in its turn as the economy recovered following sterling's exit from the ERM in 1992.

Thus the experience of 18 years of effort by the Conservative Government to reduce and then merely to contain public expenditure seems to suggest that success or failure in this task depends far more upon the overall performance of the economy than specific measures to reduce benefits or improve efficiency. Why did the Conservatives fail to meet their objective of cutting public expenditure? There were perhaps two main reasons. First the Conservatives were reluctant to reduce expenditure on popular services – such as the NHS and education – used by the majority of the electorate. As Mrs Thatcher famously declared to the 1982 Conservative Party Conference: 'Let me make one thing absolutely clear. The National Health Service is safe with us' (cited Timmins, 1996: 393). A second factor was the continuing pressure for higher spending resulting from long-term social and demographic trends which were in large measure beyond the capacity of any politician to control. The net effect was to shift the balance of public expenditure towards social security, health and education. Between 1978–9 and 1996–7 the share of public spending accounted for by these 'big three' services rose from 48 per cent to 60 per cent. The main increase was in social security – up from 23 per cent to 32 per cent – while education fell slightly and health and personal social services rose from 13 per cent to 17 per cent (*Financial Times*, 3.2.98).

The large increase in spending on social security was the product of several factors. One factor to which the Conservative Government contributed directly through the shift from direct to indirect taxation and the reduction in tax on higher incomes was growing inequality: between 1979 and 1997 the number of people dependent on income support doubled from three million to almost six million (*Financial Times*, 27.1.98). A second factor was the near elimination of new council house building (met from the Housing programme) and the introduction of Housing Benefit (met from the Social Security programme). By 1997 some £12 billion a year was being paid in Housing Benefit, twice as much in real terms as in 1987 (*Financial Times*, 16.1.98, 27.1.98, 23.2.98).

A third factor was the increase in disability benefits (Incapacity Benefit and Disability Living Allowance and Attendance Allowance): between 1982 and 1997 the number of claimants rose from two million to six and a half million (of whom two million were still of working age) while the cost rose from £6 billion to £25 billion (*Financial Times*, 23.2.98). Critics argued that these benefits were being paid as a more generous substitute for unemployment benefit. More sympathetic commentators pointed to employers' increasing demands upon the workforce which meant that many older or mildly incapacitated people were no longer able to find work in the way that they might have done a couple of decades earlier. A final factor was the increasing incidence of family breakdown: by 1997 lone parent families contained about 20 per cent of dependent children compared with only 4.5 per cent in 1960s, and lone parent benefit accounted for £10 billion (*Financial Times*, 12.9.94, 6.1.98).

It is important to correct two possible misconceptions. First of all, the increase in Social Security's share of public expenditure was due neither to unemployment (which was not much higher in the mid-1990s than in the late 1970s) nor to the increase in old age pensioners (because of the unlinking in 1980 of benefits from growth in average earnings). Pensions accounted for only 34 per cent of the Social Security bill in 1996–7 compared with 47 per cent in 1979–80 (*Financial Times*, 23.2.98). A second misconception is that the Social Security programme was 'out of control': in fact expenditure on Social Security peaked at 13.6 per cent of GDP in 1993–4 and had fallen to 12.4 per cent by 1996–7.

Despite their failure to achieve their initial ambitions to reduce public expenditure in real terms, it would be mistaken to regard the Conservative record as entirely one of failure in their terms. During the 1970s public spending in Britain was rising at the same pace as in other members of what was then called the European Economic Community and stood at around the same level. By the mid-1990s it was close to the OECD average of 40 per cent of GDP compared with a European Union average of around 50 per cent (Heald, 1997: 169). Even though the Conservatives might not have reduced public expenditure as a proportion of GDP they did succeed in reducing, by privatisation, the number of people employed in the public sector from around seven million in 1979 to around five million by 1997. In other words, the taxpayer might still be meeting the cost of many services but the services themselves were being provided by private firms (Davis, 1998: 22).

Another way in which the Conservatives transformed the public sector was by narrowing the scope of the NHS to exclude most eye and dental care and residential care of the dependent elderly. They also succeeded in promoting throughout the public sector a new management style (the so-called New Public Management) based on private-sector practice, so that public-sector managers (in theory at least) were as focussed upon customer service and financial outcomes as their private-sector analogues. Thus the Conservatives may not have succeeded in their original objective of reducing public expenditure but they did succeed in reducing the scope of the public sector, in reducing the number of public servants and in transforming the way in which the remaining public servants went about their business (rather than discharging their duties, as might have been said in the 1970s).

While the Conservatives were transforming the public sector, what had been happening to taxation? By 1996–7 taxes and national insurance contributions had risen to almost 36 per cent of GDP compared with 34 per cent of GDP in the last year of Labour government in 1978–9. At the same time the incidence of taxation had become more regressive in so far as it bore more heavily than it had done on the poor and middle-income groups. Figures released by the House of Commons Library in 1996 showed that the proportion of income paid by a typical family, with one working spouse and a mortgage of twice the family income, rose from 31 per cent in 1978–9 to 37 per cent in 1996–7. Much-trumpeted reductions in income tax were more than offset by lower mortgage tax relief and higher National Insurance contributions and VAT. Higher earners were meeting a larger proportion of the tax bill but mainly because of growth in income inequality, faster than in any other country except New Zealand since the late 1970s (Kellner, 1996). The net effect for most of the electorate was that taxes had risen to pay for what seemed like a more restricted set of services which failed to match the expectations which had developed as a result of higher standards of service in the private sector and government initiatives such as the Citizen's Charter. It is easy to see why issues concerning tax and public spending should have come to dominate political discourse in the 1990s.

The welfare debate

In June 1993, in the annual Mais Lecture to the City University, Peter Lilley, Conservative Secretary of State for Social Security, called for 'a constructive public debate on the reform of our social security system'. He noted general agreement on the need to contain costs and update the system, which was being addressed by the Government's Long Term Review of Social Security and the Labour Party's Commission on Social Justice (Lilley, 1995: 17). Lilley's speech 'launched a burst of pamphleteering not seen for half a decade' (Timmins, 1996: 513).

Why did welfare reform assume such prominence at this moment? Tax had been the key issue in the 1992 election. Labour concluded that they were defeated because of plans (announced in the notorious 'shadow budget' on the steps of the Treasury by Shadow Chancellor John Smith) to increase tax to pay for improved public services. The Conservatives discredited themselves by promising tax cuts and then imposing unprecedented increases to correct the massive budget deficit that materialised after the election: the then Shadow Chancellor Francis Maude acknowledged that the Conservatives 'lost the people's trust on tax' after 1992 (*Financial Times*, 18.2.99). Labour concluded that it was no longer possible to increase public spending if that meant tax increases. The Conservatives concluded that the only way to deliver tax cuts was by reducing welfare spending. Another factor was growing concern about a declining work ethic and the emergence of a so-called 'underclass' of young, unemployed men and single mothers dependent on state benefits.

The ensuing debate attracted an unusually large range of distinguished participants across the political spectrum. Participants on the Right included: Conservative ministers, notably Peter Lilley and Kenneth Clarke, Chancellor from 1993 until 1997; neo-Thatcherites like John Redwood and (while still at the Department of Employment before it was wound up in 1994) Michael Portillo and libertarian Right-wing backbenchers such as Alan Duncan, author of *Saturn's Children* (1995); Chris Patten, Governor of Hong Kong, who argued that the rapid economic growth enjoyed by the East Asian 'tiger' economies owed much to low taxation and public spending; and also intellectuals such as the *Financial Times*'s Sam Brittan and Robert Skidelsky, biographer of Keynes and Chairman of the Social Market Foundation think-tank.

Important participants from the Centre were the Commission on Wealth Creation and Social Cohesion and the Joseph Rowntree Foundation Inquiry into Income and Wealth, which both published their reports in 1995 (Dahrendorf, 1995; Barclay, 1995). The first was set up by the Liberal Democrats and chaired by the veteran politician/academic Ralph Dahrendorf. His colleagues included Frank Field, Labour Chairman of the House of Commons Social

Services Committee, and Will Hutton of *The Guardian* – both important contributors to the debate in their own right. The second was chaired by Peter Barclay with Howard Davies, then Director General of the CBI, and John Monks, General Secretary of TUC, among its members. Labour participated only indirectly, through the Commission for Social Justice, set up by John Smith in 1992 and reporting in 1994, and the freelance efforts of Frank Field.

This mid-1990s debate was important for two reasons: first, in delineating an emerging consensus that extended from Kenneth Clarke and Peter Lilley among the Conservatives, through the Centre represented by the people brought together by Dahrendorf and Barclay, and on to a broad spectrum of opinion on the Left; and, second, in isolating opponents on the Right who favoured radical cuts in the welfare state (that had eluded the Conservatives for 18 years) and those on the Left (like the veteran sociologist Peter Townsend and former Cabinet Minister Barbara Castle) who continued to see public spending and taxation as engines of redistribution. Nick Ellison has described the Social Justice Report and the Dahrendorf Report as 'useful vehicles for generating ideas that effectively moved the normative core of Centre–Left welfare ideology further from the traditional association with Keynesian principles towards a set of priorities that endorsed certain elements in Conservative social policy' (Ellison & Pierson, 1998: 37). Dahrendorf has recently observed that some of the main themes in Tony Blair's 'Third Way' were adumbrated in his 1995 report (Dahrendorf, 1999).

Frank Field explained the premise underlying this emerging consensus in a speech to the UK Cooperative Council in November 1996: 'One of the great questions facing all governments, but particularly a Labour one, is how can adequate common services be provided when taxpayers are understandably restive over current levels of tax' (Field, 1997: 78). The options were well captured in the key chapter, 'A Tale of Three Futures', in the Commission on Social Justice Report (1994: 95–6). The first was described as 'Investors' Britain' which would 'combine the ethics of community with the dynamics of a market economy', as 'the extension of economic opportunity is not only the source of economic prosperity but also the basis of social justice'. The aim would be to enhance national competitiveness by investment in people, through the creation of a high quality workforce. The second was described as 'Deregulators' Britain' which would involve encouraging 'dynamic entrepreneurs' who, 'unshackled by employment laws or social responsibilities', would develop 'new businesses and open up new markets', with 'no limit to how high earnings at the top will rise – and no limit to how low wages at the bottom will fall'. The aim in this instance would be to achieve national competitiveness through cutting wages and public expenditure, while being prepared to accept growing 'social exclusion', the existence of 'two nations'. The final option was described as 'Levellers' Britain' which would involve 'a strategy for social justice based primarily on redistributing wealth and incomes rather than trying to increase opportunities and compete in world markets'. Such a strategy was seen as unconcerned with competitiveness and therefore unrealistic in a world in which no society could isolate itself from global economic forces.

These tendentious categories were more than simply party labels. The Labour Party could be seen as divided between Investors and Levellers; the second is a caricature of what Tony Blair would present as Old Labour. The Conservatives increasingly could be seen as divided between Deregulators and Investors. Thus the outcome of the welfare debate was to identify a new consensus centred on the question of reconciling national competitiveness and social cohesion (both key terms in this debate) in a manner reminiscent of the national efficiency movement (discussed in Chapter 3).

Components of the consensus

This new consensus was based on containing the public spending total while shifting the balance towards services used by most of the electorate, to be achieved through controlling demands on the social security budget mainly by encouraging claimants to re-enter the labour market (welfare to work) and by modernising public services in order to raise productivity and improve service quality. We shall proceed to look at each of these elements in turn.

Containment

The last Conservative Budget Statement published in November 1996 showed that public expenditure had risen from a low point of

38 per cent of GDP in 1988–9 to 43.5 per cent in 1992–3; it forecast a reduction to 41.25 per cent of GDP in 1996–7 and 39 per cent of GDP in 1998–9. Clarke's last Budget speech set 'a target of 40 per cent or below for the share of national income that goes on public spending' (*Financial Times*, 27.11.96). The 1997 Conservative Manifesto repeated this commitment for government 'to spend less than 40 per cent of our national income' (Conservative Central Office, 1997: 7).

The Labour Manifesto famously (or notoriously) committed an incoming Labour Government to 'stick to planned public spending allocations for the first two years of office' – that is, until April 1999 (Labour Party, 1997: 13). Gordon Brown's Budget Statement in March 1999 announced a £2 billion shortfall on Conservative plans, claiming to have converted a budget deficit of £28 billion to a forecast £1 billion surplus in 1998–9 (*Financial Times*, 10.3.99). The Labour Government has always been coy about public expenditure as a proportion of GDP – stressing instead the rule-based approach (golden rule and sustainable investment rule) described in Chapter 8 – but the *Financial Times*'s Martin Wolf concluded that Total Managed Expenditure (TME, the new definition of public expenditure covering current and capital spending) was set to remain at around 40 per cent of GDP (Wolf, 1999a).

The Government has abandoned the annual public spending round instituted in the early 1960s in favour of multi-year limits covering three-year periods. Plans for the three years 1999–2002 were published in 1998; plans for the next three years will be published in 2000. Spending plans for the three years beginning April 1999 show TME as proportion of GDP rising from 40 per cent 1999–2000 to 40.6 per cent 2001–2 (HM Treasury, 1998a: 113). Thus so far Labour can claim to have succeeded in stabilising public expenditure at around 40 per cent in contrast to the sharp fluctuations under the Conservatives. However, continuing success in this area will depend on avoiding the 'boom and bust' economic cycle of the 1980s and early 1990s.

Shifting the balance

The last Conservative Budget Statement claimed that the Government's priorities were the NHS, education and combatting crime. Clarke argued in his last Budget speech for keeping 'the rest of public spending within the tightest possible limits, in order for us to spend more on the services people really care about – education, combatting crime and on our National Health Service' (*Financial Times*, 27.11.96). The Conservative Manifesto pledged to continue to provide real increases in spending on the NHS (Conservative Central Office, 1997: 55).

The Labour Manifesto stressed that 'education will be our number one priority', followed by a commitment to 'rebuild the NHS' and to be 'tough on crime and tough on the causes of crime' (Labour Party, 1997: 4). The 1998 Comprehensive Spending Review covering 1999 to 2002 allocated over 50 per cent of the increase in public expenditure to education and the NHS – allowing 5.1 per cent for education and 4.7 per cent for the NHS compared to 1.8 per cent for other programmes (HM Treasury, 1998a: 13–14). Thus Labour plans to continue the Conservative pattern of shifting resources to public services used by the majority of the electorate.

Welfare reform

Within a constrained total, the only way in which resources can be diverted to electorally popular services such as education and the NHS is by reducing the proportion available for other services. Lilley's main concern in 1993 was about the share going to social security: 'the DSS budget is huge, has grown rapidly and is set to continue outstripping national income in the future'. It had risen from 18 per cent of government spending in 1979 to 31 per cent in 1993–4 – an annual growth in real terms of 3 per cent which was set to increase to 3.3 per cent over the rest of the decade. 'It is clear that the underlying position of spending outstripping national income cannot be sustained indefinitely' (Lilley, 1995: 13–14).

Lilley believed that reform was 'best carried out sector by sector rather than by the "big bang" approach' (Lilley, 1995: 21), hence his strategy of incremental change largely by reducing the number of people entitled to claim benefits, whether by withdrawing support for future rather than existing claimants (such as the withdrawal of Income Support for mortgage interest from November 1995) or by tightening eligibility rules (as for Incapacity Benefit, for which stricter medical tests were imposed from April 1995, and the Jobseeker's Allowance, introduced in October 1996, which confined support to the first six months rather than the first year of unemployment and imposed stricter tests of availability to work).

The Jobseeker's Allowance was a key element in a shift in emphasis towards a view of social security as an instrument in an active labour market policy – in moving people from welfare to work. Lilley's Mais Lecture stressed 'the value of making unemployment benefits conditional and providing active help to people to return to work' (Lilley, 1995: 12). His lecture to the Social Market Foundation in 1995 pointed to

> growing concern about welfare dependency. More people accept that dependency on benefits can be debilitating, and that benefits can become a trap. So reinforcing incentives to work, save and take control of one's own life, has been a central objective of my reforms.
>
> (Lilley, 1995: 44)

Kenneth Clarke summed up the Conservative approach in his last Budget speech: 'Dependency impoverishes us all. The welfare system should provide a safety net... But it must never become a way of life. We do not want our social security system to be undermined by resentment' (*Financial Times*, 27.11.96). He announced several measures for reducing the number of claimants including a compulsory programme of interviews for people unemployed for more than two years, 100 000 new places on Project Work, and a new scheme entitled Contract for Work under which private contractors would help people to find work.

By 1997 the Conservative Government had introduced a wide range of schemes such as: Workstart, a pilot scheme for 100 000 people which offered an employer £60 subsidy for six months to take on someone unemployed for more than two years; the Job Finder's Grant of £200 paid to long-term unemployed on obtaining work; Work Trials which allowed an unemployed person to claim benefits for the first 15 days, taking the risk out of taking a new job; and Job Match under which an unemployed person could claim £50 a week for six months on taking a part-time job (Toynbee, 1997). The 1997 election manifesto announced plans to extend this programme nationwide as well as a new Britain Works scheme involving private and voluntary sectors to 'get people off welfare into work' (Conservative Central Office, 1997: 11). Another arm of Conservative welfare policy was in-work benefits such as Family Credit designed to encourage people to take low-paid jobs.

Thus the Conservative record invites scepticism about Labour's claims to 'break the mould of the old passive benefit system' (Department of Social Security, 1998a: 24). Former Conservative Cabinet Minister John Biffen was being fairer in describing Clarke, just before the last election, as 'rapidly becoming the John the Baptist of New Labour' (Biffen, 1997 – I owe this reference to Alan Hooper). Labour's distinctive contribution has lain in the central place of welfare reform in their overall programme and the clear focus on welfare as an instrument of labour market policy. As Blair wrote in his Foreword to the Department of Social Security Green Paper published in October 1998: 'There is no greater challenge than reform of the welfare state ... Reform must be rooted in principle ... work for those who can and security for those who cannot' (Department of Social Security, 1998b: iii). The previous Green Paper written by Frank Field while still Minister for Welfare Reform stated 'Work is at the heart of our reform programme' (DSS, 1998a: 3). Work is at the centre of the comprehensive programme of 'New Deals' – for young people aged 18 to 24, for the long-term unemployed aged over 25, for disabled people, and for lone parents – and related measures such as the Minimum Wage and Working Families Tax Credit designed to encourage people to take low-paid jobs. Alastair Darling, appointed Secretary of State for Social Security after the dismissal of Harriet Harman and Frank Field in July 1998, has returned to the path of incremental reform charted by Peter Lilley (Wintour & Thomas, 1999) but the signs are that spending on social security is speeding up again after slowing in the last years of Conservative Government (*The Economist*, 13.2.99).

Improving efficiency

At least since the crisis of the mid-1970s familiarised the notion of the relative price effect which vitiated the volume planning which lay at the heart of the Public Expenditure Survey system introduced in the early 1960s, politicians have been aware of the difficulty of raising productivity in labour-intensive public services provided by professionally-qualified people such as teachers and doctors endowed with a high degree of discretion. A main theme of Thatcher's final term and of the Major Government was the reform of public services, which has been aptly described as bringing the market to the state (that is, by introducing market mechanisms) where it was not possible to take the state to market (that is, through privatisation) (Ellison & Pierson, 1998: 5). We have seen this process in action in central government in Chapter 6, with the creation of executive agencies and the contracting out of peripheral services. Parallel developments in local government included the extension of Compulsory Competitive Tendering, large-scale voluntary transfers of council housing, mainly to housing associations, and local management of schools. The NHS and local authority personal social services have seen the introduction of the purchaser/provider split in the case of NHS hospital trusts in 1990, followed by GP fundholding and community care packages in 1991.

This new approach to public-sector management has become known as the New Public Management (in contradistinction to the old public administration). It involves three main components: private-sector-style management of public bodies competing in quasi-markets and subject to external audit and inspection. William Waldegrave, Conservative Minister for Public Services after 1992, pointed to 'a remarkable new consensus on public service issues' in a 1993 pamphlet (Waldegrave, 1993a: 8). Elsewhere he argued that what mattered was 'not whether those who run our public services are elected, but whether they are producer-responsive or consumer-responsive' (Waldegrave, 1993b: 13). The Labour Government made the same point in its second White Paper on public spending plans for 1999–2002: 'What really matters is the effectiveness and efficiency of the service the public receives' (HM Treasury, 1998b: 1).

Labour is committed to the continued restructuring of public services along private sector lines. The 1997 Manifesto claimed that 'efficiency and value for money are central' (Labour Party, 1997: 12). The Government has offered higher public spending in return for improved service: 'Our aim is to put more money into our public services in return for modernisation' (Blair, 1998a: 10–11) – 'money in return for modernisation' as Brown put it when announcing the results of the Comprehensive Spending Review in July 1998 (*Financial Times*, 15.7.98).

One feature of Labour policy on public service efficiency has been the extension of independent inspectorates as a means of enforcing tighter quality control on public service professionals. OFSTED (the Office for Standards in Education) set up by the Conservatives in 1993 has come to be seen as a model by Labour: 'Just as schools are inspected by OFSTED so we want all public services to have proper scrutiny to ensure they are providing excellent services' (Blair, 1998a: 87). The Government has extended the same principles to the NHS by establishing in April 1999 the National Institute for Clinical Excellence (NICE) to assess the clinical effectiveness and cost-effectiveness of treatments, supported by the Commission for Health Improvement (CHIMP) responsible for inspecting hospitals and primary care groups (in both NHS and the private sector) to ensure that they are following NICE guidelines (*Financial Times*, 4.2.99, 23.3.99). In the Social Services the Government plans to establish a General Social Care Council to act as a disciplinary body for care workers with regional inspectorates for private care homes (*Financial Times*, 30.11.98). In local government it is setting up a new housing inspectorate responsible for auditing the performance of every local authority within five years and with 'real power to tackle poor management' (Blair, 1998a: 62). From September 2000 a new General Teaching Council will have the power to register and 'strike off' state school teachers (Walker, 1999). All of these bodies are part of 'a growing army of waste-watchers, quality checkers, "sleazebusters" and other regulators'. By 1995 no fewer than 134 separate bodies were responsible for regulating the public services, employing almost 14 000 staff and costing £766 million to run (Hood *et al.*, 1998: 61–2). This apparatus forms an important part of the regulatory state discussed in Chapter 7. By 1999 the Labour Government had created about a dozen new inspectorates and inspection was being described as 'the fastest growing area of public expenditure' (Timmins, 1999c). Concern has been growing about the lack of coordination among these inspectorates and the questionable value for money of their efforts.

A second feature has been the introduction of Public Service Agreements between departments and Treasury, described by

Gordon Brown as 'effectively a contract with the Treasury for the renewal of public services' and an important aspect of the Government's conditional approach to resources for public services: 'money in return for modernisation' in Brown's words (*Financial Times*, 15.7.98). The White Paper published in December 1998 set more than 500 performance targets covering all departments and several multi-departmental initiatives. Progress is to be monitored by a Cabinet Committee chaired by the Chancellor (HM Treasury, 1998b: 2). The Treasury will be advised by a new Public Services Productivity Panel made up of industrialists and management consultants (*Financial Times*, 16.2.99). The Government recently announced that each panel member would be asked to study one area of public service, including civil service staffing and pay, the police and state education, and to report to the Chancellor within six months (*Financial Times*, 9.8.99).

Thus all four main components of Labour Government policy on the public services represent a continuation of policies launched by the Conservative Government. This is not to say that there no differences. Labour's New Deal is much more comprehensive than the fragmentary Conservative initiatives which it replaced. Recent budgets demonstrate a new commitment to redistribution in favour of poorer families. An analysis of Clarke's last Budget by the independent Institute of Fiscal Studies found that the richest 10 per cent of taxpayers gained most while the poorest 10 per cent suffered a modest loss (Johnson, 1996) whereas an analysis of Brown's 1999 budget found the largest gains among the poorest 10 per cent while the richest 10 per cent suffered a modest loss, repeating the pattern of the 1997 and 1998 budgets (McCrae, 1999). Nonetheless, continuity is much more evident than change. Moreover, the Conservative Opposition has signalled its acceptance of Labour's broad priorities. Shortly before being defenestrated by William Hague, the deputy leader Peter Lilley declared that problems in health, education and welfare would not be solved by the free market. These services would remain in state hands, and funding would increase (*Financial Times*, 26.4.99). The then Shadow Chancellor Francis Maude pronounced the next day: 'I want to make this absolutely clear, without ambiguity, without scope for distortion: in opposition we will support, and in government we will implement, the increases in health and education spending announced by Gordon Brown' (*Financial Times*, 27.4.99).

Conclusion

The 1990s have seen the emergence of a new consensus about the role of the state, based on the notion of national competitiveness in a global economy. In 1997 both the Conservative and the Labour Manifestos embraced the modish notion of globalisation. The Conservative Manifesto expressed the party's ambition to make Britain 'the unrivalled Enterprise Centre of Europe' (Conservative Central Office, 1997: 7) while the Labour Manifesto pointed to the need to equip the country for the new world economy, to 'build a new partnership with business to improve the competitiveness of British industry for the 21st century' (Labour Party, 1997: 1, 15).

The recent joint statement by Labour and the German Social Democratic Party talked about 'a newly defined role for an active state. The top priority must be investment in human and social capital' – just what the Commission for Social Justice meant when describing 'Investors' Britain'. The objective of European social democrats should be to 'make the European economy more dynamic', to offer 'Europe a chance to catch up with the United States' (Blair & Schröder, 1999: 12, 11)

The substance of the emerging consensus has been nowhere better captured than in Bob Jessop's notion of the Schumpeterian Workfare State (Jessop, 1994: 24). The reference to Schumpeter is based on his characterisation of capitalism in terms of 'the perennial gale of creative destruction' and his stress on the creative role of the entrepreneur (Schumpeter, 1943: 84). Workfare describes the increasing role of the state in shaping an effective workforce – what is meant by the modish and apparently neutral term 'human capital'. As Blair and Schröder put it: 'The most important task of modernisation is to invest in human capital' (1999: 8).

Jessop has described 'the distinctive objectives' of the Schumpeterian Workfare State as being

> to promote product, process, organisational, and market innovation in open economies in order to strengthen as far as possible

> the structural competitiveness of the national economy by intervening on the supply-side; and to subordinate social policy to the needs of labour market flexibility and/or to the constraints of international competition.
>
> (Jessop, 1994: 24)

The contrast is with the Keynesian Welfare State concerned to ensure full employment by demand management and to ensure that all citizens share in the fruits of economic growth (*ibid.*, 17).

Blair and Schröder illustrate Jessop's characterisation of an emerging Schumpeterian Workfare State when they call upon European social democrats to 'formulate and implement a new supply-side agenda for the left' (Blair & Schröder, 1999: 10). Here is a positive conception of the role of the state which goes beyond mere retrenchment; as Blair and Schröder put it: 'The state should not row, but steer: not so much control, as challenge' (7). 'Flexible markets must be combined with a newly defined role for an active state. The priority must be investment in human and social capital' (12). They point to a need to 'promote a go-ahead mentality and a new entrepreneurial spirit at all levels of society', which requires 'a competent and well-trained workforce eager and ready to take on new responsibilities' and 'a social security system that opens up new opportunities and encourages initiative, creativity and readiness to take on new challenges' (8).

A change in the role of the state requires change in the structure and ethos of the state: 'Within the public sector bureaucracy at all levels must be reduced, performance targets and objectives formulated, the quality of public services rigorously monitored, and bad performance rooted out' (Blair & Schröder, 1999: 7). As Blair writes in his pamphlet on the Third Way: 'Public servants must do more than administer assets; their job is to generate greater public value from our stock of public assets' (Blair, 1998b: 17). This stress on the entrepreneurial role of the public sector explains Blair's widely-reported criticisms of public services. But it also raises the question of whether it is reasonable to expect public servants in state employment, handling public money, to behave like entrepreneurs – or whether an entrepreneurial spirit could be introduced only by much more radical restructuring of the public services. We shall return to this point in the Conclusion.

10

Twilight of Ukania: Territorial Politics in Britain

Introduction

Chapters 3 to 5 sought to chart the creation of one consensus during the 1940s and its eventual breakdown in the mid-1970s crisis, to be replaced ultimately with a new form of consensus during the 1990s, while Chapters 6 to 9 sought to chart that process in rather more detail through a closer examination of four key policy areas involving the role of the state – the reconstruction of the central government machine, the privatisation of large parts of the public sector, the management of the economy, and the control of public expenditure and reform of the welfare state. This chapter and the next examine two other elements in the cumulative crisis of the mid-1970s – the emergence of strong national movements in Wales, Scotland and Northern Ireland, and British entry into what was then called the European Economic Community. Both of these developments form part of the story of Britain's relative economic decline in so far as that decline eventually posed challenges to the British state and the British national identity that had emerged during the eighteenth century – the first from within that state and the second from an emerging supranational formation from which Britain found that it could no longer stand aside.

'Constitutional issues are now at the heart of political debate', pronounced Tony Blair in an article on the British Constitution in September 1996 (Blair, 1996b: 35). He is now presiding (if that is the right word) over what it has become almost a cliché to describe as the most important programme of constitutional reform since the 1830s (see, for example, Bogdanor, 1999: 1, and Timmins, 1999a) or even since the seventeenth century (Stephens, 1999). Moreover, as Robert Hazell, perhaps the main authority on the subject and an important agent in the development of ideas being drawn upon by the Government, has stressed, 'Devolution is a process, not an event' (Hazell, 1999: 8). Blair has described his Government's programme as 'the biggest programme of change to democracy ever proposed', and Sir Richard Wilson, as Cabinet Secretary and Head of the Civil Service, literally his right-hand man at the Cabinet table, has talked about the UK and the civil service as being at 'the beginning of a very big wave of change' (Hazell, 1999: 1; Timmins, 1999a).

This is not the place to provide yet another account of a huge programme of change (see Bodganor 1999, Hazell, 1999, and Blackburn & Plant, 1999 for exhaustive treatments of this programme, the historical background and its possible future ramifications). This programme is still at an early stage and has been developing so rapidly that events are almost certain to overtake any detailed account before it can be published. So far it has involved the creation of a new Parliament in Scotland, with wide law-making and limited tax-raising powers, the creation of an Assembly for Wales with purely executive powers, and power-sharing for Northern Ireland. The Government has also incorporated the European Convention on Human Rights into UK law. Looking ahead, elections will be held in May 2000 for a Mayor of London and a new Greater London Assembly to which he or she will be accountable. Hereditary peers have been eliminated from the House of Lords and a Royal Commission has delivered proposals for a second chamber without a hereditary component. The traditional first-past-the-post voting system was modified for elections to the Scottish Parliament and the Welsh Assembly and a wholly proportional system was introduced for elections to the European Parliament in June 1999. The Government is committed to a referendum on proposals for adding a proportional element to elections to the House of Commons. Local authorities are being encouraged to experiment with central government-style Cabinet systems (in place of all-party committees) and major cities may acquire elected mayors on the London model. Devolution to Scotland and Wales has stimulated pressures for regional assemblies in some parts of England.

These innovations add up to a complete transformation of territorial politics in Britain with consequences that cannot be predicted (Hazell, 1999, examines the possibilities) but whose cumulative impact is certain to be great. By the term 'territorial politics' we mean a concern with

> relations between the central political institutions in the capital city and those interests, communities, political organisations and governmental bodies outside the central institutional complex, but within the accepted boundaries of the state, which possess, or are commonly *perceived* to possess, a significant geographical or local/regional character.
>
> (Bulpitt, 1983: 52)

In the context of the United Kingdom the centre equates with Parliament and the Whitehall headquarters of Government departments and the Periphery with the Regional Offices and Executive Agencies of Government departments, local authorities and non-departmental public bodies (so-called quangos) throughout England, Scotland, Wales and Northern Ireland, and finally, of course, the Welsh Assembly, the Scottish Parliament and the Northern Ireland executive.

The purpose of this chapter is to try to explain why constitutional issues – territorial politics – have risen to the top of the current political agenda. It begins by looking at the development of the United Kingdom and the particular character of territorial politics in what has been called the last *ancien régime* in Europe (Stone, 1983: 18). It goes on to look at the emergence of territorial issues in the late nineteenth and early twentieth centuries during the transition to modern mass democracy described in Chapter 2 and tries to account for their temporary disappearance in the 1920s. Finally it examines the re-emergence of territorial issues in the 1960s and the 1970s and the failure of Conservative attempts to settle those issues.

The development of the United Kingdom

The United Kingdom differs from other European states such as Germany or Italy in so far as it was never formally constituted in modern times and from older states such as France in so far as it has not developed a single national identity. It bears closest resemblance to Spain which, as the Spanish monarchy founded in 1469, was the product of the union of the crowns of Castile and Aragon. Like Spain, the UK is the product of continuous development since the Middle Ages. Unlike Spain, the last time it experienced major political upheaval was in the seventeenth century.

The UK is essentially the product of the English conquest of the rest of the British Isles: an 'English empire' (Bulpitt, 1983: 75). England had the advantage of size and strategic position (being close to mainland Europe while Wales, Scotland and Ireland were isolated from each other and the rest of Europe). The English monarchy has been highly centralised since the conquest of the Saxon kingdom in 1066 by a few thousand Norman knights and the subsequent need to subdue the hostile majority of the population. Parliament developed during the Middle Ages as a means of associating local elites with the monarchy. Wales and Ireland fell prey to England before they could be united under their own monarchs, while the Scottish monarchy developed under constant threat from England.

The period from 1500 to 1800 saw the gradual replacement of previous systems of indirect rule with formal union: with Wales through the Act of Union of 1536; with Scotland through the union of the crowns under James I (and VI of Scotland) and the Act of Union of 1707; and with Ireland through the Act of Union of 1800. Each Act of Union involved the extension of representation in the Westminster Parliament, thus providing a means for the local elites to gain access to the law-making body for the kingdom as a whole. Each was also associated with internal dissension and external vulnerability. Union with Wales took place in the context of Henry VIII's break with Rome. Union with Scotland took place following the Revolution of 1688 which displaced the legitimate ruler of Scotland and England and in the middle of war with Louis XIV of France who was committed to restoring the Stuarts and ready to foment rebellion to that end. The 1707 Act brought advantages to the rulers of both countries: England secured itself against French invasion through Scotland; the Scots secured the Protestant supremacy and a junior partnership in the powerful joint enterprise of Britain while preserving their own religious establishment and legal system. Union with Ireland took place after years of desperate war with revolutionary France and in the aftermath of the Irish Rebellion of 1798 which, fortunately for the British Government, failed to be reinforced by a narrowly averted French invasion (Bulpitt, 1983: 89–93).

The development of the English state as a 'dual polity' provided a means of incorporating Wales, Scotland and Ireland. A 'dual polity' is one in which the Centre and Periphery have little to do with each other: central government seeks to avoid entanglement in local affairs – thought of as 'low politics' – in order to concentrate on foreign policy and war – thought of as 'high politics'. This kind of polity developed in England as a result of the defeat of attempts by Charles I and James II to establish an absolute monarchy on the French model. Parliament provided a means of incorporating local elites in the national policy-making while leaving them free to run local affairs as Justices of the Peace (*ibid.*: 97).

Thus the UK, as it emerged in its final form at the beginning of the nineteenth century, in the early stages of the industrial revolution and under the impact of democratic revolution in France, was essentially the product of pre-industrial, pre-democratic, pre-nationalist times, a polity founded on collaboration between aristocratic elites in England, Scotland, Wales and Ireland (with the limitation that the Irish elite was the narrowly-based Protestant Ascendancy). This process did not involve the creation of a common institutional framework (except in England and Wales) and the British identity that emerged during the eighteenth century was emphatically Protestant and therefore excluded the majority of the Irish population (Colley, 1992: 52–3). The United Kingdom of Great Britain and Ireland was an 'English empire' which allowed considerable freedom to local elites and allowed the imperial ruling class to concentrate on high politics. This form of polity was bound to come under challenge in an era of nationalism and mass politics.

The first challenge

The prolonged transition from Pitt's 'parliamentary dictatorship' (Halévy's phrase) to mass democracy involved a threat to the territorial settlement established in a pre-democratic era. That challenge was most intense in Ireland, because of religious conflict within the local elite and the economic oppression of the Catholic tenant farmers. The Catholic middle class was ready and able to mobilise their co-religionists among the tenant farmers in the predominantly rural south and west of the country while the Protestant elite eventually found a mass following among the Protestant working class in the industrial north.

The long transition to democracy, beginning with the 1832 Reform Act and ending with the introduction of universal suffrage following the First World War, was associated with three main crises of territorial government. The first – in the late 1820s and early 1830s – was associated with the disintegration of the coalition assembled by Pitt which – with brief intervals – had governed the country since the 1790s and the arrival of a Whig ministry committed to parliamentary reform. Pitt had been obliged by George III to withhold the civil rights for Catholics promised as a condition of union. Mass agitation aroused by the Catholic Association led by Daniel O'Connell obliged the Government of the Duke of Wellington in 1829 to grant those civil rights (Catholic Emancipation). This concession finally split the Pittite coalition and precipitated the fall of Wellington's Government in 1830, thus opening the way to the First Reform Act and the extension of local self-government to the emerging industrial cities of the north and midlands through the Municipal Reform Act of 1835. O'Connell's followers helped to sustain the Whig ministry through the 1830s.

The possibility that Catholic Emancipation might suffice to satisfy Irish Catholic grievances was undermined by the continued economic helotry of Irish tenant farmers and the suffering of the famine in the 1840s. The second crisis of territorial government was precipitated by the extension of the vote to the majority of agricultural workers by the Third Reform Act of 1884. The election of 1885 was the first in which the majority of Irish men could vote and it resulted in the return of a well-disciplined phalanx of 85 Irish Nationalist MPs led by Charles Stewart Parnell. Gladstone's decision to introduce legislation for Irish Home Rule precipitated division within the Liberal Party and the fall of his Government in 1886. Liberal division provided the opportunity for the Conservatives under Lord Salisbury to impose their own territorial settlement through the system of county councils introduced in 1888 which lasted until the 1960s in London and the 1970s elsewhere. The Liberals won office again in 1892 and introduced a second Home

Rule Act, only to have it rejected by the House of Lords in 1893. Gladstone retired not long afterwards and the Government led by Lord Rosebery hung on for only another year until 1895.

The third crisis of territorial government was precipitated in 1910, when the second general election of that year left the Liberal Government dependent on the votes of the Irish Nationalists and therefore obliged to introduce a third Home Rule Bill, and ended only in the creation of the Irish Free State in 1921. The introduction of the Third Home Rule Bill, which would have resulted in a Dublin Parliament for the whole of Ireland, provoked strong resistance among the Ulster Protestants which was exploited by the Conservatives to undermine the authority of the Liberal Government. The ensuing deadlock led to inconclusive discussion about a federal solution to the problem of Ireland – known as 'Home Rule All Round' – with an Imperial Parliament in London and national Parliaments in England, Wales, Scotland and Ireland (with perhaps separate ones for Northern and Southern Ireland). These discussions foundered on English objections that federalism would weaken the government of the UK and Irish Nationalist suspicion of it as a diversionary tactic (Bogdanor, 1999: 44–7). The third Home Rule Bill finally reached the statute book shortly after the outbreak of war in 1914 but was suspended for the duration with a commitment to make special provision for Ulster. The Easter Rebellion of 1916 changed everything. The constitutional Nationalists were displaced by Sinn Fein in the general election of 1918 which precipitated the armed struggle that ended in 1921 with the division of Ireland between the Irish Free State and the province of Northern Ireland ruled from Stormont by the Ulster Unionists allied with the Conservative Party.

The purpose of British Governments throughout this prolonged crisis was to retain the dual polity, to free the Centre to pursue the high politics of diplomacy and war in an age of imperial rivalry among the great powers, while leaving low politics to the periphery, whether to the new multi-purpose local authorities throughout the UK or devolved government in Ireland (and possibly also Wales and Scotland). A wholesale reconstruction of the territorial government of the UK was a distinct possibility in the critical few years before 1914. There were three main reasons why this first challenge to the traditional dual polity of the UK was averted. The first was the onset of the era of world wars – Hobsbawm's Age of Catastrophe – which contributed to a revived sense of British patriotism which lingered until the disappearance of empire in the 1960s. A second was the partition of Ireland which removed the Irish Question from the agenda of high politics, and thus any stimulus to change in the territorial government of the rest of the UK, until the revival of 'the troubles' in Northern Ireland in 1968. A third was the replacement of the Liberal Party by the Labour Party which displaced constitutional with distributional issues in political debate and divided the electorate on class rather than national lines.

Thus from the early 1920s until the late 1960s, British politics were dominated by two 'unionist' parties. This was the heyday of the dual polity: Whitehall and Westminster concentrated on high politics (war and diplomacy, and latterly arms-length Keynesian economic management), leaving low politics to largely depoliticised local authorities (and without enquiring too closely into Unionist gerrymandering in Ulster).

The second challenge

After the best part of half a century the question of the territorial distribution of power returned to the agenda in the 1960s. Plaid Cymru won their first seat in the House of Commons at the Carmarthen by-election in 1966. The Scottish Nationalist Party followed by winning their first seat in the Hamilton by-election in 1967. Edward Heath responded by committing the Conservatives in 1968 to a devolved assembly for Scotland while the Labour Government set up a Royal Commission on the Constitution in 1969 (Bulpitt, 1983: 174). In the 1970 General Election the SNP won 11 per cent of the vote and 1 seat. In February 1974 they won 22 per cent of the vote and 7 seats, and in October 1974 30 per cent of the vote and 11 seats – more than in the 1997 election when they won 6 seats on 22 per cent of the vote (Bogdanor, 1999: 121, 234).

Scottish nationalism was fuelled by the memory of several centuries of statehood, relinquished voluntarily in 1707. Welsh nationalism was essentially a cultural phenomenon, concentrated in the Welsh-speaking areas of Northern and Western Wales. In the 1970 election Plaid Cymru won 11 per cent of the vote but lost Carmarthen. In February 1974 they won 2 seats and another seat in

October 1974, all on the 11 per cent of the vote won in 1970 (Bogdanor, 1999: 156).

The irruption of nationalist politics was most dramatic in Northern Ireland. The campaign of civil disobedience launched by the Northern Ireland Civil Rights Association in 1968 rapidly degenerated into inter-communal violence to which the Labour Government responded with the introduction of troops in 1969. The appearance of British troops rapidly resulted in the revival of armed struggle by the Provisional Irish Republican Army which broke away from the so-called Official IRA on this issue. Twenty people were killed in 1970, rising to 172 in 1971 and a horrific 467 in 1972 following the introduction of internment in August 1971 and the shooting of 14 demonstrators by the Parachute Regiment on 'Bloody Sunday' in January 1972 (Whitehead, 1985: 161–4). The Conservatives responded later in 1972 by suspending (and then abolishing) the Northern Ireland Parliament at Stormont and imposing direct rule from London when the Unionists refused to hand over responsibility for law and order. The Unionists in their turn brought down by direct action in March 1974 the power-sharing executive negotiated by Heath at Sunningdale in 1973.

Even in England the attempt by the Heath Government to intervene in the traditional local authority discretion over council house rents led to the refusal by Clay Cross Council to raise council rents as required by the Housing Finance Act of 1972. This incident was a prelude to mounting concern about local authority spending which led Wilson to set up an inquiry into local government finance in the summer of 1974 and Heath to enter the October election campaign with a promise to abolish the local authority rating system. In the spring of 1975 the Secretary of State for the Environment Anthony Crosland delivered his famous warning to local authorities that the party was over. All of these developments were harbingers of the much greater conflicts in the 1980s between the Conservative Government and the Labour 'municipal Left' which culminated in the Poll Tax debacle of 1990.

The explanation for this sudden reappearance of territorial politics in the late 1960s and early 1970s lies in the accumulating debility of successive British Governments in the face of external and internal challenges. 'Politically speaking, the key to these neo-nationalist renaissances lies in the slow foundering of the British state' (Nairn,

1977: 46). We can point to two key factors. First was the absolute decline in British power and independence, beginning with the humiliation of Suez in 1956 and continued by the withdrawal from empire in the late 1950s and early 1960s (with further humiliation at the hands of Rhodesia's Ian Smith in the mid-1960s) and the tortuous process of negotiating entry to the European Economic Community, beginning in 1961 and concluding only in 1973. Second was the growing consciousness of relative economic decline, brought home in especially humiliating fashion by the 1967 devaluation of sterling.

The dual polity broke down when the Centre began to interfere in matters that had previously been left to the Periphery in order to try to strengthen its position in high politics by improving economic performance. The failure of attempts by Conservative and Labour Governments in the 1960s and 1970s to improve the performance of the British economy through a variety of detailed interventions led to a collapse of authority manifested most acutely in 1974 in the defeat of the Heath Government at the hands of the National Union of Mineworkers and the destruction of the Northern Ireland power-sharing executive at the hands of Protestant strikers organised by the paramilitary Ulster Defence Association. The SNP manifesto for the second general election of 1974 could claim with some justice that 'London has lost confidence in its ability to master events. There is a hint of Weimar in the English autumn' (cited Bulpitt, 1983: 180).

The Labour Government which retained office after the second election of 1974 lacked a stable majority which put it at the mercy of minor parties (Liberals, Scottish Nationalists, Plaid Cymru and Ulster Unionists). For a couple of years after the IMF crisis it relied on the Liberals through what became known as the Lib–Lab pact. It won the cooperation of local authorities in achieving large spending cuts through a 'partnership' which involved shelving the tougher Rate Support Grant regime proposed by the Department of the Environment in evidence to the Layfield Committee on Local Government Finance (1976). The Government won the compliance of the Unionists by increasing Northern Ireland's representation in the House of Commons to a level comparable to Wales and Scotland. And it won the temporary compliance of the nationalists by legislating for devolved assemblies, subject to referendums. The

Government was eventually brought down in 1979 by defeat in a vote of confidence put down by the SNP following the failure of the Scottish referendum to deliver the necessary 40 per cent of the electorate in support of devolution. Thus the crisis of territorial governance formed a key part of the general crisis of the mid-1970s.

The Conservative record

The Conservative Government made a determined effort to restore the dual polity – to regain autonomy for the Centre – but with only limited and temporary success. Ironically they were much less successful in curbing local authority spending through confrontation than Labour had been through reliance on partnership. The frustrations of the early 1980s led to the Poll Tax which contributed largely to the fall of Thatcher in 1990. The Council Tax introduced in 1993 took the sting out of local taxation as a political issue. The Conservatives weakened the autonomy of local authorities through selective capping of local taxation introduced in 1985 and general capping introduced in 1991 (Butler *et al.*, 1994: 43, 164). The role of local authorities in providing services was reduced through a range of measures including: the abolition of the Greater London Council and Metropolitan County Councils; compulsory competitive tendering; the sale of much of the existing stock of council houses and the curtailment of new building in favour of Housing Associations; and the transfer of much education (including polytechnics, further education colleges and grant-maintained schools) to new bodies accountable to central rather than local government. But success in this quarter was achieved at the price of reducing the Conservatives to the position of third party in local government (after Labour and the Liberal Democrats) by 1997, and by increasing the involvement of central government bodies – albeit at arms length from ministers – in providing local services. The creation of Government Offices for the Regions in 1994 has strengthened the ability of the Centre to intervene in the Periphery but they could also serve as a executive arm for possible Regional Assemblies. So the balance sheet in England was distinctly ambiguous.

By contrast, Conservative efforts to restore the authority of the Centre in Wales, Scotland and Northern Ireland resulted only in an erosion of electoral support for their own party and a weakening of the traditional union state. In Scotland in the 1955 election the Conservatives had won a majority of the vote and a majority of seats. In 1979 they could still win 22 seats on 31 per cent of the vote (compared with Labour's 44 seats on 42 per cent of the vote) but in 1997 they won only 18 per cent of the vote and lost all 11 seats won in 1992 (Bogdanor, 1999: 132, 194). Labour has been dominant in Wales since it replaced the Liberals as the second party in the House of Commons after the First World War but even between 1979 and 1992 the Conservative vote remained stable at around 30 per cent, delivering 11 seats in 1979 and 6 in 1992 (Bogdanor, 1999: 195). In 1997 the Conservatives won only 20 per cent of the vote and no seats (*Financial Times*, 2/3.5.97). In Northern Ireland the Conservatives failed in their efforts to marginalise Sinn Fein/IRA. Mrs Thatcher was obliged to acknowledge a Southern dimension in the 1985 Anglo-Irish Agreement while Major laid the ground for the 1998 Good Friday Agreement by acknowledging that Britain had 'no selfish interest' in remaining in the province. Finally, they failed to halt a growing regional dimension in the governance of the European Union. Regional aid now accounts for about 35 per cent of the EU budget, with a growing role for regions represented in the Committee of Regions set up in 1995 under the 1992 Treaty of Maastricht.

Conclusion

This chapter has argued that the UK developed as an 'English empire' – an affair of elites which was bound to face challenge during the transition to representative government in the nineteenth century and mass democracy in the twentieth century. The first challenge which culminated in the period 1885 to 1921 was blunted by the creation in the 1880s and 1890s of a counter-ideology of unionism and imperialism and then overcome – for a couple of generations – by the challenge of war, the removal of the Irish Question from high politics by partition in 1921, and the replacement of the Liberals, with their strong electoral base in the so-called 'Celtic fringe', by Labour with its much broader class base and appeal. Thus territorial issues were effectively suspended from the 1920s until the 1960s. A second challenge arose at that point as a result of 'the slow foundering of the British state' which by the mid-1970s had reached the point of comprehensive crisis. The union settlement was stabilised temporarily by the Conservatives but finally foundered with their comprehensive defeat in 1997.

The British state is now at the beginning of a major transformation whose opening stages were outlined in the introduction to this chapter. The outcome will remain uncertain for some time and the union is likely to be fully tested at its weakest point in Scotland only when there are governments of differing complexions in London and Edinburgh. The constitutional changes put in train by the Blair Government may or may not herald the end of the UK – 'the break-up of Britain'. So far Spain has survived the creation of a quasi-federal system of government in which Galicia, Andalusia and the Basque Country and Catalonia have greater powers than other regions (so-called Autonomous Communities). Regions can have the best of both worlds – self-government at home, with largesse from national government and a stronger hand in dealing with the EU. The creation of a new tier of regional governments can be seen as one aspect of the variable geometry emerging with the expansion of the European Union: what has been called a 'new medievalism' (Marquand, 1991) – a patchwork quilt of overlapping jurisdictions, a hollowing out of the national state under challenge from below as well as from above by the development of the European Union. We shall turn to that subject in our next chapter, for, as Vernon Bogdanor has remarked, 'European Union and devolution offer complementary challenges to the profoundly unitary nature of the British state' (1999: 2).

11
Missed Chances: Britain and the European Union

Introduction

Looking back over more than half a century since the Second World War, the question of Britain's relations with the developing process of European integration can be seen as the dominant issue in post-war British politics. In the late 1940s Britain stood at the peak of its prestige in Europe as a result of its part in the war – far above defeated Germany and humiliated France. Now Britain stands on the fringe of a European Union dominated since the 1950s by a Franco-German partnership.

Relations between Britain and the developing EU over this half-century show a persistent pattern of what Roy Denman (a senior civil servant involved in negotiations for entry in the early 1970s and then an official of the European Commission until his retirement in 1989 after serving as its Ambassador to the United States) has called 'missed chances' (Denman, 1996). The first was Britain's failure to take part in the foundation of the European Coal and Steel Community (ECSC, precursor of the EU) in the early 1950s. According to Hugo Young, this failure cost Britain the leadership of Europe which it had enjoyed since 1945 (Young, 1998: 68). A second was Britain's withdrawal from negotiations at Messina on the creation of what became the European Economic Community to which it had been invited on the same basis as existing members of the ECSC. Failure to join the EEC at the outset meant that Britain eventually had to join on unfavourable terms. Later, more arguable, lost opportunities have been the failure to join the European

Exchange Rate Mechanism until 1990, when Britain might have joined at a more favourable time in the mid-1980s, and the decision in 1991 to opt out of progress towards the single currency set out in the Treaty of Maastricht.

This chapter attempts to explain this persistent record of failure by the British political class to come to terms with the reality of European integration. It begins with a brief account of the origins and development of the EU and goes on to address the following questions:

- why did Britain not take part in the foundation of the ECSC and the EEC in the 1950s?
- why did Britain change its mind so quickly and apply to join in 1961?
- why did Britain fail to enter the EEC until 1973 and what were the consequences of delay?
- why has Britain been such an 'awkward partner' (to quote the title of a book by Stephen George) since joining in 1973?

It concludes with an assessment of British prospects under a Labour Government committed to improving Britain's relations with Europe.

The origins and development of the EU

The origins of the EU go back further than one might think, perhaps as far as the Roman Empire which covered the entire territory occupied by the present 15 member states apart from Scandinavia, Germany and Ireland, and left a memory of grandeur and unity which has haunted later generations. The borders of the Holy Roman Empire founded by Charlemagne in 800 coincided with those of the founder members (France, West Germany, Italy, Belgium, Luxembourg and the Netherlands) to such an extent that General de Gaulle (then in temporary retirement) was moved to describe the ECSC as 'giving modern economic, social, strategic and cultural shape to the work of the Emperor Charlemagne' (cited Monnet, 1978: 287). The boundaries of the Napoleonic Empire corresponded closely with those of Charlemagne's. The nineteenth-century Concert of Europe involved regular meetings of the rulers of the Great Powers which resembled meetings of the European

Council which have taken place regularly since 1974. The industrial revolution stimulated a number of free trade treaties between France, Italy, the North German Confederation (precursor to the German Empire founded in 1871) and Britain in the mid-nineteenth century and several experiments in monetary union. A major war aim of the Central Powers (Germany and Austria–Hungary) in the First World War was the creation of a customs union (*Mitteleuropa*) embracing Belgium, Italy and northern France, and the Nazis had plans for what they called a European Economic Community under German control. On a more benign note, the close relationship between the German Chancellor Gustav Stresemann and the French Prime Minister Aristide Briand in the late 1920s, before the rise of the Nazis, foreshadowed future close relations between post-war German and French leaders.

The more immediate origins of the EU can be found in the special circumstances of the aftermath of the Second World War. The wars that dominated the first and climactic years of the Age of Catastrophe were widely seen as the calamitous result of economic autarky and political and national rivalry and there was a widespread feeling of 'never again'. Europe in 1945 was in a mood to rebuild from the ground up; this was 'year zero'. Most of Europe – with the very significant exception of Britain – had endured disastrous defeat and occupation which had demonstrated the weakness and vulnerability of even the traditional 'great powers' like France, Germany and Italy. The hardening lines of the Cold War division of Europe led the United States to encourage greater cooperation among the Western European countries against a common external threat from the Soviet Union and an internal threat from strong Communist Parties in France and Italy. The Americans found a receptive audience among the leaders of their Western European partners in the Cold War – the West German Chancellor Konrad Adenauer, the Italian Prime Minister Alcide de Gasperi and the French Prime Minister and Foreign Minister Robert Schuman. All were Christian Democrats and all were hostile to nationalism. All six signatories of the Treaty of Paris in 1951 setting up the ECSC belonged to Christian Democrat parties. The six founding states shared a common need to consolidate new and fragile liberal democracies in what Alan Milward has described as 'the European Rescue of the Nation State' (Milward, 1992). This political role helps to explain the subsequent attraction of the EU for emerging liberal democracies, first in Southern Europe in the 1970s and today in Central and Eastern Europe – and its more limited appeal to the well-established democracies of Britain and Scandinavia. Thus there were in Western Europe in the late 1940s a whole series of powerful, readily understandable factors which help to explain the origins of the EU in the form of the ECSC.

It is important to recognise that the ECSC, and by extension further developments in European integration, have always been primarily political in their motivation. Jean Monnet, who drafted the famous Plan of 1950 which bears the name of the French Foreign Minister Robert Schuman, saw it as the first step towards European Federation (Monnet, 1978: 272, 295). Konrad Adenauer records in his memoirs that Schuman told him that 'the aim of his proposal was not economic but highly political' (*ibid.*: 303) and he commended the Schuman Plan to the West German Bundestag in 1950 in those terms: 'The importance of this project is above all political, and not economic' (cited Nugent, 1999: 37). The British Government also recognised the political implications at the outset: the minutes of the Cabinet discussion of the Schuman Plan record that

> Mr Morrison [Deputy Prime Minister] said that the proposal might have been primarily economic in its origins but it clearly had most important political implications. Sir Stafford Cripps [Chancellor of the Exchequer] agreed that these were the most alarming features of the proposal. It looked like a challenge to the United States and the United Kingdom.
>
> (Cited Denman, 1996: 187)

No-one can accuse the British of lack of foresight: it was simply that they disliked what they foresaw so accurately.

The reader can find detailed accounts of the development of the EU in many places (see especially Nugent, 1999, and Dinan, 1999). The main milestones can be summarised briefly. The Treaty of Paris of 1951 created a single market in coal and steel presided over by a new supra-national High Authority (precursor to the European Commission) of which Monnet was the first President. The ECSC was one of a series of initiatives in the direction of European unity.

It was more modest than others such as the Council of Europe or the Committee for European Economic Cooperation, in so far as it was confined to particular sectors of industry, yet more ambitious in so far as it went beyond the inter-governmental nature of those other bodies by creating the supra-national High Authority and a new body of law superior to national law.

The Treaty of Paris was followed in 1957 by the two Treaties of Rome founding the European Economic Community (EEC) and the European Atomic Energy Community (EURATOM). The proclaimed aim was to establish 'a common market and progressively approximate the economic policies of Member States' (cited Nugent, 1999: 43). It involved the removal of tariff barriers between the Member States and the creation of a single external tariff which was in place by 1968. All three Communities were combined in the European Community in 1967.

Since then the original EEC comprising just six states has been enlarged to include Britain, Ireland and Denmark (in 1973), Greece (1981), Spain and Portugal (1987), the former East Germany as part of reunited Germany (1990) and Austria, Finland and Sweden (1995). 1979 saw the launch of the European Monetary System (EMS) as the precursor of Economic and Monetary Union (EMU). 1987 saw the ratification of the Single European Act providing for an extension of majority voting in the Council of Ministers (the main decision-making forum) and the Single Market programme for removing existing barriers to the free movement of goods and capital by 1992. It was followed in 1992 by the Treaty on European Union (the Treaty of Maastricht) establishing the EU and providing for a Common Foreign and Security Policy and Cooperation in Justice and Home Affairs (both based on inter-governmental cooperation) as well as a phased approach to the creation of a single currency introduced in 1999 in 11 member states and presided over by a new European Central Bank.

The development of the EU has known two main creative periods: in the 1950s and early 1960s and from the mid-1980s until the early 1990s. Both periods coincided with economic booms. The relative stagnation of the 1970s and early 1980s, and again in the mid-1990s, coincided with recessions. The economic recovery across most of Europe in the late 1990s bodes well for the two major current issues facing the EU – the successful establishment of the single currency and the conclusion of membership negotiations with ten Central and Eastern European countries formerly under Communist rule.

Why did Britain not take part in the 1950s?

Britain decided not to take part in the Schuman Plan in 1950 and then withdrew in late 1955 from the talks at Messina which resulted in the Treaties of Rome in 1957. In the late 1950s the British Government tried unsuccessfully to persuade the Six to set up a wider European free trade area (with no common tariff) and then set up a rival European Free Trade Area (EFTA) in 1960 which included Austria, Denmark, Norway, Portugal, Sweden and Switzerland as well as Britain.

The reasons were several. British politicians of both main parties in the late 1940s and at least until after the Suez crisis of 1956 continued to entertain residual notions of Britain's status as a great power. Alone among the major European states, it had never been defeated or occupied. It had been one of the 'big three' at wartime and post-war conferences and until the late 1950s it was the largest economy in Europe. Apparently Ernest Bevin would commonly ask his officials, 'What would Lord Curzon [Foreign Secretary in the 1920s] do if he were in my shoes' (cited Shaw, 1996: 44).

British politicians and their senior advisers shared a common commitment to the Empire and the 'special relationship' with the United States. De Gaulle in his memoirs quotes a statement by Churchill in June 1944 in the presence of Ernest Bevin and Anthony Eden (British Foreign Secretaries in their turn for most of the subsequent decade): 'Here is something you [de Gaulle] should know: whenever we have to choose between Europe and the open sea, we shall always choose the open sea. Whenever I have to choose between you and Roosevelt, I shall always choose Roosevelt' (cited Lichtheim, 1974: 366). British foreign policy was guided in this period by Churchill's doctrine of the three spheres of British influence (Europe, the USA and the Empire/Commonwealth). Britain's main trading links were still with the Empire which took 40 per cent of its exports in 1948 (George, 1998: 15) and sterling held a special status (shared only with the US dollar) as a reserve currency.

We have already seen that the Labour Government recognised and disliked the political implications of the Schuman Plan. Britain still had the largest coal and steel industries in Europe and was unwilling to sacrifice Government control over those industries so soon after they had been nationalised. Their attitude is well-captured in Herbert Morrison's oft-quoted comment on the Schuman Plan: 'It's no damn good – the Durham miners won't wear it' (cited George, 1998: 20).

Finally, one cannot discount sheer prejudice. The Schuman Plan and the ECSC were the creations of Catholic politicians whereas Britain in 1950 was still an emphatically Protestant country. The Labour Party has been famously said to owe more to Methodism than to Marx. Ernest Bevin was heard to mutter 'black crows' when he encountered Catholic priests, and his junior colleague at the Foreign Office Kenneth Younger saw the ECSC as 'just a step in the consolidation of the Catholic "black international"' (Young, 1998: 50–1).

Basically Britain (and here we are talking about all shades of political opinion at all social levels) saw itself as occupying a different league to other European countries. Britain was still attached to the principle of national sovereignty which seemed to have been strengthened rather than undermined by the Second World War. It took a later generation to recognise that Britain had ended the war as 'a warrior satellite of the United States, dependent for life itself on American subsidies' (Barnett, 1995: 3). Britain's collective psychology at the time was well caught by Jean Monnet: 'Britain had not been conquered or invaded; she felt no need to exorcise history' (Monnet, 1978: 306).

Why did Britain apply to join in 1961?

Monnet claims to have predicted the British about-turn even at the time of the Schuman Plan. His memoirs quote a conversation with Stafford Cripps in which he said, 'I hope with all my heart that you will join in this from the start. But if you don't, we shall go ahead without you. And I'm sure that, because you are realists, you will adjust to the facts when we have succeeded' (Monnet, 1978: 308).

Monnet was prescient in identifying so early a persistent pattern still evident today in British policy on the single currency. In 1961, little more than three years after the foundation of the EEC at the beginning of 1958 and only a year after the establishment of the rival EFTA in 1960, the Conservative Prime Minister Harold Macmillan applied to join in 1961. The reasons were several. The 'what's wrong with Britain' books discussed in Chapter 4 had created a growing awareness of Britain's relative economic decline compared with the Six. Andrew Shonfield's *British Economic Policy since the War*, the first of the genre, began by citing comparative figures for economic growth between 1952 and 1956 for Britain and members of the ECSC (Shonfield, 1958: 14). Between 1950 and 1960 the British economy grew by an annual average of 3 per cent compared with West Germany's 8 per cent, Italy's 6 per cent and France's 5 per cent (Young, 1998: 106).

Another factor was declining confidence in Britain as a great power. The Suez debacle, when Britain was obliged to withdraw from a joint enterprise with France by American withdrawal of support for sterling, revealed the extent of Britain's dependence on the USA. France drew the conclusion that it could act independently only as part of a larger European political entity whereas Britain concluded that it could not act independently of the USA. The retreat from empire which had stalled following the granting of independence to the Indian Sub-Continent in 1948 was resumed in the late 1950s with independence for Ghana and Malaya in 1957 and Nigeria in 1960 (Young, 1998: 139). In the same year Macmillan delivered his famous speech in South Africa pointing to a 'wind of change' blowing through Africa. In the early 1960s Britain was engaged in a wholesale liquidation of its African empire. Other factors were evidence of the growing importance of trade with the Six rather than with the Commonwealth and anxiety about being excluded from this market, as well as US pressure to join the EEC and failure to win support for alternative plans for a looser free trade area.

These factors combined to produce a gradual realisation of Britain's loss of great power status and growing isolation. The U2 incident in 1960, when the Soviets walked out of the Paris Summit, after shooting down an American spy-plane, destroyed what Leo Pliatzky has described as Macmillan's 'attempt to gain a niche in history by acting as a bridge between the American and Russian superpowers... I had an eye-witness description of the Prime

Minister sitting in No 10 with his foreign policy in ruins around him and asking himself what he was going to do for a foreign policy' (Pliatzky, 1982: 45). Macmillan confided to his diary about his fear of Britain being 'caught between a hostile (or at least less and less friendly) America and a boastful, powerful "Empire of Charlemagne" – now under French but later bound to come under German control' (cited Young, 1998: 122). The British Government was now ready to contemplate closer ties with previously patronised European states.

Finally, there were sound tactical reasons. The application to join the EEC can be seen as part of Macmillan's modernisation programme, as a way of refreshing the image of the Conservatives after ten years in office.

> To put the matter another way, the bid was launched because senior Conservative leaders were frightened: frightened of a new world order openly dominated by the superpowers, frightened of Europe's higher economic growth and its potential as a third force in the world, and frightened about the Conservative Party's electoral future.
>
> (Bulpitt, 1996: 236)

It was, in short, a central aspect of the response to the problem of relative economic decline that had emerged as a key domestic political issue in the early 1960s.

Why did Britain fail to enter the EEC until 1973 and what were the consequences of delay?

The first part of the question can be answered with one man's name: de Gaulle, President of France since 1958, who turned down Britain's first application in 1963 because he saw Britain as a 'Trojan Horse' for the USA. He disliked the 'special relationship' between Britain and the USA, which he saw as one of tutelage. His veto followed quickly upon Macmillan's agreement with President Kennedy at Nassau which left Britain dependent on the USA for its military nuclear technology. France, by contrast, was set upon developing its own nuclear technology. Before delivering his veto, De Gaulle had already cleared his lines with Adenauer who, for his own reasons, had no love for Britain; and he followed it quickly by inviting the West German Chancellor to Paris to sign the Treaty of Friendship between France and Germany. Henceforth the development of the EU would be based largely upon this Franco-German partnership – 'not so much a community as a two-state hegemonic alliance' (Bulpitt, 1996: 220).

Harold Wilson's Labour Government renewed Britain's application in 1967 for much the same reasons as Macmillan launched the first application – as an attempt to regain the initiative after the collapse of the growth strategy in 1966. But de Gaulle vetoed this application for much the same reasons as the earlier one. De Gaulle was succeeded in 1969 by his former Prime Minister Georges Pompidou who declared that he was ready to contemplate a widening and deepening of the EEC that might include Britain. The Conservative Government elected in 1970 renewed the British application and Heath managed to convince Pompidou of his clear commitment to Europe rather than the USA in a way that Wilson might not have been able to accomplish. The Treaty of Accession was signed in 1972 and Britain (along with its close trading partners Ireland and Denmark) joined the EEC at the beginning of 1973.

The 12-year gap between Britain's first membership application in 1961 and eventual entry in 1973 had several consequences. First of all, it allowed Germany and France to shape the EEC in its formative years in ways that suited them and thus to cement the partnership which has dominated the development of the EU since then. De Gaulle summed up the situation with his usual pith: 'France and Germany are Europe; the others are just the vegetables' (cited Barber, 1997). Secondly, Britain entered from a position of weakness: it had to accept rules shaped by others, notably the Common Agricultural Policy and unfavourable budgetary arrangements, thus storing up trouble for the future. By 1973 the British economy, and Britain's weight in the world at large, was relatively weaker than it had been in the early 1960s. To cap it all, Britain had the misfortune of entering the EEC at the end of Hobsbawm's Golden Age, between the collapse of the Bretton Woods system of fixed exchange rates and the first oil price rise. Thus Britain did not share in the economic gains made by the original Six, which left their citizens with a generally favourable view of the EEC. The circumstances of British entry meant that membership became associated instead with VAT, decimalisation and higher food prices.

Membership of the EEC was presented to the British electorate in the early 1970s in a way that stored up trouble for the future. Instead of being presented as a political venture, with long-term consequences for the way in which the country conducted its affairs, entry was presented largely in terms of the economic benefits from joining a mere trading body – a 'Common Market'. Such disingenuousness might have been justified in part by the way in which de Gaulle had managed during the 1960s to subvert the federalist intentions of the EEC's founders, but it involved a culpable dishonesty about the implications for British sovereignty which has been seized upon ever since then by the opponents of European integration. As such it was symptomatic of the accumulating collapse in confidence on the part of Britain's governing elite – a collapse which would become ever clearer in the next few years.

Why has Britain been such an 'awkward partner'?

Since joining the EEC Britain's relations with its partners have been dominated by a succession of wrangles. Problems over the British contribution to the Community budget dominated the first ten years of membership. The Labour Government took office in 1974 with a commitment to renegotiate the terms of membership which it had denounced as unsatisfactory while in opposition, and then to invite the electorate to pass judgement in a referendum on the renegotiated terms. The Government managed to secure some largely cosmetic changes which were accepted by the electorate in a referendum in 1975, but the process of negotiations did much to sour relations with other Member States.

The argument was taken up again by Mrs Thatcher in 1979 because the conditions for rebating Britain's contribution agreed by the Labour Government when the transition period ended in 1979 did not apply because Britain's balance of payments remained positive as a result of North Sea oil. The ensuing dispute dragged on until 1984 with the effect of further souring relations between Britain and its European partners. The conclusion of this dispute was followed by a brief period of good relations with France and Germany in the early years of the Single Market initiative launched in 1985 by the new President of the European Commission Jacques Delors with strong support from his deputy Lord Cockfield appointed by Britain. During this period Britain conceded a significant weakening in the ability of individual Member States to obstruct developments which they disliked as the price of securing the rapid implementation of the free market reforms which it favoured. These concessions would redound to the British Government's disadvantage once the thrust of Delors' policy in the direction of a single currency became clear in the late 1980s.

In 1988, as Thatcher recalled in her memoirs, 'The agenda in Europe began to take an increasingly troublesome shape' (Thatcher, 1995: 737) and relations deteriorated rapidly once again. The main objects of Mrs Thatcher's hostility were Delors' plans, backed by France and Germany, for further economic integration including a single currency and for a 'social dimension' to complement the single market. Delors won a standing ovation for a speech at the TUC conference in 1988 which prompted Mrs Thatcher's riposte, in a famous speech at Bruges, that 'We have not successfully rolled back the frontiers of the state in Britain only to see them reimposed at a European level, with a European super-state exercising a new dominance from Brussels' (*ibid.*: 744). Her opposition to the entry of sterling to the ERM destroyed relations with her two key lieutenants Geoffrey Howe and Nigel Lawson, leading ultimately to her outburst 'No, no, no' over EMU at Question Time in the House of Commons in October 1990 which precipitated Howe's resignation and her own downfall. The link between her fall and developments in the EU permanently soured her disciples' attitude towards European integration.

The consequences of this implication of the EU in the fall of Thatcher became clear not long after John Major's victory in the 1992 election. Major took office in 1990 with the declared aim of putting Britain back 'at the very heart of Europe', as he put it, and he enjoyed a brief period of good relations with an avuncular Helmut Kohl, Chancellor of the newly reunified Germany and the most powerful politician in Europe (Young, 1998: 424). By securing an opt-out from the single currency at the Maastricht summit in December 1991 Major was able to mollify Conservative opponents of further European integration without alienating other European leaders. Thus he entered the 1992 election campaign with a united party behind him. 'Black Wednesday' in September 1992, when sterling was forced out of the ERM by a tidal wave of speculation, broke the central plank of the Government's economic policy and left Major vulnerable to sniping from the Thatcherite Right on the backbenches and in his own Cabinet. 'As an external shock it ranked with de Gaulle's veto in 1963 and the sterling crisis of 1976. Only the 1931 crisis had more immediate and intense political consequences' (Bulpitt, 1996: 248). Continuing divisions over Europe were a key factor in undermining Major's authority and worsening relations with the rest of the EU (for example, by using the EU as a scapegoat for problems over BSE – 'mad cow disease' – in 1996).

How are we to explain the difficult relationship between Britain and its European partners, during nearly a quarter of a century since Britain joined the EEC in 1973 to the catastrophic electoral defeat of the Conservatives in 1997, brought on more by divisions over Europe than by any other factor? We have already pointed to the lasting consequences of Britain's delay in entering the EEC, which meant that Britain played no part in devising the rules in a club dominated by its historic rivals France and Germany. This was the source of the disputes over the budget which dominated the first ten years of British membership. Moreover, Britain was never going to be able to accept happily the duumvirate of France and Germany in a way that other Member States might.

A second factor was the historic British suspicion of foreigners conveyed in expressions such as 'Wogs begin at Calais' or 'Fog in Channel; Continent isolated'. Britain as an island has always been able to indulge in a semi-detached relationship with the rest of Europe that has never been open to countries like France and Germany. British politicians of both parties have often been tempted to play the nationalist card, as Gaitskell did in 1961 when invoking 1000 years of history being put at risk or Wilson did in the early 1970s when denouncing the entry terms negotiated by Heath, or as Thatcher did over the budget ('I want my money back') and Major did over BSE ('Beef Wars'). Hitherto most politicians have been reluctant to make a public show of sympathy for European integration, as witnessed by Blair's fear of antagonising the Murdoch press in the run-up to the 1997 election. This willingness of mainstream politicians to defer to or even to exploit popular suspicions of foreigners has few parallels in other European countries outside the neo-Fascist or unreconstructed Communist fringes.

A third factor has been the absence of consensus over European integration either *within* the two main parties or *between* those parties. Within the Conservative Party, the old imperialist and the newer free-market Right have always been hostile to the EEC and now the EU. Within the Labour Party, the warring followers of Gaitskell and Bevan shared a common suspicion of the EEC, and the Bennite Left remained hostile to the EU until their numbers and influence began to fade following the 1983 electoral defeat and Mitterrand's U-turn in the same year. Strong feelings over Europe have threatened party unity, within the Labour Party in the 1970s and early 1980s, culminating in the SDP breakaway in 1981, and among Conservatives in the 1990s. These divisions have meant that party leaders from Wilson to Major have always had to temporise and equivocate in order to reconcile differences within their own parties and have always been tempted to exploit divisions within the opposing party for tactical reasons. For example, one important reason for the change in the Labour Party's attitude to Europe in the late 1980s was the scope that it afforded for exploiting divisions within the Conservative Party. The elections to the European Parliament in 1989 were the first to be lost by the Conservatives under Thatcher's leadership. 'Largely, though not entirely, because Mrs Thatcher was anti-Europe, Labour became pro-Europe' (Young, 1998: 474). The same factor may be at work today in Conservative criticisms of Labour over the single currency. By contrast, most other Member States have enjoyed a much wider consensus over European integration.

A fourth factor has been the nature of the British political system and British party politics. The absence of a written constitution and the tradition of Parliamentary sovereignty invests an unusual degree of power in the governing party. The two main British political parties have been accustomed to governing alone rather than in coalitions. By contrast, politicians from other Member States are used to operating within the confines of written constitutions, and to brokering deals in coalitions with other parties. Hence they are better able to cope with the constant negotiation involved in EU politics.

A fifth factor has lain in Britain's closer ties to the USA as result of a common language and a similar type of free-market capitalism as well as the personal ties between leading politicians on both sides of the Atlantic – in the past between Macmillan and Kennedy, Wilson and Johnson, Thatcher and Reagan, and today between Blair and Clinton. If we recall Churchill's three circles, the ties to one (the Empire and Commonwealth) may have largely gone but the ties to a second (the USA) remain as strong as ever under Blair. The one-sided 'special relationship' with the USA always threatens to be stronger than relations with other European politicians. Heath – with closer ties to the West German Chancellor Brandt and the French President Pompidou than to Nixon – still remains an exception to this pattern.

A sixth and perhaps the most important factor has been the failure of British politicians (with only partial exceptions such as Heath and Jenkins) to convey any sense of idealism about the project of European integration, unlike some of the founding figures such as Adenauer and Schuman, or even later figures such as Mitterrand and Kohl. This contrast, perceived in 1950 by Monnet, has been well-put by Hugo Young in his magisterial history of Britain's relations with Europe:

> For the makers of the original 'Europe' ... their creation was a triumph. Out of defeat, they produced a new kind of victory. For Britain, by contrast, the entry into Europe was a defeat, a fate she had resisted, a necessity reluctantly accepted, the last resort of a once-great power, never for one moment a climactic or triumphant engagement with the construction of Europe.
>
> (Young, 1998: 2–3)

Thus there are deep-seated reasons for Britain's difficulty in adjusting to membership of the EU.

Conclusion

Tony Blair has made clear that one of his ambitions is to overcome the sour legacy inherited from John Major and to forge a new consensus on Britain's relations with Europe. Accepting the award of the Charlemagne prize at Aachen in May 1999, he pronounced: 'I have a bold aim that over the next few years Britain resolves once and for all its ambivalence towards Europe' (Bennett, 1999). What are the prospects for achieving this ambition?

On the one hand, one can point to an emerging political consensus on a constructive engagement with Europe. Since the late 1980s there has been a general support for the EU within the Labour Party; no longer is it seen as an obstacle in the way of achieving a uniquely British form of socialism, as in the days of Bevin, Gaitskell and Benn, but more as a check on an unbridled free-market capitalism on the American model admired by the Conservative Right. There has always been strong support for the EU among Liberals (and now Liberal Democrats) and on the Left of the Conservative Party (represented by Heseltine, Clarke and Chris Patten). The Europhobes to whom the present Conservative leadership defers are more marginal than ever before, whatever encouragement they might have drawn from the results of the 1999 elections to the European Parliament.

Blair is obviously much more at ease with other European politicians than any of his predecessors except Heath, as witnessed by his speech in French to the French National Assembly in 1998 and the award of the Charlemagne prize in 1999 for his 'outstanding contribution to European unification' (Young, 1998: 491; Bennett, 1999). He has demonstrated his strong personal commitment to engagement with the EU by launching a full-scale policy review in the summer of 1998 (*Financial Times*, 1.7.98) and by calling on Ministers and Permanent Secretaries to strengthen ties with their EU counterparts (*Financial Times*, 2.12.98). Despite reported cool relations with Lionel Jospin, the Socialist Prime Minister of France, he has won French support for a joint security initiative launched at St Malo in December 1998 (*Financial Times*, 5/6.12.98). He has also taken full advantage of a close political alignment between the governments of the four main Member States (France, Britain, Italy and Germany). Britain's Foreign Secretary Robin Cook was responsible for chairing the working party which drew up the manifesto for the European Socialist parties in the 1999 elections to the European Parliament (*Financial Times*, 7.1.99). Having taken the lead in proposing Romano Prodi as the new President of the European Commission, Blair will be in a strong position in arguing for reform of the Commission and for an agenda favourable to Britain (*Financial Times*, 25.3.99). Both of the British members of the new Commission, Chris Patten and Neil Kinnock, are likely to play a prominent part in its work.

On the other hand, Blair still seems to have more personal and political sympathy for US President Bill Clinton and his New Democrats than for European Socialist parties (although the German Chancellor Gerhard Schröder and the Italian Prime Minister Massimo D'Alema seem to share his interest in a 'third way' between neo-liberalism and social democracy – and Jospin has taken a notably pragmatic position in key policy areas such as privatisation). More importantly, Blair may be inhibited in pursuing a distinctive agenda within the EU by Britain's exclusion from the single currency and the constraints on his room for manoeuvre as a result of the Government's commitment to a referendum before entry (effectively forced on Labour by the Conservative commitment) and a lingering fear of the Murdoch press.

Two issues are likely to be decisive in enabling Britain to play as full a part in the EU as Blair would like. The first, obviously, is entry to the single currency. In his statement to the House of Commons in February 1999 Blair made clear that his Government sees no constitutional or political difficulties: 'We have, as a government, resolved the political issues, in favour of the principle of joining, should the economic tests be met... It is conditional. It is not inevitable' (*Financial Times*, 24.2.99). At the same time, the Government published a national changeover plan which would require a period of about three years between a positive vote in a referendum and the replacement of sterling notes and coins by the euro. The expectation is that a referendum would follow a Labour victory in the next general election which is unlikely to take place earlier than 2001, so Britain is unlikely to enter the single currency before 2004.

The second factor is the war in Kosovo. The EU has been committed since the Treaty of Maastricht to developing a Common Foreign and Security Policy, leading eventually to a common defence policy and ultimately a common defence. So far the CFSP has amounted to little, mainly because of long-standing differences between the EU's two main military powers, Britain and France, over the relationship between the EU's defence policy and the Atlantic Alliance. The St Malo declaration demonstrated a willingness on the part of both countries to resolve those differences in developing a distinct European arm of NATO, capable of acting independently from the USA. Blair's speech at Aachen stressed the need for the EU to modernise its defence capability through 'greater integration in the defence industry and procurement. If we were in any doubts about this before, Kosovo should have removed them' (Bennett, 1999). This is an area in which Britain would be able to take the initiative, offsetting its laggard role in the single currency.

At the moment, Blair's dominance of British politics seems likely to continue for at least a second full parliamentary term – for the first time in the history of the Labour Party. In that event, by the time the Conservative party regain power, the question of Britain's relations with Europe is likely to have been finally resolved by British entry into the single currency and the construction of a new diplomatic and military dimension to the EU which together would involve a decisive shift towards the supra-national (rather than intergovernmental) dimension within the EU which would render unthinkable any lessening of Britain's commitment. In this most decisive fashion the Blair Government is likely to preside over the consolidation of a new consensus on what has been the most divisive issue in British politics since the Second World War.

Conclusion: Towards Managerial Society?

Between crisis and consensus

'In Britain, at any rate, the sole consensus possible is around the *status quo*. It is only by abjuring consensus politics that a new *status quo* can be secured around which a new consensus can develop', writes Nigel Lawson near the end of his mammoth but indispensable memoirs (1992: 1036). No doubt he would shun the term, but Lawson was pointing to the dialectic between crisis and consensus in twentieth-century British politics that forms the subject of this book: only through crisis did one consensus emerge which was in turn destroyed and replaced in another crisis. The consensus politics of the 1990s emerged from the crisis of the mid-1970s just like the post-war consensus was a product of the much more severe crisis of 1940. Labour now occupies the terrain shaped by the Conservatives during the 1980s and 1990s just like the Conservatives in 1951 inherited terrain shaped by Labour. Looking back, the inter-war consensus embodied in the National Government of 1931–40 was the product of an earlier crisis beginning in the 1880s (Langan & Schwarz, 1985).

This dialectical movement between crisis and consensus has taken place against the background of continuing relative economic decline since the first 'great chasm' in the development of modern British society in the 1870s and 1880s (Harris, 1994: 252). New Labour set its project in this context just as Conservatives like Thatcher and Lawson did in the late 1970s, at the end of the second such 'great chasm' beginning in the 1960s. The British governing elite in the late nineteenth century was far too preoccupied with the challenge of an emerging mass democracy, to say nothing of

Britain's imperial entanglements, to give much attention to the question of relative economic decline until the Boer War brought home the important military and diplomatic consequences. The ensuing concern with national efficiency in the face of economic challenges from Germany and the USA was rapidly overtaken by the much more intense challenge of war in 1914.

The external challenge of war coincided with an internal challenge from the working class. Victory in the First World War was soon seen to require the conciliation of labour and an enlarged role for the state through rationing and rent control. Trade union membership grew from four million to eight million during the war, and in 1918 the Labour Party emerged as the main Opposition in the House of Commons. The Russian Revolution and abortive revolutions in Germany and Hungary dramatised the threat of socialist revolution in the shape of the bogey of Bolshevism.

These developments aroused intense concern among the British middle classes at large and among Liberal and Conservative politicians and senior officials and bankers. British politics in the inter-war years can be seen as series of attempts to meet the challenge of Labour. Lloyd George's attempt to create an anti-socialist Centre party collapsed in 1922 and Lloyd George was consigned to the political wilderness. Baldwin's Conservative Government attempted to return to pre-war normalcy by restoring the Gold Standard in 1925, leading to the General Strike of 1926 which demonstrated that the wage cuts needed to restore the competitiveness of British exports could be achieved only at unacceptable social cost. The Conservatives' failure to improve Britain's economic performance resulted in political defeat in 1929 but they returned to power in 1931 as the mainstay of the National Government erected on the ruin of the second minority Labour Government. The National Government's sweeping election victories in 1931 and 1935 were based on the weakness of the Labour Party and the decay of the traditional working class. A modest economic recovery during the 1930s, based on devaluation and protection, held out a prospect of a third victory in the general election due by 1940.

However, the Conservative hegemony of the inter-war years was destroyed by a renewed military challenge, even more severe than in 1914. The failure of appeasement in 1939 and military defeat in Norway in early 1940 discredited the Conservatives and brought

Labour to power in what Dalton shrewdly characterised as the Churchill–Labour coalition. National survival, let alone victory, required the conciliation of Labour. Mobilisation for total war led to a revival of the traditional working class whose position had been eroded in the inter-war years. It also undermined opposition to higher taxation and public spending. The crisis of 1940 laid the foundation for the Labour victory in 1945 and the post-war consensus.

The post-war consensus was based on the assumption that the economic problems of the 1920s and the 1930s had been solved. US aid and economic liberalisation overcame the perceived threat of another post-war slump, as in 1920. The techniques of arms-length Keynesian economic management seemed to guarantee growth without unemployment or inflation. Britain's long-term relative economic decline was masked in the first post-war decade by an unexpectedly rapid economic recovery and by the temporary eclipse of European competitors whose recovery became increasingly evident in the late 1950s.

The reemergence of the problem of relative economic decline set the context for the modernisation strategy embraced by Macmillan in 1961. Key ingredients in what Sam Brittan described as 'the reappraisal of the 1960s' (1971: 227) included economic planning, incomes policy, the public expenditure planning system, EEC membership and a 'dash for growth'. This strategy was continued in its essentials by Wilson after 1964 and Heath after 1970. It assumed that governments commanded the means for raising economic performance without sacrificing full employment and price stability. This confident assumption was undermined by a succession of political and economic failures which resulted in the collapse of the post-war consensus in the mid-1970s crisis and the rise of Thatcherism. The Conservatives won the opportunity to set the terms of a new consensus because of divisions on the Left. The revival of the Labour Party under Blair was based on overcoming divisions on the Left and exploiting growing divisions within the Conservative Party.

New Labour

Blair has always scorned ideology and doctrine. Like Thatcherism, New Labour is best understood as a form of statecraft, 'in which ideas and principles are subordinated to political calculation, the pursuit of office and the management of power' (Gamble, 1988: 141). The much-touted 'Third Way' is a much more threadbare cloak for Blair's ambitions than the doctrines of Hayek and Friedman embraced by Thatcher in the 1970s.

Blair has never hidden his ambition to assemble a new progressive coalition as the basis for lasting power. The opening item in a collection of speeches published in 1996 was a lecture delivered on the fiftieth anniversary of Labour's 1945 election victory. In it Blair stressed the extent to which Attlee's victory was based on 'a strong political consensus'. He described his own 'ultimate objective' as being to create 'a new political consensus of the left-of-centre... To reach that consensus we must value the contribution of Lloyd George, Beveridge and Keynes and not just Attlee, Bevan or Crosland'. Attlee's Government succeeded in a way that no subsequent Labour government had done because it was 'willing to draw on the resources of the whole progressive tradition' whereas later Labour governments had been unable to maintain 'the coalition forged in 1945... To create the conditions in which Labour is once again capable of leading a governing consensus – in which it is truly the "people's party" – we have to learn the lessons of 1945', that is, to convey 'a clear sense of national purpose, to win the battle of ideas' and to 'mobilise all people of progressive mind' (Blair, 1996a: 5–13). Blair returned to this theme in his speech to the 1997 Labour Party Conference when he described his heroes as being Keynes, Beveridge and Lloyd George as well as Ernie Bevin, Nye Bevan and Attlee (*The Guardian*, 1.10.97) and in his 1998 Fabian Society pamphlet on the 'Third Way' when he described its aim as being to unite 'the two great streams of left-of-centre thought – democratic socialism and liberalism – whose divorce did so much to weaken progressive politics across the West' (Blair, 1998b: 1).

All political parties operate with a conception of the people which offers a viable base for winning and maintaining power. The Gladstonian Liberal Party was aiming at respectable, independent-minded artisans while Salisbury's Conservatives aimed at suburban bank clerks; the Labour Party of Harold Wilson aimed at technicians and junior managers, while Thatcher's Conservatives aimed at small businessmen and shopkeepers. The weakness of Labour in the 1980s lay in aiming at trade union activists when unions were in retreat under the impact of economic change and a hostile government, just like Lloyd George's weakness lay in aiming at independent artisans when socialist shop stewards had assumed their mantle of radicalism. Blair's conception of the people involves an attempt to combine the traditional Labour appeal to the working class and the Conservatives' appeal to the middle class. Blair's 'man of the people' is the self-employed electrician – so-called 'Sierra Man' – evoked in a famous passage in his speech to the 1996 Labour Party Conference:

> I recall vividly the exact moment that [sic] I knew the last election was lost. I was canvassing in the Midlands, on an ordinary suburban estate. I met a man polishing his Ford Sierra. He was a self-employed electrician. His dad always voted Labour, he said. He used to vote Labour, too. But he had bought his house now. He'd set up his own business. He was doing quite nicely. 'So I've become a Tory', he said ... In that moment he crystallised for me the basis of our failure ... People judge us on their instincts of what they believe our instincts to be. And that man polishing his car was clear. His instincts were to get on in life. And he thought our instincts were to stop him.
>
> (Cited Fielding, 1997: 24)

'Sierra Man' is probably a fictional construct out of the same stable as 'Bill Andrews' and 'Steve Stephenson' and the rest of the cast in Mandelson and Liddle's *The Blair Revolution* (1996: 60–9, 110–23) but he gives a clear indication of Blair's target audience. It forms a link with his conception of Labour as 'the people's party' with an aspiration to 'represent all the British people' set out in his first speech to the Labour Party Conference after being elected Leader in 1994 (1996a: 35). It is expressed in breath-taking form in the claim in the 1997 Manifesto that 'New Labour is the political arm of none other than the British people as a whole', excluding only 'the privileged few' (Labour Party, 1997: 4–5).

This inclusive conception of the people is reflected in key themes in Blair's political discourse.

- **Inclusion** Blair's introduction to the collection of speeches published in 1996 proclaims his commitment to 'one nation' politics: 'We live as one nation, and must act as one too... There is a big idea left in politics. It goes under a variety of names – stakeholding, one nation, inclusion, community – but it is quite simple. It is that no society can ever prosper ... unless all its people prosper' (1996a: x). This inclusiveness is reflected in his conception, set out in his speech to the 1995 Party Conference, of Britain as a 'young country', free from 'a class system unequal and antiquated' (1996a: 69), and in his celebration, in a speech to the IPPR conference in January 1999, of a 'new larger, meritocratic middle class... A middle class that will include millions of people who traditionally may see themselves as working class, but whose ambitions are far broader than those of their parents or grandparents' (White, 1999).

- **Partnership** Blair proclaimed in his speech to the 1994 Party Conference that economic revival could not be accomplished by 'state control' or 'market dogma' but only by 'a dynamic market economy based on partnership between government and industry, between employer and employee, and between public and private sector' (1996a: 40). Partnership was a key theme in his 1998 pamphlet on the Third Way: it mentions government partnership with private and voluntary sector, New Labour's partnership with business, partnership between public and private sector and partnerships among different parts of the public sector (1998b: 7, 8, 14, 15, 16).
- **Pragmatism** Blair's pragmatism was stated most bluntly in the report on the Government's first year in office: 'What matters is what works' (1998a: 30). This bald statement was elaborated upon in the pamphlet on the Third Way which rejects both the 'fundamentalist Left' with its belief that 'the state could replace society' and a New Right veering to the other extreme in its hostility to the state. Government needs to be guided by values rather than ideology: 'Without [values], we are adrift. But in giving them practical effect, a large measure of pragmatism is essential. As I say continually, what matters is what works to give effect to our values' (1998b: 4).

Blair draws constant parallels with business. His speech to the 1994 Party Conference condemns the Conservatives for incompetence in failing to understand that a nation, like a community, must work together: 'Go and look at a company that is succeeding. It will treat its workforce not as servants but as partners. They will be motivated and trained and given a common purpose' (1996a: 36). The most egregious example appears in the Government's first annual report which compares Labour's election victory to a successful takeover: 'Changing a government is like sweeping away the entire senior management of a company' (1998a: 6). David Marquand has pointed to Blair's 'rhetoric of a management consultant' (1998) and Will Hutton to his combination of 'managerialism and the big tent consensus' (1999). Underneath the rhetoric about a Third Way lies the banal and stale conception of 'UK plc', with the Cabinet as a Board of Directors and the Prime Minister as Managing Director: the epitome of managerialism. Anthony Barnett has summed up Blair's project as 'corporate populism' (Barnett, 1999: 27). The term 'UK plc' can be found in several places in the 1998 report of the Management Consultancies Association (Management Consultancies Association, 1998: 1, 4, 5).

Blair's embrace of managerialism reflects the transformation of the Labour Party since 1945 and more recent changes in the public sector. The pre-1914 Labour Party was a party of the manual working class, supported by manual workers and led by manual workers or former officials of trade unions representing manual workers. The foundation of Labour as a major national party in 1918 resulted in a gradual transformation of the Party, beginning at the top. Members of the professional middle class accounted for 25 out of 65 Labour ministers between 1916 and 1951, second only to former union officials (Perkin, 1989: 256). Since 1964 Labour Cabinets have been dominated by the professional middle class: former union officials like Ray Gunter and Frank Cousins were as unsuccessful as ministers under Wilson in the 1960s as former businessmen like John Davies were under Heath. Only 18 out of 118 ministers in Blair's Government were union officials; of the rest, 26 worked in education, 17 in industry (presumably as managers), 16 as lawyers, 15 in the media and 14 in local government (Wintour, 1999).

Changes at ministerial level reflected change among the parliamentary rank and file. In 1951 former manual workers still accounted for 37 per cent of Labour MPs compared with 14 per cent from the private-sector professional middle class (all lawyers) and 21 per cent from the public-sector professional middle class (two-thirds from education) (Adonis & Pollard, 1997: 111). In 1974 manual workers accounted for 28 per cent of the Parliamentary Party while in 1997 this proportion had fallen to 13 per cent compared with 60 per cent from the public-sector middle class (including the voluntary sector, trade unions and political organisers) and only 9 per cent from the private sector (Criddle, 1997: 205–6).

Meanwhile the social composition of local party activists was transformed by the gradual decline of Labour as a mass party in the 1950s and 1960s. By the late 1960s and early 1970s there was widespread comment about an influx of young, university-educated public sector professionals, often from working-class backgrounds and inspired by the ideals of the New Left, into moribund local parties (Panitch & Leys, 1997: 26–30). They were the main supporters of the Labour New Left during the 1970s and early 1980s. Much of the public-sector middle class, alienated by the Labour Left as well as the Conservatives, was drawn in the early 1980s to the SDP which has been described as 'the political voice of public sector professionals... Their social equivalents of the mid 1990s ... transferred *en masse* to Labour ... in a fit of political enthusiasm reminiscent of the early days of the SDP' (Adonis & Pollard, 1997: 119, 121).

Finally, there has been a change among voters. Already in the early 1980s commentators were pointing to the growing importance of the division between private and public sector in explaining voting behaviour (Dunleavy & Husbands, 1985: 21–2). Until the 1980s most of the public-sector middle class voted Conservative. In the 1980s they turned temporarily to the SDP (Adonis & Pollard, 1997: 118). In 1997 they returned to Labour; as we have seen, the largest swings to Labour were among the middle class. It is reasonable to suppose that the 1997 victory was based on an alliance between Labour's traditional working-class support and the public-sector professional middle class returning to Labour after the divisions of the 1980s.

Adonis and Pollard point to New Labour's 'hegemonic hold over the public sector' (1997: 122) but it is no more than the culmination of a long process of change dating back to the late 1960s among activists and even earlier within the Parliamentary Party. The conflict between the Left and Right culminating in the disastrous split in 1981 reflected divisions within the public-sector middle class. The transformation of the Labour Party begun under Kinnock and completed under Blair reflects a transformation of the public-sector middle class since the early 1980s and its embrace or acceptance of a managerial ethos.

From class society to professional society

These relatively recent changes need to be seen in the context of long-term social and economic changes which have been described persuasively by Harold Perkin in *The Origins of Modern English Society 1780–1880* (1969) and *The Rise of Professional Society: England since 1880* (1989). For him, the Industrial Revolution saw the 'birth of a new class society', based on 'vertical antagonism between a small number of horizontal groups, each based on a common source of income' (1969: 176). Class conflict took the form of a conflict between ideals: 'a conscious image of the class in its relation to rival classes, and of the ideal society in which it would find its rightful place' (219).

> The class ideal thus sublimated the crude material self-interest of the competition for income, sanctified the role of class members by the contribution they made to society and its well-being, and so justified the class and its claim to a special treatment within the social framework. It had a twofold function: first, to act as a catalyst in the formation and growth of class ... second, to operate as an instrument of propaganda or psychological warfare *vis-à-vis* the other classes... In other words, it was a means of educating both the class itself to class-consciousness, and the rest of society to accept it at its own valuation.
>
> The class which was most successful in this educational and moral struggle, in uniting its own members and imposing its ideal upon others, would win the day and have most influence in determining the actual society in which all had to live and in approximating it more or less closely to its own ideal.
>
> (219–20)

Class conflict was thus primarily 'a struggle for the minds and hearts of men. It was a struggle between ideals' – in the early nineteenth century, between the aristocratic ideal of paternal responsibility for lower orders in a hierarchical society, the entrepreneurial ideal of active capitalism in a competitive society, and the working-class ideal of cooperative labour in an egalitarian society (237, 221, 231). Members of what Perkin describes as the 'forgotten middle class', the non-capitalist or professional middle class of journalists, academics, lawyers and officials, played a key role in formulating the class ideals. It was they who sublimated the economic interests of the other three classes by 'infusing into them large doses of the professional ideal ... a functional ideal' of disinterested service in 'a society based on expertise (skilled labour by hand and brain) and selection by merit (from each according to his ability)' (261, 264–5).

Perkin interprets the last two centuries in the light of this framework of class conflict sublimated into a conflict between ideals fought out at various levels: social, economic, intellectual and political. Recalling the six phases in the development of British capitalism described in Chapter 1, the Industrial Revolution was dominated by the conflict between three contending ideals culminating in what Perkin calls 'the triumph of entrepreneurial ideal' by the end of the 1840s. The second phase – from the 1850s to the 1870s when Britain could plausibly be described as 'the workshop of the world' – saw what Perkin described as 'the rise of a viable class society' in which aristocratic politicians like Palmerston were content to rule in the interests of the manufacturing middle class and a labour movement dominated by trade unions representing skilled workers had ceased to challenge capitalism. Traversing some of same ground, David Cannadine has argued that mid-Victorian society tended to be seen in terms of an ordered hierarchy rather than two or three contending classes as in previous decades. This was the context in which the vote was extended to much of the urban working class in 1867, partly as a way of avoiding the politics of class conflict (Cannadine, 1998: 95–101)

The third phase – that period from the 1870s until 1914 which saw the onset of relative economic decline – saw what Perkin describes as 'the zenith of class society' in which each of the three main classes achieved its 'advanced capitalistic form' based on its relation to the means of production and these classes became more sharply segregated from each other (Perkin, 1989: 27). This period, as we have seen, coincided closely with the transition to mass democracy, when politics increasingly came to be perceived, once again, in terms of contending classes (Perkin, 1989: 41; Cannadine, 1998: 109). The same period also saw the development of a professional middle class based on the growth of state employment and an increasing divergence between the professional ideal and an entrepreneurial ideal weakened by the rise of *rentier* capital and a resurgence of working-class militancy. Members of the professional middle class played key roles in formulating both the New Liberal and Fabian critiques of liberal capitalism. The impact of the professional ideal can be seen in the movement for national efficiency and the social reforms of the last Liberal Government. For Perkin as for Dangerfield (1935), the First World War overtook a society on the verge of crisis (Perkin, 1989: 121, 85, 111, 130, 159, 168, 171).

The fourth phase – the Age of Catastrophe from 1914 until the late 1940s which saw the collapse of Britain's commercial preeminence – also witnessed the transition from what Perkin describes as the segregated class society of the late nineteenth century to what he calls a professional society, that is, one 'structured around career hierarchies rather than class, one in which people find their place according to trained expertise and the service they provide rather than the possession or lack of inherited wealth or acquired capital' (Perkin, 1989: 359). The crisis of class society which culminated in the General Strike of 1926 was averted 'not by the triumph of the government and employers over a potentially revolutionary labour movement ... but by the common interest of professional managers, professional union leaders, and increasingly professional politicians and civil servants in keeping the system going and avoiding crises' (217). The Second World War represented 'a triumph for the triple entente between government, employers and workers' (321). The war was decisive in laying the foundations for the post-war consensus by sealing the alliance between the working class and the professional middle class. The commercial middle class had been weakened by the defeat of appeasement and the apparent triumph of planning undertaken by the professional middle class. Ross McKibbin has come to much the same conclusion about the significance of the Second World War and Labour's 1945 victory in marking the triumphant recovery of a traditional working class (1998: 535–6).

The fifth phase – the Golden Age from the late 1940s until the mid-1970s crisis – has been described by Perkin as one in which professional society reached a 'plateau of attainment' but also saw an increasing 'bifurcation of the professional ideal' between the public-sector and private-sector middle classes (Perkin, 1989: 405, 437–8).

The post-war consensus embodied a belief that social and economic problems could be solved through professional expertise just as military and organisational problems had been solved in wartime. The failure of Keynesian policies led to increasing sectional conflict over resources. Perkin interprets Thatcherism as a revival of the entrepreneurial ideal by the private-sector middle class while Labour's shift to the Left involved an alliance of at least parts of the public-sector middle class and the working-class under the banner of a revived working-class ideal (Perkin, 1989: 464–8).

The sixth phase – one of shock therapy applied by the Conservatives after 1979 with the aim of reversing relative economic decline – is interpreted by Perkin in terms of a

> confrontation between the two rival factions of the professional ideal... It was not a reaction *against* professional society but a rounding of the private sector professionals who ran the great corporations and their academic and journalistic supporters upon the public sector professionals.
>
> (471, 473)

The free-market ideology of the New Right provided intellectual armoury for private sector managers seeking to increase their authority and financial reward.

Thus, as Perkin sums up in a striking phrase, 'the struggle between the public and private sector professions is the master conflict of professional society' (10). For him,

> The main issue in British politics is which version of the professional social ideal is to be applied to British society, the public sector ideal of an egalitarian, caring and compassionate state run by well-paid professionals or the private sector ideal of equal opportunity for those able to climb the corporate ladder of success and compete in the struggle for survival of the fittest corporations.
>
> (Perkin, 1989: 518)

At that time the Labour Party was still engaged in its long march from New Left to New Labour (Panitch & Leys, 1997); the Conservatives had yet to embark on the wholesale reconstruction of the public services which was the hallmark of Thatcher's third term of office and of Major's Government. We can now see that Perkin was posing a false dilemma; what has happened is that the public sector professions have either embraced or had imposed upon them the disciplines implicit in the private sector professional ideal.

Towards managerial society

When Perkin was writing in the late 1980s the conflict between the public- and private-sector middle class was still unresolved. Since then there have been three important developments. First has been the continued reconstruction of the public-sector along private-sector lines. Faith in markets as an external economic discipline was one strand of Thatcherism. Another strand stressed sound management as an internal discipline. This faith in management was well put by Michael Heseltine in 1980: 'Efficient management is the key to [national] revival... And the management ethos must run right through our national life – private and public companies, civil service, nationalised industries, local government, the National Health Service' (cited Pollitt, 1993: 3).

We have seen in Chapter 6 how the Conservative Government began to transform the civil service in the early 1980s. Michael Heseltine as Secretary of State for the Environment from 1979 to 1983 played a key role: his officials developed the prototype management information and management accounting systems (MINIS and MAXIS) that spread throughout Whitehall in the mid-1980s under the aegis of the FMI. So-called Rayner scrutinies created an internal constituency for management reform among a younger generation of middle- and senior-ranking officials while the FMI enhanced the role of management consultants as external change agents. This process culminated in the Next Steps initiative which began to be implemented only from around 1989.

These changes to the central government machine were accompanied by parallel developments in other parts of the public sector. Local government began to be transformed in the early 1980s with the introduction of compulsory competitive tendering for directly employed manual workers and the establishment of the Audit Commission with a remit to encourage improvements in efficiency, economy and effectiveness in local authority services (Peat Marwick,

1986a: 7–8). During the same years the NHS experienced the introduction of Rayner reviews on the central government model and of general managers, following a report by Roy Griffiths, Managing Director of Sainsburys. One leading firm of management consultants which benefited hugely from these changes commented: 'As a result of the Griffiths Report, management style has changed from that of consensus management to one much more akin to a business management model' (Peat Marwick, 1986b: 45).

But these changes were still in their early days and still encountering considerable resistance from local authority and NHS professionals and unions at the time Perkin was writing. These conflicts remained unresolved and the scale of Conservative ambitions for the public services was not yet clear. Since 1988 these developments have gone much further. The Next Steps proposals have been fully implemented within central government, and market testing followed after 1992. Local authorities have been transformed from service providers to 'enablers' by the extension of CCT to financial, housing, property and leisure management services as well as direct labour, to say nothing of the erosion of their responsibility for education. Social workers have been transformed into purchasers and managers of 'care packages'. The NHS has seen the introduction of the purchaser/provider split with the creation of GP fundholders and NHS hospital trusts.

By the early 1990s academics began to analyse these changes as components of what came to be called the New Public Management (as distinct from the old public administration, a term that has been consigned to history) (Hood, 1991; Pollitt, 1993; Dunleavy & Hood, 1994). Mandelson and Liddle stressed that 'pressure for efficiency improvements' from the public services would be constant because of the tendency for 'the underlying cost of any given level of public services ... always [to] rise faster than inflation' (1996: 150). The 1997 Labour Manifesto made clear that 'efficiency and value for money' would be 'central' for the new Government (Labour Party, 1997: 12).

A second development has been the emergence of 'a new élite of top professionals and managers' enjoying exceptionally high incomes: what Adonis and Pollard have called 'the Super Class'. Until around 1980 the top echelons of the public and private sector professions enjoyed comparable prestige and levels of reward. Since then rewards in the top echelons of the private sector professions engaged in London-based financial services – banking, accountancy, law and management consultancy – have drawn away from those available to the rest of the professions. Able and ambitious private sector professionals can now earn very much more than their former peers in the public sector. Adonis and Pollard view Perkin's 'master conflict' between the public- and private-sector middle class as 'essentially a transitory phase in the construction of the Super Class' (1997: 69). The high incomes earned by the Super Class can readily be transformed into capital. Thus Adonis and Pollard are pointing to a symbiosis between the peaks of the private-sector professional middle class and the capitalist class comparable to the symbiosis between the aristocracy and corporate capital in the emerging plutocracy of late Victorian England (Perkin, 1969: 428–37). The difference is that this 'new class' can justify their high earnings as the legitimate rewards for effort and ability.

Tony Blair matches Lloyd George in his admiration for business leaders whom he has appointed in large numbers to his Government and to over 300 task forces. A recent article in *The Economist* (14.8.99) observed that '28 of Britain's biggest 100 public companies – the FTSE-100 – have donated either their chairman or their chief executive as part-time advisers to the government, in one capacity or another'. Not so widely remarked has been the third of our developments since the late 1980s, that of growing links between the Super Class and the new Labour leadership. Three of Blair's closest associates – his wife Cherie, his mentor the Lord Chancellor Derry Irvine and his former flatmate and Cabinet Office Minister Charles Falconer – as QCs belong to the Super Class in which City barristers are among the highest earners (Adonis & Pollard, 1997: 83). Labour has developed close links with management consultants, notably the 'Big Five' accountancy-based firms. One of these firms, Andersen Consulting, organised training seminars for the Shadow Cabinet at Templeton College and helped to finance the IPPR. Two others – Deloitte & Touche and KPMG – carried out studies of the Party's administrative systems, with KPMG recommending out-sourcing its membership system to the private sector (Donkin, 1997; *Financial Times*, 26.5.99). David Gardner, assistant general-secretary in charge of organisation, is currently on secondment to KPMG (*Financial Times*, 9.9.99).

This growing affinity with the Super Class can be seen in the trajectories of some key figures close to Tony Blair. Tom Sawyer, appointed General Secretary of the Labour Party by Blair in 1994 with a remit to introduce private-sector best practice as recommended by Deloitte & Touche, was a supporter of Tony Benn in the early 1980s when working as a trade union official (Panitch & Leys, 1997: 187). So too was Patricia Hewitt, now Minister of State at DTI but Head of Research with Andersen Consulting from 1994 to 1997 after serving as Deputy Director of the IPPR since its foundation in 1989 and before then in Peter Mandelson's Shadow Communications Agency (Anderson & Mann, 1997: 52). Margaret Hodge, now junior Minister at the Department for Education and Employment with responsibility for private sector initiatives in school education, achieved notoriety as Leader of Islington Council and a prominent member of the urban Left in the mid-1980s. From 1994 to 1996 she worked as senior consultant for Price Waterhouse, another member of the 'Big Five', now merged with Coopers & Lybrand (Barnett & Bright, 1999). The story of Peter Mandelson's home in Notting Hill can be seen almost as a morality play about the aspirations of New Labour to join the Super Class and the accompanying political risks. Enough has been written about the links between New Labour and the world of political consultancy illustrated by the scandal surrounding Derek Draper – which also touched Roger Liddle, co-author with Mandelson of that key New Labour text *The Blair Revolution*.

These developments – the transformation of the public services along private-sector lines, the emergence of a Super Class of high-earning private sector professionals, and the forging of links between this group and leading lights of New Labour – create problems for Labour in government so long as it remains 'the party of the public professionals' (Adonis & Pollard, 1997: 106). The Blair Government faces a problem in reconciling its commitments to tight controls on public spending and a continuing drive for efficiency in public services with the expectations of the public-sector middle class from which it draws its main support. The summer of 1999 saw evidence of increasing discontent among rank-and-file public-sector professionals such as university lecturers, school teachers and junior doctors, and Government impatience with public sector resistance to change.

Tony Blair's unscripted outburst during a speech to the British Venture Capitalist Association in July attracted wide comment:

> One of the things I would like to do, as well as stimulating more entrepreneurship in the private sector, is to get a bit of it into the public sector as well. I mean people in the public sector are more rooted in the concept of 'if it's always been done this way, it must always be done this way' than any group of people that I've ever come across. You try getting change in the public sector and public services – I bear the scars on my back after two years in government. Heaven knows what it will be like if it is a bit longer.
>
> (Watt, 1999)

Blair returned to this theme in his speech to the Party Conference in September 1999, casting teachers and doctors among the 'forces of conservatism' against which the Government was striving (*The Guardian*, 29.9.99)

A Government committed to control of public spending and 'money in return for modernisation' cannot afford to relax its constraints on public sector pay in general and therefore to offer rewards for the general run of public sector professionals comparable to those available in the private sector. Yet resentment among the public sector middle class threatens the Government's ability to deliver improvements in public services and thus its chances of winning a second term in office. As the next election approaches, the Government needs to find some way of stimulating improvements in public services while at the same time satisfying the aspirations of the public-sector middle class.

Judging from Blair's outburst to the venture capitalists, the Government seems to be pinning its hopes upon awakening an 'entrepreneurial spirit' among public servants. He seems to have been influenced by some of the ideas in Charles Leadbeater's *Living on Thin Air* (1999) published in July with a prominent puff from Blair describing the author (a former regular with *Marxism Today*) as 'an extraordinarily interesting thinker [whose] book raises critical questions for Britain's future'. Much of the book is an account of the 'new economy' based on knowledge rather than fixed assets but the last few chapters discuss ways of restructuring the public sector.

For example, Leadbeater describes how Norma Redfearn, a headteacher in the impoverished district of Walker on Tyneside, enhanced the local community by involving parents in a range of activities based on the school:

> Norma Redfearn is a knowledge entrepreneur, working in the public sector. And she is not alone. Throughout the public sector a new breed of managers are [*sic*] emerging who understand that their job is to generate more value from the public assets they are stewards of. The public sector does not need more restructuring or rationalisation; it needs reviving and renewing. That means more than running the public-sector machine faster to deliver more output from fewer resources. The problem is not just that the public sector is inefficient. The problem is that it does not produce enough value; it seems to consume resources, not replenish them. The public sector will only start to generate more value on the public's behalf when it becomes better able to learn, adapt and innovate.
>
> (204)

However, Leadbeater admits in a discussion of biotechnology that 'innovation prospers when it is rewarded' (173). He acknowledges that there are fundamental structural reasons why public services as presently constituted do not breed entrepreneurs:

> Public servants enjoy few of the incentives of innovators in the private sector. Successful private-sector innovators make more profit or win promotion within their company. Successful innovators in the public sector, who, for instance, find a cheaper way to deliver a service, may find themselves rewarded with a lower budget or more work for the same pay. It is little wonder that there is so little innovation in the public sector: the space for innovation is minimal, the costs of failure are alarming, the incentives are feeble, the personal rewards uncertain and the pay-off from success only comes in the long term.
>
> (208)

Leadbeater clearly recognises the problem but offers no structural solutions. He concludes rather lamely that 'we need to develop a new cadre of public-sector managers capable of acting entrepreneurially; without spelling out how (216). Blair admitted in an interview with *The Observer* (5.9.99) that

> It is far harder to change the way a public service works because it doesn't have the great machine that the market is always creating for change in the private sector... Let's be honest about it, the private sector, in its reward and motivation, has moved on apace. The public sector is still incredibly inflexible.

Nevertheless the solution seems clear enough: the way to generate entrepreneurial activity in the public services is by offering the same opportunities of reward for innovation, for adding value, as in the private sector. There are signs that the Labour Government is feeling its way towards a solution of this problem in the same way as the Conservative Government in the early 1980s was feeling its way towards a solution to the problems of the nationalised industries in the shape of privatisation. Ingredients in that solution in the field of education policy would be higher financial rewards for successful headteachers, the introduction of performance-related pay for teachers, and the entry of private companies like Nord Anglia and Capita into school education. These changes will create opportunities for able and ambitious teachers, by becoming headteachers or joining private educational contractors, to raise their incomes to levels comparable with those being earned in the private sector while also providing them with mechanisms for raising the performance of their (shall we say) less energetic colleagues. Meanwhile OFSTED will provide a formidable weapon for achieving public objectives in an increasingly privatised service.

The ultimate logic of change along these lines is to extinguish the division between the public-sector and private-sector professions through the creation of a common managerial culture, what Paul Hirst has described as 'a bureaucratic monoculture spanning the public and private domains' (1996: 104). Just as the consensus forged in the 1940s was based on the triumph of the professional ideal of disinterested functional service in a professional society composed of 'career hierarchies of specialised occupations, selected by merit and based on trained expertise' (Perkin, 1989: 2), so the consensus forged in the 1990s is based on overcoming the conflict between the public- and private-sector professional ideals through the triumph of the managerial ideal in a managerial society.

The term 'managerial society' was coined by James Burnham to describe the outcome of the 'managerial revolution' in the form of a society ruled by the managers of major industries taken into state ownership. He saw the managers as replacing capitalists as the ruling class and managerial society as 'a new form of exploiting, class society' (Burnham, 1941: 72, 80, 127). Perkin, by contrast, was quite clear that 'the professionals are not just another ruling class' on Burnham's model but rather that 'the professional hierarchies cut across the horizontal solidarities of class in the warp and weft of the social fabric' (1989: 2–3). It is in this 'weaker' sense that the term managerial society is being used – to describe a society in which wealth, power and status are determined not by success in controlling the market for services as in Perkin's conception of professional society (6–7), but by success in meeting the demands of the market. A common subjection to market forces is shaping the bureaucratic monoculture discerned by Hirst. Managerial society is one in which individuals and organisations alike are subject to the disciplines of competition and the drive to innovate. The managerial ideal of efficiency replaces the professional ideal of trained expertise. It leaves no room for elaborate vertical divisions which, in Perkin's conception, moderated the starker horizontal divisions of a class society. Instead, by requiring a single hierarchy based on proven competence in meeting the demands of the market place rather than paper qualifications and with financial rewards to match, it is likely to reinforce class divisions and increase social inequality.

This is the society sketched at the end of Leadbeater's book, one divided between 'so-called "knowledge workers": mobile, skilled, affluent, independent, hard-working, ambitious, environmentally conscious, people who can trade on their skills, expertise and intellectual capital' and 'the knowledge-poor and immobile' (Leadbeater, 1999: 228–9). Blair's speech to the IPPR in January 1999 (White, 1999) showed that he and Leadbeater share an essentially optimistic vision of the emerging society in which an aspirational middle class of 'knowledge workers' comprises an increasing majority of the population with a diminishing minority of the 'socially excluded'. There must be some plausibility in this vision when, according to a recent poll reported in *The Guardian*, two-thirds of the workforce define themselves as 'managers' of one kind or another (Andrews, 1999a: 20). However, within this 'middle-class' 'managerial' majority it is possible to discern a potential division between the Super Class described by Adonis and Pollard (1997) and a mass of insecure and stressed, and more modestly rewarded, self-employed service workers and subordinate managers.

David Cannadine has argued persuasively in an account of changing perceptions of class in Britain over the last two hundred years that perceptions of social structure are politically constructed and open to dispute (1998: 188). As well as Blair's optimistic vision, it is equally possible to imagine a future in which the Super Class constitutes a beleaguered minority among an increasingly resentful majority, as in Michael Young's conception of meritocracy (Young, 1961) or Nye Bevan's conception of 'managerial society' in which the citizen might become 'the passive creature of supposed supermen, even though these present themselves in the guise of public servants' (cited Perkin, 1989: 444). In that case, today's political consensus may contain the seeds of a future crisis of managerial society.

References

Addison, P. (1994), *The Road to 1945: British Politics and the Second World War*, Pimlico

Adonis, A. & S. Pollard (1997), *A Class Act: the Myth of Britain's Classless Society*, Hamish Hamilton

Anderson, P. (1964), 'Origins of the Present Crisis', in P. Anderson, *English Questions*, Verso, 1992, 15–47

Anderson, P. & N. Mann (1997), *Safety First: The Making of New Labour*, Granta

Andrews, G. (1999a), 'New Left and New Labour: Modernisation or a New Modernity', *Soundings*, 13, 14–24

Andrews, G. (1999b), 'The Three New Lefts and Their Legacies', in Andrews *et al.*, 1999, 66–84

Andrews, G., R. Cockett, A. Hooper & M. Williams (eds) (1999), *New Left, New Right and Beyond*, Macmillan

Bacon, R. & W. Eltis (1976), *Britain's Economic Problem: Too Few Producers*, Macmillan

Bagehot, W. (1867), *The English Constitution*, Oxford Classics, Oxford University Press, 1928

Balogh, T. (1959), 'The Apotheosis of the Dilettante', in Thomas, 1959, 72–115

Barber, L. (1997), 'Vegetable-eater', *Financial Times*, 12 November

Barclay, P. (1995), *Joseph Rowntree Foundation Inquiry into Income and Wealth*, Joseph Rowntree Foundation

Barnett, A. (1999), 'Corporate Control', *Prospect*, February, 24–9

Barnett, A. & M. Bright (1999), 'Labour accused of "crony deals"', *The Observer*, 30 May

Barnett, C. (1972), *The Collapse of British Power*, Methuen

Barnett, C. (1995), *The Lost Victory: British Dreams, British Realities 1945–1950*, Macmillan

Barnett, J. (1982), *Inside the Treasury*, André Deutsch

Beer, S. H. (1982), *Britain against Itself: the Political Contradictions of Collectivism*, Norton

Beer, S. H. (1998), 'Liberalism Rediscovered', *The Economist*, 7 February, 23–5

Bennett, R. (1999), 'Blair vows to put UK at the heart of Europe', *Financial Times*, 14 May

Bevins, A. (1999), 'Shape up or you're sacked', *The Express*, 4 August

Biffen, J. (1997), 'We are all Conservatives now', *Tribune*, 7 February

Blackburn, R. & R. Plant (eds) (1999), *Constitutional Reform: the Labour Government's Constitutional Reform Agenda*, Longman

Blair, T. (1996a), *New Britain: My Vision of a Young Country*, Fourth Estate

Blair, T. (1996b), 'Democracy's Second Age', *The Economist*, 14 September, 33–5

Blair, T. (1998a), *the government's annual report 97/98*, Cm 3969, The Stationery Office

Blair, T. (1998b), *The Third Way: New Politics for the New Century*, Fabian Society

Blair, T. (1998c), 'Speaking Mandarin', *Prospect*, December, 10

Blair, T. & G. Schröder (1999), *Europe: the Third Way, Die Neue Mitte*, Labour Party/SPD

Bogdanor, V. (1999), *Devolution in the United Kingdom*, Oxford University Press

Booker, C. (1970), *The Neophiliacs: a Study of the Revolution in English Life in the Fifties and Sixties*, Fontana

Briggs, A. (1959), *The Age of Improvement 1783–1867*, Longman

Briggs, A. (1965), *Victorian People*, Penguin

British Broadcasting Corporation (1991), 'Pandora's Box: a Fable from the Age of Science. Everybody Wants to Rule the World'

British Broadcasting Corporation (1997a), 'The Great Sell Off: the Gamble'

British Broadcasting Corporation (1997b), 'Black Wednesday'

Brittan, S. (1964), *The Treasury under the Tories 1951–1964*, Penguin

Brittan, S. (1971), *Steering the Economy: the Role of the Treasury*, Penguin

Bruce-Gardyne, J. & N. Lawson (1976), *The Power Game: an Examination of Decision-making in Government*, Macmillan

Bulpitt, J. (1983), *Territory and Power in the United Kingdom*, Manchester University Press

Bulpitt, J. (1986), 'The Discipline of the New Democracy: Mrs Thatcher's Domestic Statecraft', *Political Studies*, 34, 19–39

Bulpitt, J. (1996), 'The European Question', in Marquand & Seldon, 1996

Burk, K. & A. Cairncross (1992), *'Goodbye, Great Britain': the 1976 IMF Crisis*, Macmillan

Burn, W. L. (1964), *The Age of Equipoise: a Study of the Mid-Victorian Generation*, George Allen & Unwin

Burnham, J. (1941), *The Managerial Revolution*, John Day

Burrows, R. & B. Loader (eds) (1994), *Towards a Post-Fordist Welfare State?*, Routledge

Butler, D., A. Adonis & T. Travers (1994), *Failure in British Government: the Politics of the Poll Tax*, Oxford University Press

Butler, D. & D. Kavanagh (1997), *The British General Election of 1997*, Macmillan

Cabinet Office (1994), *The Civil Service: Continuity and Change*, Cm 2627, HMSO

Cabinet Office (1998), *Next Steps Report 1997*, Cm 3889, The Stationery Office

Cabinet Office (1999), *Modernising Government*, Cm 4310, The Stationery Office

Cairncross, F. & A. Cairncross (eds) (1992), *The Legacy of the Golden Age: the 1960s and Their Economic Consequences*, Routledge

Campbell, C. & G. K. Wilson (1995), *The End of Whitehall: Death of a Paradigm?*, Blackwell

Cannadine, D. (1998), *Class in Britain*, Yale University Press
Chapman, L. (1978), *Your Disobedient Servant*, Chatto & Windus (revised edition published by Penguin, 1979)
Churchill, W. S. (1938), *The World Crisis 1911–1918*, Odhams
Clark, A. (1998), *The Tories: Conservatives and the Nation State 1922–1997*, Weidenfeld & Nicolson
Clarke, P. (1992), *A Question of Leadership*, Penguin
Clutterbuck, R. (1978), *Britain in Agony: the Growth of Political Violence*, Faber & Faber, revised edition published by Penguin 1980
Cockett, R. (1995), *Thinking the Unthinkable: Think-tanks and the Economic Counter-Revolution 1933–1983*, Fontana
Colley, L. (1992), *Britons: Forging the Nation 1707–1837*, Yale University Press
Commission on Social Justice (1994), *Social Justice: Strategies for National Renewal*, Vintage
Conservative Central Office (1997), *You can only be sure with the Conservatives*
Cormack, P. (ed.) (1978), *Right Turn*, Leo Cooper
Coyle, D. (1997), 'Britain, the "envy of Europe", races up the competitiveness league', *The Independent*, 21 May
Crewe, I. (1996), '1976–1996', in A. Seldon (ed.), *How Tory Governments Fall: the Tory Party in Power since 1783*, Fontana, 1996
Criddle, B. (1997), 'MPs and Candidates', in Butler & Kavanagh, 1997
Cronin, J. E. (1991), *The Politics of State Expansion: War, State and Society in Twentieth-Century Britain*, Routledge
Dahrendorf, R. (1995), *Report on Wealth Creation and Social Cohesion in a Free Society*, Commission on Wealth Creation and Social Cohesion
Dahrendorf, R. (1999), 'Whatever happened to liberty?', *New Statesman*, 6 September, 25–7
Dangerfield, G. (1935), *The Strange Death of Liberal England*, MacGibbon & Kee, 1966
Davies, G. (1998), 'How Labour gained from its shift to the centre', *The Independent*, 9 February
Davis, E. (1998), *Public Spending*, Penguin
Dell, E. (1997), *The Chancellors: a History of the Chancellors of the Exchequer, 1945–90*, HarperCollins
Denman, R. (1996), *Missed Chances: Britain and Europe in the Twentieth Century*, Cassell
Department of Social Security (1998a), *New Ambitions for Our Country: a New Contract for Welfare*, Cm 3805, The Stationery Office
Department of Social Security (1998b), *A New Contract for Welfare: Principles into Practice*, Cm 4101, The Stationery Office
Department of Trade and Industry (1998), *Our Competitive Future: Building the Knowledge Driven Economy*, Cm 4176, The Stationery Office
Dinan, D. (1999), *Ever Closer Union: an Introduction to European Integration*, Macmillan
Donkin, R. (1997), 'Organised Labour', *Financial Times*, 23 July
Dowding, K. (1995), *The Civil Service*, Routledge
Drewry, G. (1999), 'The Civil Service', in Blackburn & Plant, 1999, 154–72

Dunleavy, P. (1991), *Democracy, Bureaucracy and Public Choice: Economic Explanations in Political Science*, Harvester Wheatsheaf

Dunleavy, P. & C. Hood (1994), 'From Old Public Administration to New Public Management', *Public Money & Management*, July–September, 9–16

Dunleavy, P. & C. T. Husbands (1985), *British Democracy at the Crossroads: Voting and Party Competition in the 1980s*, Allen & Unwin

Efficiency Unit (1988), *Improving Management in Government: the Next Steps*, HMSO

Ellison, N. & C. Pierson (eds) (1998), *Developments in British Social Policy*, Macmillan

Feigenbaum, H., J. Henig & C. Hamnett (1998), *Shrinking the State: the Political Underpinnings of Privatisation*, Cambridge University Press

Field, F. (1997), *Reforming Welfare*, Social Market Foundation

Fielding, S. (1997), 'Labour's Path to Power', in A. Geddes & J. Tongue (eds), *Labour's Landslide: the British General Election 1997*, Manchester University Press, 1997

Foster, C. D. & F. J. Plowden (1996), *The State under Stress: Can the Hollow State Be Good Government?*, Open University Press

Fry, G. K. (1997), 'The Conservatives and the Civil Service: "One Step Forward, Two Steps Back"?', *Public Administration*, 75(4), 695–710

Fulton, J. (1968), *The Civil Service: Volume 1*, Cmnd. 3638, HMSO

Gamble, A. (1988), *The Free Economy and the Strong State: the Politics of Thatcherism*, Macmillan

Gamble, A. (1994), *Britain in Decline: Economic Policy, Political Strategy and the British State*, Macmillan

Gamble, A. (1995), 'The Crisis of Conservatism', *New Left Review*, 214, 3–25

Garrett, J. (1972), *The Management of Government*, Penguin

George, S. (1998), *An Awkward Partner: Britain in the European Community*, Oxford University Press

Gerth, H. H. & C. Wright Mills (eds) (1948), *From Max Weber: Essays in Sociology*, Routledge & Kegan Paul

Gowan, P. (1987), 'The Origins of the Administrative Elite', *New Left Review*, 162, 4–34

Gray, J. (1996), *After Social Democracy*, Demos

Halévy, E. (1937), *A History of the English People in 1815*, Penguin

Hall, S. (1979), 'The Great Moving Right Show', in Hall & Jacques, 1983

Hall, S. & M. Jacques (eds) (1983), *The Politics of Thatcherism*, Lawrence & Wishart

Harris, J. (1994), *Private Lives, Public Spirit: Britain 1870–1914*, Penguin

Hay, C. (1996), *Re-Stating Social and Political Change*, Open University Press

Hazell, R. (ed.) (1999), *Constitutional Futures: a History of the Next Ten Years*, Oxford University Press

Heald, D. (1997), 'Controlling Public Expenditure', in D. Corry (ed.), *Public Expenditure: Effective Management and Control*, The Dryden Press

Healey, D. (1990), *The Time of My Life*, Penguin

Heffernan, R. & M. Marqusee (1992), *Defeat from the Jaws of Victory: Inside Kinnock's Labour Party*, Verso

Hencke, D. (1996), 'Thin times in Whitehall', *The Guardian*, 8 February
Hennessy, P. (1989), *Whitehall*, Secker & Warburg
Hennessy, P. (1992), *Never Again: Britain 1945–1951*, Jonathan Cape
Hennessy, P. (1999), 'Tony's bane', *The Guardian*, 9 July
Hicks, U. K. (1954), *British Public Finances: Their Structure and Development 1880–1952*, Oxford University Press
Hirst, P. Q. (1996), 'Democracy and Civil Society', in Hirst & Khilnani, 1996
Hirst, P. Q. & S. Khilnani (eds) (1996), *Reinventing Democracy*, Blackwell
HM Treasury (1991), *Competing for Quality*, Cm 1730, HMSO
HM Treasury (1998a), *Modern Public Services for Britain: Investing in Reform*, Cm 4011, The Stationery Office
HM Treasury (1998b), *Public Services for the Future: Modernisation, Reform, Accountability*, Cm 4181, The Stationery Office
Hobsbawm, E. J. (1962), *The Age of Revolution 1789–1848*, Mentor
Hobsbawm, E. J. (1969), *Industry and Empire*, Penguin
Hobsbawm, E. J. (1975), *The Crisis and the Outlook*, Birkbeck College Socialist Society
Hobsbawm, E. J. (1989), *Politics for a Rational Left*, Verso
Hobsbawm, E. J. (1994), *Age of Extremes: the Short Twentieth Century 1914–1991*, Michael Joseph
Hood, C. (1991), 'A public management for all seasons?', *Public Administration*, 69(1), 3–19
Hood, C., O. James, G. Jones, C. Scott & T. Travers (1998), 'Regulation Inside Government: Where New Public Management Meets the Audit Explosion', *Public Money & Management*, April–June, 61–8
Hooper, A. (1999), 'A Politics Adequate to the Age: the New Left and the Long Sixties', in Andrews *et al.*, 1999
Howe, G. (1995), *Conflict of Loyalty*, Pan
Hudson Institute (1974), *The United Kingdom in 1980: the Hudson Report*
Hurd, D. (1979), *An End to Promises: Sketch of a Government 1970–74*, Collins
Hutber, P. (ed.) (1978), *What's Wrong with Britain?*, Sphere
Hutton, W. (1995), *The State We're In*, Jonathan Cape
Hutton, W. (1999), 'Is cutting benefits the right way to welfare reform?', *The Observer*, 23 May
Jackson, T. (1999), 'Reflections of knowledge worker', *Financial Times*, 27 April
Jacques, M. (1979), 'Thatcherism – Breaking Out of the Impasse', in Hall & Jacques, 1983, 40–62
Jenkins, P. (1989), *Mrs Thatcher's Revolution: the Ending of the Socialist Era*, Pan
Jenkins, S. (1996), *Accountable to None: the Tory Nationalisation of Britain*, Penguin
Jessop, B. (1994), 'The Transition to Post-Fordism and the Schumpeterian Workfare State', in Burrows & Loader, 1994, 13–37
Jessop, B., K. Bonnett, S. Bromley & T. Ling (1984), 'Authoritarian Populism, Two Nations, and Thatcherism', *New Left Review*, 149, 32–60
Johnson, C. (1991), *The Economy under Mrs Thatcher 1979–1990*, Penguin
Johnson, P. (1996), 'High earners gain the most', *Financial Times*, 27 November

Kaletsky, A. (1999), 'Inevitability of EMU entry has begun to disintegrate', *The Times*, 8 June

Kavanagh, D. (1985), 'Whatever Happened to Consensus Politics?', *Political Studies*, **33**(4), 529–46

Kavanagh, D. (1994), 'A Major Agenda', in Kavanagh & Seldon, 1994, 3–17

Kavanagh, D. & P. Morris (1994), *Consensus Politics from Attlee to Major*, Blackwell

Kavanagh, D. & A. Seldon (eds) (1994), *The Major Effect*, Macmillan

Kellner, P. (1996), 'The Tory Report', *The Independent on Sunday*, 6 October

Kellner, P. (1998), 'Blair points way to "one-nation" parties', *The Observer*, 27 December

Kellner, P. & N. Crowther-Hunt (1980), *The Civil Servants: an Inquiry into Britain's Ruling Class*, Macdonald

Kemp, P. (1996), 'Whitehall's quiet revolution', *The Independent*, 19 February

Kennedy, P. (1988), *The Rise and Fall of the Great Powers: Economic Change and Military Conflict from 1500 to 2000*, Unwin Hyman

Keswick, T. (1999), 'Let us face it: Thatcher's legacy is Blair's Britain', *The Guardian*, 20 April

Keynes, J. M. (1919), *The Economic Consequences of the Peace*, Harcourt, Brace and Howe, 1920

King, A. (ed.) (1976), *Why is Britain Becoming Harder to Govern?*, BBC

Koestler, A. (ed.) (1963), *Suicide of a Nation? An Enquiry into the State of Britain*, Hamish Hamilton

Kuper, S. (1997), 'Tory reforms "may have halted decline"', *Financial Times*, 17 March

Labour Party (1997), *new Labour because Britain deserves better*

Langan, M. & B. Schwarz (eds) (1985), *Crises in the British State 1880–1930*, Hutchinson

Lawson, N. (1992), *The View from No. 11: Memoirs of a Tory Radical*, Bantam

Layfield, F. (1976), *Local Government Finance*, Cmnd 6453, HMSO

Leadbeater, C. (1999), *Living on Thin Air: the New Economy*, Viking

Lichtheim, G. (1974), *Europe in the Twentieth Century*, Cardinal

Likierman, A. (1988), *Public Expenditure*, Penguin

Lilley, P. (1995), *Winning the Welfare Debate*, Social Market Foundation

Lowe, R. (1997), 'The Core Executive, Modernisation and the Creation of PESC, 1960–64', *Public Administration*, 75(4), 601–15

Macaulay, T. B. (1854), 'Report on the Indian Civil Service', in Fulton, 1968, 119–28

Majone, G. (1996), 'A European Regulatory State', in J. J. Richardson (ed.), *European Union: Power and Policy-Making*, Routledge, 1996

Major, J. (1991), *The Citizen's Charter*, Cm 1599, HMSO

Management Consultancies Association (1998), *President's Statement and Annual Report*

Mandelson, P. & R. Liddle, *The Blair Revolution: Can New Labour Deliver?*, Faber & Faber

Margetts, H. (1996), 'The Implications for Democracy of Computerisation in Government', in Hirst & Khilnani, 1996

Marquand, D. (1988), *The Unprincipled Society: New Demands and Old Politics*, Fontana
Marquand, D. (1991) 'The New Medievalism', in Marquand, *The New Reckoning: Capitalism, States and Citizens*, Polity, 1997
Marquand, D. (1992), *The Progressive Dilemma: From Lloyd George to Kinnock*, Heinemann
Marquand, D. (1998), 'Can Labour kick the winning habit?', *New Statesman*, 23 October, 25–7
Marquand, D. & A. Seldon (eds) (1996), *The Ideas That Shaped Post-War Britain*, Fontana
Marr, A. (1996), *Ruling Britannia: the Failure and Future of British Democracy*, Penguin
Marwick, A. (1970), *Britain in the Century of Total War: War, Peace and Social Change 1900–1967*, Penguin
Marwick, A. (1998), *The Sixties: Cultural Revolution in Britain, France, Italy and the United States, c. 1958–c. 1974*, Oxford University Press
Mazower, M. (1999), *Dark Continent: Europe's Twentieth Century*, Penguin
McCrae, J. (1999), 'Gainers are at the bottom of the scale', *Financial Times*, 10 March
McKibbin, R. (1998), *Classes and Cultures: England 1918–1951*, Oxford University Press
McKinsey Global Institute (1998), *Driving Productivity and Growth in the UK Economy*
Milward, A. S. (1992), *The European Rescue of the Nation State*, Routledge
Monnet, J. (1978), *Memoirs*, Collins
Moss, R. (1975), *The Collapse of Democracy*, Temple Smith
Mount, F. (1992), *The British Constitution Now: Recovery or Decline?* Heinemann
Nairn, T. (1977), 'The Twilight of the British State', *New Left Review*, 101–2, 3–61
Northcote, S. H. & C. E. Trevelyan (1854), 'Report on the Organisation of the Permanent Civil Service', in Fulton, 1968
Nugent, N. (1999), *The Government and Politics of the European Union*, Macmillan
Olson, M. (1982), *The Rise and Decline of Nations*, Yale University Press
Panitch, L. & C. Leys (1997), *The End of Parliamentary Socialism: From New Left to New Labour*, Verso
Peacock, A. T. & J. Wiseman (1961), *The Growth of Public Expenditure in the United Kingdom*, George Allen & Unwin
Peat Marwick (1986a), *Financial Management in the Public Sector: a Review 1979–84*
Peat Marwick (1986b), *Current Issues in Public Sector Management*
Perkin, H. (1969), *The Origins of Modern English Society 1780–1880*, Routledge & Kegan Paul
Perkin, H. (1989), *The Rise of Professional Society: England since 1880*, Routledge
Pimlott, B. (1988), 'The Myth of Consensus', in *Frustrate Their Knavish Tricks: Writings on Biography, History and Politics*, HarperCollins

Pimlott, B. (1993), *Harold Wilson*, HarperCollins
Pirie, M. (1988), *Privatisation: Theory, Practice and Choice*, Wildwood House
Pliatzky, L. (1982), *Getting and Spending: Public Expenditure, Employment and Inflation*, Basil Blackwell
Plumb, J. H. (1969), *The Growth of Political Stability in England 1675–1725*, Penguin
Plowden, W. (1994), *Ministers and Mandarins*, Institute for Public Policy Research
Pollitt, C. (1993), *Managerialism and the Public Services: Cuts or Cultural Change in the 1990s?*, Blackwell
Redwood, J. (1980), *Public Enterprise in Crisis: the Future of the Nationalised Industries*, Basil Blackwell
Rhodes, R. A. W. (1994), 'The Hollowing Out of the State: the Changing Nature of the Public Service in Britain', *Political Quarterly*, 65(2), 138–51
Richards, D. (1997), *The Civil Service under the Conservatives 1979–1997: Whitehall's Political Poodles?*, Sussex Academic Press
Richards, S. (1996), 'New Labour – New Civil Service?', *Political Quarterly*, 67(4), 311–20
Riddell, P. (1991), *The Thatcher Era: And Its Legacy*, Blackwell
Riddell, P. (1996), *Honest Opportunism*, Indigo
Ridley, N. (1973), *Industry and the Civil Service*, Aims of Industry
Ridley, N. (1992), *'My Style of Government': the Thatcher Years*, Fontana
Sassoon, D. (1997), *One Hundred Years of Socialism: the West European Left in the Twentieth Century*, Fontana
Saunders, P. & C. Harris (1994), *Privatisation and Popular Capitalism*, Open University Press
Schumpeter, J. A. (1943), *Capitalism, Socialism and Democracy*, Unwin
Searle, G. R. (1971), *The Quest for National Efficiency: a Study in British Politics and Political Thought, 1899–1914*, Basil Blackwell
Searle, G. R. (1993), *Entrepreneurial Politics in Mid-Victorian Britain*, Oxford University Press
Sedgemore, B. (1980), *The Secret Constitution: an Analysis of the Political Establishment*, Hodder & Stroughton
Seldon, A. (ed.) (1978), *The Coming Confrontation: Will the Open Society Survive to 1989?*, Institute of Economic Affairs
Shanks, M. (1961), *The Stagnant Society: a Warning*, Penguin
Shannon, R. (1976), *The Crisis of Imperialism 1865–1914*, Paladin
Shannon, R. (1999), *Gladstone: Peel's Inheritor, 1809–1865*, Penguin
Shaw, E. (1996), *The Labour Party since 1945*, Blackwell
Shonfield, A. (1958), *British Economic Policy since the War*, revised edition published as Penguin Special 1959
Skidelsky, R. (1970), *Politicians and the Slump: the Labour Government of 1929–1931*, Penguin
Skidelsky, R. (1975), 'The future of the state', *New Society*, 2 October
Skidelsky, R. (1992), *John Maynard Keynes: the Economist as Saviour 1920–1937*, Macmillan

Skidelsky, R. (1995), *The World after Communism: a Polemic for Our Times*, Macmillan
Skidelsky, R. (1996a), 'Welfare without the state', *Prospect*, January, 38–43
Skidelsky, R. (1996b), 'The Fall of Keynesianism', in Marquand & Seldon, 1996, 41–66
Skidelsky, R. (1997), *Beyond the Welfare State*, Social Market Foundation
Smith, D. (1987), *The Rise and Fall of Monetarism*, Penguin
Stephens, P. (1996), *Politics and the Pound: the Conservative Struggle with Sterling*, Macmillan
Stephens, P. (1999), 'Missing emotions', *Financial Times*, 9 April
Stone, N. (1983), *Europe Transformed 1878–1919*, Fontana
Taylor, A. J. P. (1961), 'Lloyd George: Rise and Fall', in *Essays in English History*, Penguin, 1976
Taylor, A. J. P. (1970), *English History 1914–1945*, Penguin
Terry, F. (1996), 'The Private Finance Initiative – Overdue Reform or Policy Breakthrough?', *Public Money & Management*, January–March, 9–16
Thain, C. & M. Wright (1995), *The Treasury and Whitehall: the Planning and Control of Public Expenditure, 1976–1993*, Clarendon Press
Thatcher, M. (1995), *The Downing Street Years*, HarperCollins
Thomas, H. (ed.) (1959), *The Establishment*, Ace Books, 1962
Thompson, E. P. (1968), *The Making of the English Working Class*, Penguin
Timmins, N. (1996), *The Five Giants: a Biography of the Welfare State*, Fontana
Timmins, N. (1999a), 'UK constitution faces "fundamental" change', *Financial Times*, 6 May
Timmins, N. (1999b), 'An explosive mixture', *Financial Times*, 22 July
Timmins, N. (1999c), 'Another inspector calls', *Financial Times*, 12 August
Titmuss, R. M. (1958), *Essays on 'The Welfare State'*, Unwin
Tocqueville, A de (1835 & 1840), *Democracy in America*, HarperPerennial, 1988
Toynbee, P. (1997), 'Labour's Big Idea – will it really work?', *The Independent*, 7 July
Vincent, J. (1972), *The Formation of the British Liberal Party 1857–68*, Penguin
Waldegrave, W. (1993a), *Public Service and the Future: Reforming Britain's Bureaucracies*, Conservative Political Centre
Waldegrave, W. (1993b), *The Reality of Reform and Accountability in Today's Public Service*, Public Finance Foundation
Walker, D. (1999), 'Self service', *The Guardian*, 26 July
Watt, N. (1999), 'Blair berates old Labour "snobs"', *The Guardian*, 7 July
White, M. (1999), 'Blair hails middle class revolution', *The Guardian*, 15 January
Whitehead, P. (1985), *The Writing on the Wall: Britain in the Seventies*, Michael Joseph and Channel 4 TV
Wiener, M. (1981), *English Culture and the Decline of the Industrial Spirit 1850–1980*, Cambridge University Press
Willetts, D. (1996), *Blair's Gurus: an Examination of Labour's Rhetoric*, Centre for Policy Studies

Willetts, D. (1999), 'The paradox of class', *Prospect*, February, 64–6
Williams, M. J. (1996a), *Demolishing the Property Services Agency*, University of Hertfordshire Business School Working Papers
Williams, M. J. (1996b), *The Rise of the Consultants: External Advisers and Public Policy since 1979*, University of Hertfordshire Business School Working Papers
Williams, M. J. (1999), 'The Long Sixties in the Short Twentieth Century', in Andrews *et al.*, 1999, 144–67
Willman, J. (1994), 'The Civil Service', in Kavanagh & Seldon, 1994, 64–82
Wintour, P. (1999), 'No change is as good as a rest', *The Observer*, 1 August
Wintour, P. & R. Thomas (1999), 'The tough love revolution that's failing the poor', *The Observer*, 14 February
Wolf, M. (1997), 'Labour of prosperity', *Financial Times*, 21 January
Wolf, M. (1999a), 'Prudent housekeeper compulsive tinkerer', *Financial Times*, 10 March
Wolf, M. (1999b), 'Sick man of Britain', *Financial Times*, 2 August
Young, H. (1993), *One of Us: a Biography of Margaret Thatcher*, Pan
Young, H. (1994), 'The Prime Minister', in Kavanagh & Seldon, 1994, 18–28
Young, H. (1998), *This Blessed Plot: Britain and Europe from Churchill to Blair*, Macmillan
Young, M. (1961), *The Rise of the Meritocracy*, Penguin

Index